Music, Indigeneity, Digital Media

Eastman/Rochester Studies in Ethnomusicology

Ellen Koskoff, Senior Editor
Eastman School of Music
(ISSN: 2161-0290)

Music, Indigeneity, Digital Media

Edited by Thomas R. Hilder,
Henry Stobart, and Shzr Ee Tan

UNIVERSITY OF ROCHESTER PRESS

First published 2017

University of Rochester Press
668 Mt. Hope Avenue, Rochester, NY 14620, USA
www.urpress.com
and Boydell & Brewer Limited
PO Box 9, Woodbridge, Suffolk IP12 3DF, UK
www.boydellandbrewer.com

ISBN-13: 978-1-58046-573-1
ISSN: 2161-0290

Library of Congress Cataloging-in-Publication Data

Names: Hilder, Thomas R., 1982– editor. | Stobart, Henry, 1958– editor. | Tan, Shzr Ee, editor.
Title: Music, Indigeneity, digital media / edited by Thomas R. Hilder, Henry Stobart, and Shzr Ee Tan.
Other titles: Eastman/Rochester studies in ethnomusicology ; v. 6.
Description: Rochester : University of Rochester Press, 2017. | Series: Eastman/Rochester studies in ethnomusicology ; v. 6 | Includes bibliographical references and index.
Identifiers: LCCN 2016052378 | ISBN 9781580465731 (hardcover : alk. paper)
Subjects: LCSH: Indigenous peoples—Music—History and criticism. | Sound—Recording and reproducing—Social aspects. | Sound recordings—Social aspects. | Digital media—Social aspects.
Classification: LCC ML3545 .M895 2017 | DDC 781.6200285—dc23 LC record available at https://lccn.loc.gov/2016052378

A catalogue record for this title is available from the British Library.

This publication is printed on acid-free paper.
Printed in the United States of America.

This book is dedicated to our families, friends, and colleagues, as well as artists and cultural activists who have inspired and supported this project.

Contents

Illustrations

Acknowledgments

This book is a result of the symposium *Music, Indigeneity, and Digital Media* held at the Department of Music, Royal Holloway, University of London, in April 2010, organized by Thomas Hilder, Shzr Ee Tan, and Henry Stobart. We would like to express special gratitude to Helen Gilbert for her inspiring interdisciplinary work on Indigeneity and for generous funding for the symposium as part of her wider project on Indigeneity in the Contemporary World: Performance, Politics, Belonging, funded by the European Research Council (ERC). We are also grateful to the Faculty of Arts and Social Sciences at Royal Holloway, University of London, which offered extra funds for the symposium. Not least, we are extremely indebted to all the participants at the symposium and the contributors to this edited volume, whose tremendous experience and insight have been fundamental to our own research and the present volume. Many thanks also go to Ellen Koskoff and Julia Cook at University of Rochester Press for supporting this project and to our copyeditor Carrie Crompton for her hard and diligent work.

Music, Indigeneity, Digital Media

An Introduction

Thomas R. Hilder

This book is about Indigenous musical performance in a digital era. It addresses both the impact of digital technologies on the composition, production, and consumption of music by and for Indigenous people and the ways in which Indigenous people have utilized digital technologies to revive, repatriate, and transmit musical traditions in complex articulations of Indigeneity.[1] Bringing together the work of international scholars and musicians, this volume highlights new perspectives on contemporary Indigenous music making across five continents to reveal both striking connections and contrasts across Indigenous experiences. Indigenous communities have faced histories of genocide, coerced religious conversion, social marginalization, land dispossession, and cultural assimilation.[2] Since World War II, Indigenous activists, academics, and artists have mobilized transnationally to achieve political recognition in diverse governmental and nongovernmental institutions, develop international laws that secure Indigenous rights, and fight for rights to land and cultural heritage. The revival of Indigenous languages, cosmologies, and cultural traditions, including music, has assisted aspirations to Indigenous political and cultural self-determination. Communication technologies have long been tools for nation building and imperial expansion, as well as symbols of the supposed ascendancy of the industrialized "West."[3] The explosion of digital technologies over the last decades has also very much shaped the everyday lives of Indigenous people but in ways that complicate earlier hegemonic power structures. As Pamela Wilson and Michelle Stewart write, "Contemporary Indigenous media demonstrate the extent to which the hallmarks of an earlier regime of empire—colonization, forced assimilation, genocide, and diaspora—are being challenged and displaced by new constellations of global power."[4] Indeed, digital communication technologies have themselves transformed forms of Indigenous activism while also being adopted by Indigenous musicians to assist in cultural revival, repatriation, and transmission—processes which have helped to "decolonize" earlier media spaces and practices. In turn, those technologies have shaped musical traditions, alongside notions of Indigenous subjectivity, collectivity, and sovereignty. But digital media might also cement hegemonies through censorship, surveillance, and propaganda and magnify existing hierarchies within and between Indigenous communities along lines of gender, class, and "race."

This volume seeks to explore the opportunities and challenges presented by a range of digital media and aspects of digital culture—including the Internet, VCDs, recording studios, digital archives, YouTube—by engaging with debates from across a variety of disciplines. As scholars, activists, and musicians, we bring contrasting perspectives, theoretical approaches, and ethical priorities which are shaped by our own research contexts, working experiences, and individual subjectivities. The variety of scholarly styles and representational methods represented in this volume helps to foster an appreciation of the diversity of Indigenous contexts as well as possibilities for scholarly interventions. Nonetheless, our texts converge and overlap in many striking ways that highlight the overarching global challenges in the nexus of music, Indigeneity, and digital media. We raise broad and ambitious questions: How might digital media enable the forging of local and transnational Indigenous communities? How do digital media allow for the negotiation and transformation of representations of Indigeneity? In what ways might Indigenous music studio production revive aspects of Indigenous cosmologies? What are the implications of digital databases in archiving and repatriating Indigenous knowledge and intangible heritage? In what ways do digital media reshape notions of subjectivity, the body, and the human that might clash with—or, conversely, resonate with—Indigenous cosmologies? How might digital media enable new understandings of orality and multisensorial expression that are commensurate with Indigenous cultural performance? Drawing on the literature of Indigeneity and media, this book calls attention to new and often unpredictable dynamics of Indigenous musical cultures precipitated by digital media technologies. It recognizes and interrogates further how, as Georgina Born's work on musical mediation demonstrates, musical ontologies are embedded in social, institutional, technological, and aesthetic "assemblages."[5] Given the rapidity with which digital technologies and their theorization evolve, we seek to document, analyze, and theorize current practices of musical media in particular Indigenous contexts in order to shed light on wider global shifts in digital and Indigenous politics that suggest new horizons of Indigenous experiences, expressive cultures, and transnational activism. This chapter serves as an introduction to the multifarious and complex ways in which music, Indigeneity, and digital media intersect. The first section offers an overview of the politics of Indigeneity. In the second section, I outline key debates in the field of media studies specifically relevant to Indigenous issues. The third section provides a broader discussion of the intersection of music, Indigeneity, and digital media. Here, I introduce the case studies of the ensuing chapters by contextualizing them within five complexes of themes: (1) activism, transnationalism, sovereignty; (2) production, mediation, consumption; (3) archives, transmission, orality; (4) subjectivity, ownership, authorship; (5) cosmologies, virtuality, posthumanism.

Articulating Indigeneity in Global Modernity

Indigenous people are descendents of populations marginalized in their own land by majority populations of settler colonies founded after the advent of the age of "discovery" during the European Renaissance. As the Indigenous legal scholar James Anaya writes, "Indigenous peoples, nations, or communities are culturally distinctive groups that find themselves engulfed by settler societies born of the forces of empire and conquest."[6] While colonial contexts differ, a definition of Indigeneity was formulated by Martinéz Cobo in a UN report from 1986 which highlights a precolonial connection to colonized land, cultural distinctiveness from the dominant society, and an experience of social discrimination.[7] Indeed, empire building often involved the decimation of local populations (through violence, infectious diseases, famine), forced religious conversion, the annexing of land, the exploitation of natural resources and destruction of local ecosystems, and the imposition of imperial cultures. As a result of these histories, various aspects of Indigenous culture—including "traditional" livelihoods, languages, cosmologies, economies, natural resources, and cultural traditions—were suppressed, forbidden, or made shameful. As imagined by the paradigm of salvage ethnography in the late nineteenth and early twentieth centuries, the tangible and intangible cultural heritage of Indigenous people had to be documented, collected, and deposited in archives and displayed in museums for the sake of preserving a global heritage, or it would be lost in the global tide of modernity.[8]

Around the same time, the increasing pressure and encroachment on the rights of Indigenous communities by state authorities ignited Indigenous resistance and mobilization. Members of Indigenous communities who gained access to state education and political institutions began to fight against discrimination and campaign for the welfare and rights of their marginalized Indigenous communities, forming local and national Indigenous organizations at the beginning of the twentieth century.[9] However, Indigenous campaigns only began to be taken seriously by state authorities following the Second World War owing to a new focus on national minority concerns.[10] It was at this time that a transnational movement based on global Indigenous solidarity began to blossom. Participating in international political conferences, performing at pan-Indigenous cultural forums, and gaining wider representation in newly established international institutions (such as the United Nations), Indigenous activists voiced their history of suppression and demanded recognition of their human rights.[11] In 1989 the International Labour Organization (ILO) adopted Convention No. 169, which became the first international law to address the rights of Indigenous people.[12] Indigenous issues garnered global attention in the 1990s through various forums, such as the inauguration of the First International Decade of the World's Indigenous People (1995–2004), and the UN Permanent Forum on Indigenous Issues (UNPFII) established in 2002.[13] After years of work, the UN finally published its Declaration on the Rights of Indigenous Peoples in 2007, a document which sets a moral standard for nation states to recognize the need to enable Indigenous self-determination, respect land rights, and support cultural development.[14] As a result of local and international mobilization, Indigenous people have utilized the processes and institutions of modernity to articulate their own political agendas, and growing numbers of Indigenous populations have begun to enjoy greater political representation, as well as access to material wealth, education, and health care and the freedom to develop their own language and cultural traditions.

Despite attempts to forge a united global Indigenous community, there remains great divergence across Indigenous experiences. Communities that depend on traditional livelihoods and the fragile balance of local ecosystems are already facing the consequences of environmental devastation and global warming.[15] At the same time, various Indigenous representatives have begun to argue for their own share of economic gain from industrial uses of land resources such as mining and oil extraction. In some contexts, urban middle-class communities have begun to reclaim their Indigenous heritage, and in so doing are opening Indigenous cultures to new audiences and transforming notions of Indigeneity. Nonetheless, as Indigenous cultures become more marketable, various Indigenous commentators have critiqued the appropriation of their cultural heritage and cosmologies by profiteering outsiders unaware of local cultural sensitivities and customary law.[16] Certain trends in neoliberal politics emphasizing diversity, decentralization, and entrepreneurship have in some contexts enabled increasing forms of local (albeit fragile) political control and economic wealth that have strengthened forms of Indigenous self-determination.[17] But the increasingly unequal distribution of wealth, especially since the global financial crisis in 2008, has had strong negative consequences for many Indigenous communities already facing severe economic hardships. Owing to the increasing pressures of cultural and economic globalization, the twenty-first century has also witnessed the emergence of neo-nationalism and a rise in religious fundamentalism in many parts of the world. Not only do these conservative movements risk further marginalizing minority groups such as Indigenous people; they also often appropriate a simplified rhetoric of Indigeneity to suit their own nationalist agendas, thus engendering wider suspicion about the legitimacy of notions of Indigeneity. At the same time, there is arguably increasing inequality within and across Indigenous communities, inequality dependent upon individual state policies, marked by rural/urban divides, and often shaped along lines of "race," class, and gender.[18]

These divergent Indigenous experiences, nonetheless, offer valuable perspectives on pressing global social, cultural, and political issues. Critiquing simplistic and essentialized notions of Indigeneity, James Clifford has proposed the nuanced concept of "Indigenous articulation" for understanding diverse strategies of political activism and cultural revival that draw on cosmopolitan experiences and search for new possibilities of sovereignty in the face of changing political, social, and environmental challenges.[19] Indeed, new narratives recounted by Indigenous artists through cultural performance, including music, articulate Indigenous histories while critiquing the national and imperial histories of settler societies.[20] Indigenous scholars have also promoted notions of traditional ecological knowledge (TEK) to revalorize certain Indigenous livelihoods and cosmologies in response to environmental degradation while asserting rights to Indigenous land to resist land dispossession.[21] Likewise, Indigenous representatives have highlighted how these traditional knowledges can themselves transcend Western notions of science and technology.[22] Owing to histories of cultural dispossession, numerous Indigenous activists have called for legal solutions within international intellectual property law; some have highlighted notions of collective ownership as a form of resistance to dominant notions of commodity and copyright in global capitalism.[23] Furthermore, the struggle for self-determination by most Indigenous political organizations both draws on and challenges the liberal democratic foundations of national sovereignty, state borders, and international law.[24] Such claims are articulated in ways that, by reformulating notions of Indigenous "difference," can inspire wider social change or ensnare Indigenous communities within existing hegemonic forces or both.[25] But, as Karena Shaw has argued, Indigenous politics, rather than being marginal to contemporary politics, actually speak to the inherent paradoxes of modern political theory and are thus implicated in broader global challenges of the twenty-first century.[26] The rise of digital media in the last decades has itself shaped Indigenous activism and artistic creativity in diverse and complex ways that, as we shall see, themselves suggest emergent trends and challenges within global digital culture.

The Politics of Digital Indigeneity

The potentially destructive and liberating forces of modernity have always been present in the discourses of media. Max Horkheimer and Theodor Adorno claimed famously in 1944 that modernity resulted in the fetishization of commodities, the rationalization of society, and the alienation of the individual.[27] Reacting to both Nazism in Europe and consumer culture in the United States, they argued that the "culture industry" powered by late capitalism and mass media led to excessive consumption and cultural homogeneity, and was the root cause of capitalist exploitation, political control, and ultimately global war.[28] In contrast, the anthropologist Arjun Appadurai has argued for the transformative potential of contemporary communication technologies to inspire individual action and to imagine transnational communities that signal a postnational future.[29] Such diverging views continue today in the popular imagination, whereby new technologies, are greeted with both—in the words of Timothy Taylor—"wonderment and anxiety."[30] Within the last five years, digital media technologies have been praised for instigating social revolution (e.g., the "Arab Spring") but also condemned for their use in unprecedented forms of global surveillance (e.g., the "WikiLeaks" scandal). As technology becomes symbolic of modernity's "civilization" and "progress," in their ability to both serve and undermine nationalisms and (neo)imperialisms, digital media seem to mark the disjuncture between utopian and dystopian visions of the future of humanity.[31] Raymond Williams has pointed out contrasting tendencies in the analysis of media, with some commentators focusing on "technological determinism"—the idea that technology has the power to transform society—and others on "symptomatic technology"—the idea that technologies are products of existing social organization and historical patterns.[32] Both tendencies have been criticized for under- and overemphasizing human agency and reifying a dichotomy between humans and technology.[33] Technological determinism posits that the different eras of human history (premodernity, modernity, and postmodernity) have been brought about by revolutions in media (orality, print culture, and digital media respectively).[34] Indeed, popular and academic discourse often emphasize the revolutionary nature of digital media vis-à-vis earlier analogue media both in terms of their technological features and their impact on global society; however, this view has been critiqued for overlooking continuities and mimicking product marketing.[35] Nonetheless, many scholars agree that digital technologies have undermined long-held notions about the self, community, and power in modernist theory. As Mark Poster has argued, digital media enable "a new play of power, a new dialectics of resistance and a new configuration of politics and its theorization."[36]

One key aspect of digital culture is the creation of new networks and the reshaping of notions of community and democracy. While print and broadcast media enabled the building of national communities, the network nature of digital media has allowed decentralized subcultural and transnational communities to emerge.[37] Digital media have thus allowed Indigenous communities to sidestep national broadcast media and transform the public sphere.[38] Moreover, they have enabled Indigenous communities to mobilize within and across national boundaries to inspire local activism and engender pan-Indigenous sentiments.[39] Indeed, as Landzelius writes, "it seems a safe bet that ICTs will play an increasingly significant role in the articulation of emergent forms of Indigenous cosmopolitanism."[40] Likewise, digital media offer new ways of becoming recognized and asserting authorship over representations of Indigeneity. As scholars have noted, Indigenous people have a long history of being subjected to negative representations, and digital media enable the creation and dissemination of more positive representations.[41] Thus, the Internet can be a platform for Indigenous "articulations of alterity" that resist and subvert earlier and persisting racist representations of Indigenous communities.[42] Such discourses are suggestive of the ways in which digital media have the potential to reverse power relations between settler and Indigenous communities.

Nonetheless, digital media can also consolidate existing power hierarchies. One particularly salient issue in Indigenous contexts is the "digital divide," a term coined to highlight growing inequalities in global society with respect to access to digital technologies.[43] Indeed, Dyson, Hendriks, and Grant have warned that certain Indigenous communities face greater challenges owing to the "cost of the new technologies, the geographic isolation of many communities, low levels of computer literacy, and lack of awareness of how technologies might serve Indigenous goals and interests."[44] Lamenting the ethnocentrism of utopian discourses about the digital era but remaining wary of paternalistic discourses on the digital divide, Ginsburg urges us "to keep listening to the large percentage of the earth's population that is on the unwired side of the so-called digital divide."[45] Moreover, Evgeny Morozov has warned of the potentials of digital technologies for unprecedented forms of surveillance, censorship, and propaganda in dictatorships and supposedly liberal democracies.[46] Indeed, in a post-WikiLeaks global climate, we should not underestimate the power of governmental and commercial powers to attempt to manipulate and quash political mobilization, including Indigenous activism. As Rheingold has warned, "the Net that is a marvelous lateral network can also be used as a kind of invisible yet inescapable cage."[47] Such discourses suggest that we should remain critical of casual allusions to digital "democracy" and "freedom" and acknowledge the potential for digital media to render the struggles of Indigenous communities more volatile and unpredictable in a digital era.

Manuel Castells has discussed how common understandings of space and time become much more flexible and fluid through digital technologies.[48]

Digital media allow for almost instantaneous communication across huge distances and thus render those distances seemingly insignificant. For Indigenous communities living in remote geographical contexts, digital media have enabled networking with wider Indigenous communities, drawing on global information resources and reaching global audiences in ways that overcome the challenges caused by their physical remoteness.[49] Landzelius has suggested that digital media can perform notions of "center" and "periphery," and thus subvert a center/periphery dichotomy.[50] But Indigenous people have also experienced histories of land dispossession through imposed national and colonial conceptions of place, exploitation of natural resources, and fixing of political borders. Castells's description of digital culture as bringing about "spaces of flows" is significant, considering the ways in which Indigenous people have striven to articulate alternative conceptions of place and belonging to land that call into question a world mapped according to an Enlightenment cartographic imagination.[51] Likewise, digital media have enabled the storage of data from different historical moments in databases from which users can retrieve information at unprecedented speed.[52] Digital databases have become crucial for empowering Indigenous communities by, for example, providing opportunities for local documentation and repatriation of cultural heritage.[53] Such a fluid relationship between the present and past in digital culture creates a certain "ahistoricity," in Castells's words, which puts into question notions of linear time in a modernist temporal imagination.[54] Such "ahistoricity" is pertinent, considering Indigenous attempts to resist the perception of their cultures as "premodern" and the fact that many Indigenous cosmologies conceptualize time in ways that are at odds with Enlightenment notions of historical linearity.[55]

Furthermore, digital culture has transformed notions of the self and body. Poster has argued that the digital era renders subjectivities fluid and scattered and blurs the boundaries between public and private, as well as between the body and technology.[56] Likewise, other scholars have noted the ability of digital technology to expand the possibilities of human body and agency.[57] Donna Haraway's famous proposal of the cyborg, a technologically enhanced human, as a feminist and postcolonial strategy, has generated debates about posthumanism.[58] On the one hand, such discourses might be at odds with the need to articulate unproblematic Indigenous subjectivities in the context of human rights disputes and international law, and overlook the ways in which Indigenous communities might have been victims of technological development and industrial expansion.[59] On the other hand, they might assist in Indigenous attempts to undermine modernist notions of subjectivity (for example, in the case of copyright law) and promote alternative models of human-nature-technology relations based on Indigenous cosmologies.[60]

Digital culture also allows for new possibilities of simulation and virtuality.[61] A negative take on simulation has been offered by Jean Baudrillard, who famously argued that we have entered the era of "simulacra" and a "hyper-real" order that conceals wider political truths.[62] But digital simulation can be beneficial by providing an escape for marginalized individuals, offering opportunities for political resistance, and rendering perceptible alternative visions of reality.[63] Digital simulation also enables the convergence of different communication forms (oral, written, audiovisual) and thus the supposed reunification of the senses upon which they rely.[64] That this overcomes the logocentrism of print media and brings about forms of orality and multi-sensorialism that might chime with Indigenous traditions had already been suggested by McLuhan.[65] Indeed, as Dyson, Hendriks, and Grant write, "the graphical, video and audio facilities of media speak directly to cultures which are principally rooted in spoken language, music, dance, ceremony and visual forms of artistic expression."[66] For Indigenous communities, thus, virtual reality can support cultural revival and bring about a new sense of holistic multisensorial experience and orality that was not possible with earlier media technologies, as Cocq has argued.[67] But how does music intersect with the politics of Indigeneity and digital media? In what ways have digital media reshaped Indigenous musical performance, production, and consumption? What does Indigenous music in a digital era tell us about global politics in the twenty-first century?

Music, Indigeneity, Digital Media

Technologies of communication were significant in early understandings of Indigenous music. The phonograph, invented in 1877 by Thomas Edison, was one of the first technologies capable of recording and reproducing sound and thus became a key tool for fieldwork in the study of oral and musical traditions from the 1890s.[68] Marveled at for its ability to capture musical performance into a tangible form, the phonograph enabled researchers to collect, catalog, and analyze musical traditions that were, according to the doctrine of salvage ethnography, threatened by modernity. Yet, at the same time, the technologies of mass reproduction and consumption, through their apparently globalizing and hegemonizing tendencies, epitomized the threat to cultural diversity.[69] The phonograph, like the bourgeoning ethnographic disciplines, was caught up in practices and discourses of colonialism.[70] Oral traditions, recorded by missionaries, colonial officials and ethnographers, were subjected to transcriptions and analyses that served outdated theories of universal musical evolution and racial difference.[71] As music scholars have noted, recording technologies have not only been key in attempting to "understand" other cultures; they have been fundamental to constructing notions of "difference" between "modern" Europeans and their "Others."[72]

But how have political hierarchies changed within a digital era? Some scholars have noted how digital media, through enabling the quick global distribution of Western cultural forms, can reproduce and solidify power dynamics between privileged and underprivileged people along lines of ethnicity and gender.[73] Such issues have led René Lysloff to diagnose an era of "*virtual* colonization,"[74] mirroring what Frederick Williams had earlier termed "communications colonialism."[75] Other scholars, however, have argued that digital technologies can empower local music making through opening up new, democratic, and decentralized forms and patterns of production, distribution, and consumption.[76] Utopian and dystopian outlooks, however, often fail to account for the complexities of and differences between Indigenous experiences. This is most evident when interrogating notions of the digital divide. In this volume, Russell Wallace describes, for example, how he uses Internet platforms such as YouTube to share his music widely, yet continues to release CDs in order to reach members of his communities who have limited Internet access. But, as Beverley Diamond and I discuss in this volume, there are Indigenous communities in welfare-strong nations, such as the Sámi, for whom geographical "remoteness" does not necessarily map onto lack of access to digital musical technologies. Thus, notions of Indigenous artistic freedom and self-determination are tied to everyday practicalities around access, which can be dependent upon place, region, and national context, as well as to issues of class, gender, and "race."[77]

As we have seen, debates concerning the impact of media on society have the danger of reaffirming a problematic division between technology and humanity.[78] This is all the more pertinent in debates concerning Indigeneity, since Indigenous people have long been represented as "premodern" and lacking technological "progress," and have often faced hardships due to national and colonial deployments of technology. Indeed, notions of power, perceived on a spectrum between "technological determinism" and "symptomatic technology," obscure how technologies become intrinsic parts of Indigenous cultures.[79] Many chapters in this volume not only highlight how particular technologies have become adopted (in Landzelius's term, "Indigenized") within Indigenous musical traditions;[80] they also suggest how certain characteristics of digital culture can chime with Indigenous musical traditions, are more commensurable to Indigenous cosmologies, and thus are more conducive to assisting Indigenous cultural revival and "decolonizing" earlier media spaces and practices. Diamond, for example, highlights the importance of the musical studio for strengthening aspects of Sámi *joik* performance. Wallace describes how patterns of MIDI notes created via his synthesizer on his computer in the late 1980s rendered a visual form that reminded him of local weaving designs and landscapes. These examples point to the ways in which digital media can both support and transform Indigenous musical performance and ontologies. Nonetheless, considering histories of cultural dispossession and assimilation in Indigenous contexts, the arrival of new digital media can lead to heated debates concerning the hegemonizing forces of technology.[81] Due to the global standardization of certain technologies and formats, digital music is inherently a form of cultural hegemony, imposing certain musical aesthetics and modes of listening.[82] Indeed, despite her acknowledgment that studios can strengthen Indigenous musical aesthetics and cosmologies, Diamond views the studio as a politically sensitive site of encounter between Indigenous musical traditions and globalizing technologies. Drawing on Fredric Jameson's pessimistic outlook on cultural homogenization,[83] she raises the pertinent question: "Have Indigenous musicians and music producers been able to create and retain a distinctive 'voice' in the commodified forms that were central to this cultural flourishing?" Likewise, Linda Barwick's contribution on the Murriny Patha people of Northwest Australia concludes with the very conundrum of technological determinism: Have the people of Wadeye "hijacked" technology or has technology ensnared them? Rather than reifying a distinction between technology and culture, this thought-provoking question addresses politically charged issues of Indigenous cultural sustainability and survivance. Thus, what the examples in this volume suggest is that there is a much more fluid and complex relationship between the ways in which certain technologies become intrinsic to restoring musical traditions and in turn transforming those traditions in Indigenous modernities. Indeed, digital music can be both embraced and dismissed for the ways in which it celebrates or denigrates modernity, assists or hinders cultural revival, and supports or quashes moves toward self-determination. It is these particular challenges and conundrums of musical Indigeneity in digital culture that I interrogate in the ensuing five sections.

Activism, Transnationalism, Sovereignty

How have digital media transformed Indigenous aspirations toward self-determination through music? Considering the importance of digital media to network musicians and publics (e.g., YouTube, Facebook, musicians' websites), it is unsurprising that digital musical media have been key to strengthening inter-Indigenous dialogue and engendering local, regional, and transnational Indigenous belonging.[84] Byron Dueck has theorized that the mediation of Indigenous Canadian music can enable the imagination of Indigenous publics (and counterpublics), whose "members share experiences and hopes, a sense of a social transformation in process, and a feeling of solidarity."[85] The issue of Indigenous networking is central to Shzr Ee Tan's contribution to this collection on the music of the Amis in Taiwan. She assesses the role of new musical media in tapping into existing networks (based on kinship, village life, local and national institutions, and analog media) and bringing about new networks in Amis society that not only bridge rural/urban and homeland/diaspora divides, but also forge larger Aborigine/non-Aborigine networks. Pointing out the high use of Internet in Taiwan, she explains that a digital divide is marked less by ethnicity and geography than by generation. Indeed, younger Amis musicians and audiences have harnessed the potential of digital media for strengthening an Amis public sphere. Tan discusses, among other case studies, the young, cosmopolitan, and digitally creative Amis singer Suming. Suming, she writes, draws on a long history of "Indigenous nationalism" and "Indigenous musical activism" in the way he addresses political issues, revives local traditions, strengthens language, and engages in education and outreach through his songs, music videos, participation at cultural and political events, and exploitation of online platforms. Building on the concept of musical "ecosystems" explored in her monograph,[86] Tan reveals how Suming creates, transforms, and plays with notions of "virtual networks," through creative work that attempts to bridge generational divides and addresses both Indigenous and non-Indigenous audiences. But Tan is cautious of overemphasizing the impact of digital technology, arguing instead that new media become enmeshed within existing Amis and national social, institutional, and media structures. What this highlights, then, is that Indigenous musical networks enabled by digital culture might indeed nurture, strengthen, and transform imagined communities that challenge notions of citizenship and bypass state boundaries. But these networks are embedded in offline local, national, and international social and institutional structures and the everyday realities of rural, urban and cosmopolitan Indigenous life. Moreover, they may be strongly shaped along rural/urban, generational and class divides. Digital media thus become part of, augment, and in turn reconfigure the complex and contradictory work toward Indigenous sovereignty.

Gaining political recognition and achieving authorship over Indigenous representations have been central aspects of working toward sovereignty, aspects that have also been rendered more circuitous since the arrival of digital technologies. Within Indigenous contexts, musical performance has long been a site where Indigenous artists can demand wider recognition and have an impact on images of Indigeneity. Thus it is no surprise that Internet platforms such as YouTube can both reify and transform notions of Indigeneity as well as engender what Michelle Bigenho has termed "intimate distance" between Indigenous subjectivities and international audiences.[87] This is the topic of Fiorella Montero-Diaz's chapter on Andean "fusion" music in Peru. Here, she discusses contemporary representations of Indigeneity in Peru, a country with a complex hierarchy of ethnicities, where Indigenous mobilization has been less successful than in neighboring Latin American countries, but whose society is increasingly debating Indigenous rights. Montero-Diaz's study is based on the results and analysis of a Internet survey she undertook on the reception of three YouTube videos among elite communities in Lima, in order to investigate their perceptions of Andean Indigenous culture. The videos by three famous but contrasting Peruvian artists—Miki González, Damaris Mallma, and Magaly Solier—elicited diverse responses from the 70 respondents, responses which highlight problematic but transforming notions of Indigenous "authenticity," national identity, and Andean heritage shaped by issues of language, livelihood, and location evoked within the music videos. While acknowledging that YouTube can reify stereotypes and consolidate perceived segregation, Montero-Diaz concludes that these videos offer a space for national debate and Indigenous agency. Also in the present volume, Tan highlights how a network of Internet sites (by national ministries, NGOs, tourist boards, research institutions, musicians, and fans) offers diverse representations of Amis music and musicians. She admits that "digital remediation is key to reclaiming aboriginal artists' multiple identities as musicians consciously plugged into technological developments, urban life and politics." Nonetheless, what emerges from her rich online and offline ethnographic account is that this wide and entangled network of contrasting and overlapping representations complicates notions of authorship, thus rendering the aspiration of sovereignty precarious.

Production, Mediation, Consumption

One of the most significant impacts of digital media is in the realm of Indigenous music production, mediation, and consumption. As several chapters in this volume demonstrate, these transforming aspects of digital culture reconfigure Indigenous experiences and subjectivities in multifarious ways. In his research on Andean Huayno music, Joshua Tucker explores the loaded aesthetic and political dimensions of musical production and dissemination, arguing that producers can both capitalize on as well as subvert globalizing forces.[88] Indeed, music studios can be sites where struggles for authorship and power play out between musicians, producers, and the music industry along lines of class, gender, and "race."[89] Chris Scale's work on the "recording culture" of powwow music highlights how these conflicting power relations surface in studio recording but also how studios can lead to new social dynamics and creative possibilities that benefit Indigenous artists.[90] Similarly, Karl Neuenfeldt traces a history of recording Indigenous musical performance in the Torres Strait, initially as part of ethnographic and archival projects, through the production of "quasi-commercialized field recordings," to the emergence of local recording studios and finally in-home studios by Indigenous musicians themselves.[91] Such changes, he posits, have enabled a greater control and authorship by Indigenous communities over their own musical heritage.[92] This points to the ways in which in a digital era musicians have, as noted by Theberge, become "consumers of technology," thus blurring the line between music production and consumption.[93] Indeed, these studies reveal how the growing availability and affordability of digital recording technology has transformed the power relations between Indigenous communities, majority populations, and international recording industry. The proliferation of local studios, Indigenous record labels, and the marketing of Indigenous artists themselves via Internet platforms (YouTube, Facebook, SoundCloud), while fitting into and building upon existing social, institutional and economic networks, is certainly more than simply symbolic of cultural self-determination.

Musical production, mediation, and consumption can also assist the revival of Indigenous musical traditions and cosmologies. Such issues have been the focus of research by Diamond, who has elsewhere investigated how CD recording and production by Native Americans not only have aesthetic significance, but can also be "forms of social action" with regard to local community building, cultural transmission, and transnational activism.[94] In the present volume, Diamond argues that the studio is an important site for experimenting with Indigenous creativity and the production of multiple meanings for musicians, producers, and listeners. She focuses, in particular, on issues of genre and gender, temporality and space, as well as polyvalence, highlighting how the experiences of musicians, producers and listeners, and the meanings they associate with the mentioned examples of Sámi music, can both diverge and overlap in interesting ways. On the one hand, Diamond reveals that studio recording may still pose challenges to Sámi artists in terms of vocal technique, the dialogic nature of the vocal tradition *joik*, and the common practice of *joiking* outdoors. On the other hand, she argues that Sámi studio production can help nurture and emphasize facets of vocal technique and ontologies of *joik* while also alluding to wider aspects of Sámi cosmology. Such a study attests to the creative possibilities enabled in digital musical production, offering seemingly infinite ways to both restore and transform Indigenous musical traditions and cosmologies in the twenty-first century.

One particular way in which digital studio technologies can build on Indigenous cosmologies is through playing with conceptualizations of time and place. Historical recordings, for example, can be accessed, sampled, and remixed with ease in contemporary Indigenous music production, as noted by Diamond both elsewhere and in this volume.[95] One example is the *joik* "Čálkko-Niillas" on the album *Máttaráhku Askái* by *joiker* Ulla Pirttijärvi, which brings out temporal aspects of the ontologies of *joik*: "Sámi performers . . . see the archive sample as a means of bringing the liveness of the past into the present. A significant part of traditional *joik* performance in a community context is the fact that one *joik* may be 'answered' by another." Diamond interprets this particular example as collapsing time, thus undermining universal conceptions of history.[96] Likewise, the potentials of digital media in studio production have also been harnessed by Indigenous musicians to reaffirm and expand Indigenous philosophies relating to place and environment. Drawing on Greene, Diamond also explores how Sámi CD production can "sound spatiality" by referencing places and spaces.[97] In particular, she notes the ways in which the mixing of field recordings can help in the construction of what *joiker* Wimme Saari calls "sound worlds." But these references are not necessarily simply to the Indigenous homeland; they also index other global locations encountered during travel and musical tours. Thus, Indigenous digital music production might indeed articulate attachments to place that reaffirm belonging to Indigenous land, but they can also articulate transnational belongings that bring into question essentialist notions of home.[98] In these ways, the fluid nature of space and time engendered by digital media can be harnessed by Indigenous musicians both to reaffirm Indigenous cosmologies and to articulate alternative temporalities and cosmopolitan cartographies that resist modernist categorization.

Yet we should not forget the experience of Indigenous musicians working in less wealthy parts of the globe where digital production might not reap the same level of cultural capital. This is Henry Stobart's warning at the opening of his contribution on music video production in Bolivia, a country famous for its poverty and large Indigenous population. He offers a study of the *originario* musician, producer and cultural activist Gregorio Mamani, focusing on the production of music videos on VCD (video compact disc), a commonplace format among low-income people in the global south, but little known in the global north. Following the production of three music videos, Stobart discusses issues of audiovisual aesthetics and the opportunities offered by Mamani's modest studio to take issue with hegemonic middle-class notions of "amateurish" production. Stobart is cautious of literature in music studies that has argued for the revolutionary potential of home studio technologies, suggesting we should take seriously a "low-tech aesthetic." Likewise, he is critical of literature within film studies on Indigenous film projects in Latin America that has the potential to essentialize and romanticize notions of "Indigenous aesthetics." Thus, drawing on Hutchby, Stobart proposes the notion of "creative pragmatism" to interrogate more closely both the local economics and aesthetics of Indigenous digital media production as well as the impact they have on wider Indigenous publics.[99] Such a study alerts us to the ways in which music and music video production, mediation, and consumption is enmeshed in entangled webs of technical affordances, economic wealth, local and national Indigenous imaginaries, as well as individual and collective aesthetics.

Archives, Transmission, Orality

The greater access to, distribution, and affordability of digital music technologies also allows for transforming relationships between Indigenous communities and their musical heritages. As discussed above, many Indigenous oral traditions have been recorded and subjected to various types of documentation, collecting, and archiving within a paradigm of salvage ethnography. While this has meant that there is much audio documentation of Indigenous musical heritage, Indigenous communities have in most cases had little or no access to such documentation. Owing to the fragility and limited life spans of certain analog media formats, much documentation also risks being lost or becoming obsolete. Following pressure from certain Indigenous cultural activists, there has in the last two decades been a move to digitize and repatriate archive collections to source communities.[100] Issues of archives, digitization, and access are addressed by Barwick in the present collection, where she discusses her research on *djanba*, the ceremonial song of the Murriny Patha people, in the township of Wadeye, Northwest Australia. Barwick's work draws from a collaborative project between a number of national and local institutions that set out to digitize and document recordings in a database that has become an important tool by which communities can search, access, and employ recordings in community ceremonial events.[101] By focusing on local funeral songs, she analyzes a marked change afforded by digital media in funeral practice both in the ease of playback opportunities and the emergence of newly composed songs. Reflecting on creativity, social organization, and notions of democracy, Barwick surmises that these technologies have both strengthened existing predilections toward community autonomy and potentially jeopardized clan structures and funeral traditions. Her study, thus, testifies to the ways in which digital archives can provide significant resources for Indigenous communities that can both sustain as well as transform Indigenous musical traditions and cosmologies, often in surprising and unprecedented ways.

Likewise, digital technologies can help nurture the transmission and education of Indigenous musical traditions. Scholars have highlighted the malleability of digital technologies to suit the needs of users.[102] This malleability makes digital music technologies ripe for use in what Landzelius might call "inreach" contexts, such as in Indigenous education.[103] One aspect of digital culture, its ability to bring about a new sense of orality, might be commensurate with ontologies of Indigenous musical performance, as suggested in John-Carlos Perea's chapter. Perea examines his own transition from analog to digital technologies through an autoethnographic account of powwow learning, performing, and teaching in the San Francisco Bay Area. He first discusses how he learned powwow repertoire, technique, and philosophy in the mid-1990s using audiocassettes—cassettes that were later used as an archive for repertoire by members of Perea's new group, the Sweetwater Singers, even as certain digital recording devices become available in the early 2000s. As digital recording technology became more accessible and versatile, Perea began to experiment with vocal overdubbing in 2007 in his work with the Paul Winter Consort, which enabled individual creativity to take place of group activity. Finally, Perea discusses his use of digital recording media to facilitate his teaching of American Indian music at San Francisco State University. Here, he highlights how the sociality involved in his earlier cassette recording practices means that they will always inform his contemporary practice and teaching. Thus, the cassettes form an "aural history archive" of local powwow song and "repositories of traditional knowledge" which, alongside other digital technologies and the flexibility they offer, continues to inform current practice. Moreover, Perea argues that the use of technologies in learning, performing and teaching, as well as the personal, social and aesthetic implications they have, are commensurate with the orality necessary for the transmission of Indigenous traditions. Indeed, he stresses the ever-transforming nature of his archives, necessary for the sociality and vitality of the ever-changing tradition of powwow. Elsewhere I have argued, drawing on Diana Taylor's notion of the archive and repertoire,[104] that the digitization and repatriation of sound archives to Indigenous communities can feed back into education and performance contexts that nurture new forms of orality commensurate with Indigenous musical ontologies.[105] This not only assists cultural revival but can also be a powerful articulation of Indigeneity in challenging logocentric notions of culture in modernity. What the examples in the present volume highlight, however, is more ambiguous. Firstly, they show how analog and digital technologies continue to have a complex mutual relationship that may indeed assist and transform notions of orality. Moreover, the ubiquity and legacy of the archive (both analog and digital) in global modernity suggest that new potentials for nurturing orality rest, uncomfortably or not, alongside archival ways of knowing, a dynamic which will continue to shape Indigenous musical performance.

Subjectivity, Ownership, Authorship

Concerns about the cultural heritage of Indigenous communities within a digital era have brought new understandings of subjectivity, ownership and intellectual property. The subject of Indigenous cultural heritage is politicized not only due to histories of cultural dispossession but also because Indigenous musical ontologies hold complex notions of ownership and customary law that often necessitate particular sensitivities regarding the performance and use of musical traditions. Recording technologies (both analog and digital), because they can reproduce and distribute sound in ways that complicate the relationship between composer, performer, and listener, can become politically charged when employed by musicians, producers, teachers, archivists, or ethnomusicologists. Over the last decades, the nonconsensual use of recordings of Indigenous music in global popular-music hits has led to accusations of musical "appropriation" and several high-profile court cases.[106] This has led to critiques of intellectual property laws that privilege Western notions of authorship and originality in capitalist economies over notions of collective composition, group ownership, and orality common in Indigenous cultures.[107] Indigenous musicians and communities have addressed these challenges in diverse ways, sometimes adopting and sometimes challenging international copyright laws. Wallace reminds us in the present volume that "technology needs an informed, consensual, and contextual agreement with cultural practitioners. I, as a traditional singer, need to know that the music I share will not be used to sell beer or put into any other context that might bring harm to the songs." Nonetheless, he is wary of resorting to narrow definitions of ownership: "As an individual I do not own the songs but I am part of a larger community which collectively owns the songs. Some would say that the songs are part of what has gone on before and we honor those before us by keeping the songs alive and sharing them. To give the power of ownership to a select few inhibits the transmission to the future." Indeed, he recounts a project whereby his own Salish chief and council did not grant permission for him to release a recording of songs imparted to him by his mother. Thus, he poses the provocative question: "I understand the importance of protecting our songs but what is the price of doing so when so few know the songs?" Wallace's experience alerts us to the challenges for Indigenous artists and communities who both strive to maintain traditional notions of collective ownership and sharing as well as search for ways to regulate access by, and engender respectful use among wider publics.

As digital media become more pervasive, Indigenous artists have articulated more complex and divergent forms of authorship and subjectivity. Tan's monograph highlights the legacy of the mid-1990s court case surrounding Enigma's 1993 global hit "Return to Innocence," based on contemporary Amis musical performance.[108] Within the present volume, she reveals how heightened concerns of copyright within contemporary Amis society have resulted in greater remuneration for performers, complicated legal negotiations for intellectual property, and websites that safeguard content by various means. Among younger generations, nevertheless, she observes that "with constant reproduction and remediation of music, the long-debated issue of copyright is slowly becoming a moot point." On the one hand, then, the ease of musical recording, transfer, sampling, and selling in the digital world would suggest that Indigenous music is more vulnerable to cases of "appropriation." On the other hand, those Indigenous communities that participate avidly in digital culture have found creative ways of protecting and sharing Indigenous music among friends and fans that criss-cross local and transnational networks. Thus, the digital era has brought about new notions of Indigenous subjectivity, ownership, and authorship that might be seen to collude with—or challenge—the principles of Western legal notions of intellectual property.

The very foundations of copyright law are themselves being challenged by new forms of formal and informal digital musical consumption and exchange in both Indigenous and non-Indigenous contexts. Scale's study of the pow-wow recording industry has demonstrated how local and regional Indigenous labels adopt their own strategies for maintaining the fluidity of digital musical exchange while also maintaining a commitment to local ethics of sharing: "The business models of these labels revolve around a promise that the ethical self-policing that occurs on the powwow trail—with regard to song ownership, and by extension the ethical values that guide powwow people themselves—will inform and structure the relationship between drum groups and powwow record labels."[109] Meanwhile, Stobart has elsewhere discussed how the emergence of cheaper digital recording technologies and the explosion in musical "piracy" in Bolivia has led to the fall of the recording industry and simultaneous growth of small-scale producers.[110] While middle-class consumers might perceive this as a "democratization" of culture, musicians, producers, and vendors have experienced new and unpredictable opportunities and challenges.[111] Stobart's detailed analysis, thus, reminds us of the complex impact digital media has on issues of power, production, and aesthetics in national and transnational contexts and warns against simplistic and idealistic narratives. Speaking broadly about the contemporary global music market, Sterne asserts, "If we are to reimagine an alternative, better world for musicians and listeners, we will need to look past both the old monopolies over distribution and existing practices of peer-to-peer file-sharing for new models that support a robust musical culture, one not just based on buying and selling."[112] The transformation of musical creativity and consumption in a digital era thus has radical implications for the wider musical industry and notions of musical ownership, collectivity, and distribution. Considering the crisis in international copyright law in a digital era, perhaps Indigenous musical ontologies of composition, and transmission as well as articulations of protecting and sharing in a digital era—such as those suggested in Scales' case studies—can offer alternative global models of musical creativity, subjectivity, and consumption in the twenty-first century.[113]

Cosmologies, Virtuality, Posthumanism

Indigenous cosmologies, virtuality, and posthumanism, offer another matrix of themes that this volume addresses. My own contribution takes issue with Baudrillard's pessimistic account of a world characterized by "simulacra" and the "hyperreal" and instead proposes that Sámi uses of digital simulation might reveal more pertinent issues concerning Indigenous cosmologies, perceptions of reality, and the human.[114] In particular, I focus on Sámi museum exhibitions, CD-ROM software, and music production that support Sámi musical revival, cultural transmission, and the articulation of an Indigenous cosmology that challenges notions of the virtual and the real. By drawing on the literature of virtuality, I discuss how the virtual/real binary is simply a construct of positivistic trends in Enlightenment thought and that notions of alternative worlds have existed in other cultural and historical contexts.[115] Indeed, within a Sámi cosmology, reality consists of three fluid and mutually dependent realms—the human realm, the realm of the dead, and the realm of the spirits. I highlight how the three case studies all allude to these notions of separate but permeable realities and thus serve as a way of reviving a Sámi Indigenous cosmology. This leads me to argue for the wider political significance of digital virtuality: "It is in the sphere of the virtual that humans can adopt new ways of relating to the object world, develop alternative understandings of embodiment and orality, and explore diverse ways of imagining and perceiving reality." Digital media, thus, not only assist in the revival of Indigenous cosmologies but also help us reconsider more broadly how we relate to the lived-in world.

Such an argument also raises important questions concerning the relationship between humans and technology as well as nature and culture. Tina K. Ramnarine has elsewhere argued that Sámi studio composition, in response to environmental devastation and global warming in the polar regions, can be a way of articulating the interconnections between humans and nature.[116] Likewise, I highlight in this volume how the Sámi *joiker*, lawyer, and academic Ánde Somby articulates a link between humans and technology by alluding to notions of Haraway's cyborg.[117] Through discussing Somby's exploration with vocal technique, I show how the computer is positioned as a "friendly self" which highlights the potentials of Haraway's feminist manifesto for indigenous articulations.

Tan addresses notions of posthumanism, highlighting the ubiquity of digital media in contemporary Taiwanese life. She proposes that, for musicians like Suming, new media are simply "prosthetics for life at large." Indeed, we might think of digital media as part of wider social relations: "One could say that the evolving state of music and indigeneity—certainly in aboriginal Taiwan—is less a digital than postdigital issue, where new media has become a large part of an ecosystem interrogating what it means to be a human." These notions of the "posthuman" and "postdigital" raise important ethical questions about the human body and collective identities. Subjectivity, the body, and the human are politicized topics within postcolonial studies that may not fit comfortably with the notions of fractured identities and cyborgs embraced within postmodern theory and media studies.[118] Indeed, we should caution against romanticized and essentialized notions of Indigenous cyborgs, considering the ways in which technologies continue to be exploited by state authorities and multinational companies not only in the violence against and marginalization of Indigenous communities, but also in environmental degradation of Indigenous land and wider global ecosystems. Nonetheless, the case studies in this volume demonstrate how questions of the relationship between humans, nature, and technology in diverse articulations of Indigeneity are ripe for further interrogation. Indeed, as we have seen, Indigenous traditional knowledges in pre- and postdigital contexts point to new conceptualizations of science and technology, and thus, the questions posed here will undoubtedly prove to be pertinent to future studies of music, Indigeneity, and digital media.

❦   ❦   ❦

This book is a result of the symposium *Music, Indigeneity, and Digital Media* held at the Department of Music, Royal Holloway, University of London, in April 2010, organized by Shzr Ee Tan, Henry Stobart, and myself. It was sponsored by Helen Gilbert as part of her wider project on *Indigeneity in the Contemporary World: Performance, Politics, Belonging* (funded by the European Research Council) as well as the Faculty of Arts and Social Sciences at Royal Holloway, University of London.[119] Many of the presenters at the event have contributed to this volume with studies that draw on their extensive work on musical performance and practices within Indigenous communities around the world. The key questions we posed in the invitation to the symposium were framed around issues of representation and self-determination; revival and repatriation; ownership and transmission; centers and peripheries; production, mediation, and consumption; transnationalism and cosmopolitanism; and virtual ethnography. These issues were taken up, explored and developed in exciting and creative ways by each presenter, which the current contributors then developed further for the current volume. Their rich texts and theoretical insights offer important perspectives on contemporary Indigenous musical traditions, extend timely political debates, and point to emerging trajectories further into the twenty-first century. As such, it is hoped that this book can provide a useful resource for scholars in a variety of disciplines, for readers interested in Indigenous music and music technologies, and also for Indigenous musicians and cultural activists throughout the globe. But the book also hints at larger social, cultural, and political transformations that might be valuable to an even wider readership. Addressing the significance of Indigenous media use for understanding the digital age, Faye Ginsburg argues that "Indigenous media offer some other coordinates for understanding what such an interconnected world might be like outside a hegemonic order"—"examples of alternative modernities, resources of hope, new dynamics in social movements, or as part of the trajectory of Indigenous life in the twenty-first century."[120] Indeed, we hope this book can shed light on such diverse potential futures, as musical performance, Indigenous aspirations to sovereignty, and digital media continue to transform and be transformed in global modernities.[121]

Notes

1. "Digital media" is also often termed "new media" and "information and com-munications technologies" (ICTs).

2. I mainly adopt the terms "Indigenous" and "Indigeneity" in this chapter, though other contributors employ other terms (capitalized or not) including "Aboriginal," "Native," "First Nations," "American Indian," "*originario*," and "Fourth World," which might have slightly different nuances and currency in particular geographical and political contexts. I have chosen to capitalize these terms in line with scholars in Indigenous studies and in keeping with new prac-tices in North American and Australian contexts. I have left it to the discretion of the individual contributors what terms, and with lower- or uppercase, they feel are appropriate for the regional contexts they work in depending on local histories, cultural sensitivities, political activism, and scholarship.

3. Timothy D. Taylor, *Strange Sounds: Music, Technology & Culture* (New York: Routledge, 2001), 41–44.

4. Pamela Wilson and Michelle Stewart, "Indigeneity and Indigenous Media on the Global Stage," in *Global Indigenous Media: Cultures, Poetics, and Politics*, ed. Pamela Wilson and Michelle Stewart (Durham, NC: Duke University Press, 2008), 5.

5. Georgina Born, "On Musical Mediation: Ontology, Technology and Creativity," *Twentieth-Century Music* 2, no. 1 (2005): 7–36.

6. James S. Anaya, *Indigenous Peoples in International Law*, 2nd ed. (Oxford: Oxford University Press, 2004), 3.

7. Martinéz Cobo, "Report to the UN Sub-Commission on the Prevention of Discrimination of Minorities" (United Nations, 1986).

8. James Clifford, *The Predicament of Culture: Twentieth-Century Ethnography, Literature, and Art* (Cambridge, MA: Harvard University Press, 1988), 189–214.

9. Henry Minde, "The Making of an International Movement of Indigenous Peoples," *Scandinavian Journal of History* 21, no. 3 (1996): 222–30.

10. Henry Minde, "The Destination and the Journey: Indigenous Peoples and the United Nations from the 1960s through 1985," in *Indigenous Peoples: Self-Determination, Knowledge, Indigeneity*, ed. Henry Minde et al. (Delft, NL: Eburon, 2008), 52–53.

11. Ibid. 58–81.

12. Henry Minde, "The Challenge of Indigenism: The Struggle for Sami Land Rights and Self-Government in Norway 1960–1990," in *Indigenous Peoples: Resource Management and Global Rights*, ed. Henry Minde, Ragnar Nilsen, and Svein Jentoft (Delft, NL: Eburon, 2003), 97–99.

13. Russel Lawrence Barsh, "Indigenous Peoples in the 1990s: From the Object to Subject of International Law," *Harvard Human Rights Journal* 7, no. 2 (1994): 33–86.

14. United Nations, "United Nations Declaration on the Rights of Indigenous Peoples," March 2008, http://un.org/esa/socdev/unpfii/documents/DRIPS _en.pdf.

15. See Michael R. Dove, "Indigenous People and Environmental Politics," *Annual Review of Anthropology* 35 (2006): 192–208.
16. See Michael F. Brown, *Who Owns Native Culture?* (Cambridge, MA: Harvard University Press, 2003).
17. I thank Henry Stobart for this insight.
18. I thank Shzr Ee Tan for emphasizing this point in an earlier draft of this chapter.
19. James Clifford, "Indigenous Articulations," *The Contemporary Pacific* 3, no. 2 (2001): 468–90.
20. See Linda Tuhiwai Smith, *Decolonizing Methodologies: Research and Indigenous Peoples* (London: Zed Books, 1999), 19–41.
21. Fikret Berkes, *Sacred Ecology: Traditional Ecological Knowledge and Resource Management* (Philadelphia: Taylor & Francis, 1999); Roy Ellen, Peter Parkes, and Alan Bicker, eds., *Indigenous Environmental Knowledge and Its Transformations: Critical Anthropological Perspectives* (Amsterdam: Harwood Academic Publishers, 2000); Henry Minde, Ragnar Nilsen, and Svein Jentoft, eds., *Indigenous Peoples: Resource Management and Global Rights* (Delft, NL: Eburon, 2003).
22. I am grateful for one anonymous reviewer of the book manuscript for highlighting this point.
23. Darrell Addison Posey and Graham Dutfield, *Beyond Intellectual Property: Toward Traditional Resource Rights for Indigenous Peoples and Local Communities* (Ottawa, ON: International Development Research Centre, 1996).
24. Anaya, *Indigenous Peoples in International Law*, 4; Karena Shaw, *Indigeneity and Political Theory: Sovereignty and the Limits of the Political* (London: Routledge, 2008), 203–12; Duncan Ivison, Paul Patton, and Will Sanders, "Introduction" in *Political Theory and the Rights of Indigenous Peoples*, edited by Duncan Ivison, Paul Patton, and Will Sanders (Cambridge: Cambridge University Press, 2000), 1–21.
25. Kyra Landzelius, "Introduction: Native on the Net," in *Native on the Net: Indigenous and Diasporic Peoples in the Virtual Age*, ed. Kyra Landzelius (London: Routledge, 2006), 2.
26. Shaw, *Indigeneity and Political Theory*, 211.
27. Max Horkheimer and Theodor W. Adorno, *Dialectic of Enlightenment*, trans. John Cumming (London: Verso, 2010).
28. See also Paddy Scannell, *Media and Communication* (Los Angeles, CA: SAGE, 2007), 31–51.
29. Arjun Appadurai, *Modernity at Large: Cultural Dimensions of Globalization* (Minneapolis: University of Minnesota Press, 1996), 1–26.
30. Taylor, *Strange Sounds*, 201.
31. Ibid., 7–8.
32. Raymond Williams, *Television: Technology and Cultural Form* (London: Routledge, 2003), 1–25.
33. Ibid., 6.
34. Mark Poster, *The Mode of Information: Poststructuralism and Social Context* (Cambridge: Polity Press, 1990), 6.

35. Jonathan Sterne, *The Audible Past: Cultural Origins of Sound Reproduction* (Durham, NC; Duke University Press, 2003), 336.
36. Mark Poster, *The Second Media Age* (Cambridge: Polity Press, 1995), 91.
37. Andrew Chadwick, *Internet Politics: States, Citizens, and New Communication Technologies* (New York: Oxford University Press, 2006), 4; Howard Rheingold, *The Virtual Community: Homesteading on the Electronic Frontier*, 2nd ed. (Cambridge, MA: MIT Press, 2000), xxix–xxx.
38. Landzelius, "Introduction." 17–19.
39. Wilson and Stewart, "Indigeneity and Indigenous Media," 21.
40. Landzelius, "Introduction," 18.
41. Faye Ginsburg, "Rethinking the Digital Age," in *Global Indigenous Media: Cultures, Poetics, and Politics*, ed. Pamela Wilson and Michelle Stewart (Durham, NC: Duke University Press, 2008), 301; Landzelius, "Introduction," 11.
42. Landzelius, "Introduction," 2.
43. Chadwick, *Internet Politics*, 49–80.
44. Laurel Evelyn Dyson, Max Hendriks, and Stephen Grant, "Preface," in *Information Technology and Indigenous People*, ed. Dyson, Hendriks, and Grant (London: Information Science Publishing, 2007), x.
45. Ginsburg, "Rethinking the Digital Age," 293.
46. Evgeny Morozov, *The Net Delusion: How Not to Liberate the World* (London: Allen Lane, 2011).
47. Rheingold, *The Virtual Community*, 308.
48. Manuel Castells, *The Rise of the Network Society*, 2nd ed. (Oxford: Wiley-Blackwell, 2010), 407–99.
49. Dyson, Hendriks, and Grant, "Preface," xxi.
50. Landzelius, "Introduction," 12, 31.
51. Castells, *The Rise of the Network Society*, 407.
52. Lev Manovich, "Database as Symbolic Form," in *Convergence: The International Journal of Research into New Media Technologies* 5, no. 2 (1999): 81.
53. See Barwick in this volume.
54. Castells, *The Rise of the Network Society*, 259.
55. Landzelius, "Introduction," 6, 8. For discussion of the articulation of alternative notions of time, space and spirituality in Native American Film, see Michelle H. Raheja, *Reservation Reelism: Redfacing, Visual Sovereignty, and Representations of Native Americans in Film* (Lincoln: University of Nebraska Press, 2010), 203.
56. Poster, *The Mode of Information*. 14–15.
57. Chris Shilling, *The Body in Culture, Technology and Society* (London: SAGE, 2005), 177.
58. Donna J. Haraway, "The Cyborg Manifesto: Science, Technology, and Socialist-Feminism in the Late Twentieth Century," in *Simians, Cyborgs and Women: The Reinvention of Nature*, ed. Donna J. Haraway (New York: Routledge, 1991), 149–81.
59. For a discussion of the tensions between postcolonial and postmodern subjectivity, see Mahdi Teimouri, "On the Question of Overlap between the Postcolonial and the Postmodern," *Sarjana* 27, no. 2 (2012): 1–12.

60. See Tina K. Ramnarine, "Acoustemology, Indigeneity, and Joik in Valkeapää's Symphonic Activism: Views from Europe's Arctic Fringes for Environmental Ethnomusicology," *Ethnomusicology* 53, no. 2 (2009): 187–217.

61. See Miller, *Understanding Digital Culture.*

62. Jean Baudrillard, *Simulacra and Simulation* (Ann Arbor: University of Michigan Press, 1994), 1–42.

63. Tom Boellstorff, *Coming of Age in Second Life: An Anthropologist Explores the Virtually Human* (Princeton, NJ: Princeton University Press, 2008), 248; Rob Shields, *The Virtual* (London: Routledge, 2003), 13, 60, 65.

64. Castells, *The Rise of the Network Society,* 356.

65. Marshall McLuhan, *The Gutenberg Galaxy: The Making of Typographic Man* (London: Routledge & Paul, 1962), 31–32, 46; see also Coppélie Cocq, "From the Árran to the Internet: Sami Storytelling in Digital Environments," *Oral Tradition* 28, no. 1 (2013): 127; Castells, *The Rise of the Network Society,* 392; Scannell, *Media and Communication,* 138–39.

66. Dyson, Hendriks, and Grant, "Preface," xvi.

67. Cocq, "From the Árran to the Internet." 127–28, 133.

68. Erika Brady, *A Spiral Way: How the Phonograph Changed Ethnography* (Jackson: University Press of Mississippi, 1999), 1–9.

69. Ibid., 2.

70. Sterne, *The Audible Past,* 26–27.

71. Brady, *A Spiral Way,* 16, 28.

72. René T. A. Lysloff and Leslie C. Gay Jr., "Introduction: Ethnomusicology in the Twenty-First Century," in *Music and Technoculture,* ed. Rene T. A. Lysloff and Leslie C. Gay Jr. (Middletown, CT: Weslyan University Press, 2003), 3; Sterne, *The Audible Past,* 321; Taylor, *Strange Sounds,* 8.

73. Wilson and Stewart, "Indigeneity and Indigenous Media," 3.

74. René T. A. Lysloff, "Mozart in Mirrorshades: Ethnomusicology, Technology, and the Politics of Representation," *Ethnomusicology* 41, no. 2 (1997): 217.

75. Frederick Williams, *The Communications Revolution* (Beverly Hills, CA: SAGE, 1982), 195.

76. Taylor, *Strange Sounds;* Lysloff and Gay, "Introduction,"; Paul D. Greene, "Wired Sound and Sonic Cultures," in *Wired for Sound: Engineering and Technologies in Sonic Cultures,* ed. Paul D. Greene and Thomas Porcello (Middletown, CT: Wesleyan University Press, 2005).

77. For a discussion of digital music education and issues of class and gender, see Georgina Born and Kyle Devine, "Music Technology, Gender, and Class: Digitization, Educational and Social Change in Britain," *Twentieth-Century Music* 12, no. 2 (2015): 135–72.

78. Lysloff and Gay "Introduction," 3.

79. Taylor, *Strange Sounds,* 22–38; Lysloff and Gay, "Introduction," 8.

80. Landzelius, "Introduction," 2.

81. Lysloff and Gay, "Introduction," 11; Wilson and Stewart, "Indigeneity and Indigenous Media," 5.

82. Jonathan Sterne, *MP3: The Meaning of a Format* (Durham, NC: Duke University Press, 2012), 25–26.

83. Fredric Jameson, "Notes on Globalization as a Philosophical Issue," in *The Cultures of Globalization*, ed. Fredric Jameson and Masao Miyoshi (Durham, NC: Duke University Press, 1998), 54–80.

84. For a study of the "democratizing" potentials of digital media in an increasingly multicultural UK, see Georgina Born, "Digitising Democracy," *Political Quarterly* 76, no. 1 (2005): 102–23.

85. Byron Dueck, *Musical Intimacies and Indigenous Imaginaries: Aboriginal Music and Dance in Public Performance* (New York: Oxford University Press, 2013), 6.

86. Shzr Ee Tan, *Beyond "Innocence": Amis Aboriginal Song in Taiwan as an Ecosystem* (Farnham, UK: Ashgate, 2012).

87. Michelle Bigenho, *Intimate Distance: Andean Music in Japan* (Durham, NC: Duke University Press, 2012), 23–29.

88. Joshua Tucker, *Gentleman Troubadours and Andean Pop Stars: Huayno Music, Media Work, and Ethnic Imaginaries in Urban Peru* (Chicago: University of Chicago Press, 2013), 144.

89. See, for example, Louise Meintjes, *Sound of Africa: Making Music Zulu in a South African Studio* (Durham, NC: Duke University Press, 2003).

90. Christopher A. Scales, *Recording Culture: Powwow Music and the Aboriginal Recording Industry on the Northern Plains* (Durham, NC: Duke University Press, 2012). See also Christopher A. Scales, "The Politics and Aesthetics of Recording: A Comparative Canadian Case Study of Powwow and Contemporary Native American Music," *The World of Music* 44, no. 1 2002): 41–59.

91. Karl Neuenfeldt, "Notes on the Engagement of Indigenous Peoples with Recording Technology and Techniques, the Recording Industry and Researchers," *The World of Music* 49 (2007): 8–13.

92. Ibid., 7; see also Karl Neuenfeldt, "'Bring the Past to Present': Recording and Reviving Rotuman Music via a Collaborative Rotuman/Fijian/Australian CD Project," *The World of Music* 49, no. 1 (2007): 83–103.

93. Paul Theberge, *Any Sound You Can Imagine: Making Music/Consuming Technology* (Hanover, NH: University Press of New England, 1997), 4–6.

94. Beverley Diamond, "Media as Social Action: Native American Musicians in the Recording Studio," in *Wired for Sound: Engineering and Technologies in Sonic Cultures*, ed. Paul D. Greene and Thomas Porcello (Middletown, CT: Wesleyan University Press, 2005), 83–103.

95. See also Beverley Diamond, "'Allowing the Listener to Fly as They Want to': Sámi Perspectives on Indigenous CD Production in Northern Europe," *The World of Music* 49, no. 1 (2007): 23–48.

96. Beverley Diamond, "The Music of Modern Indigeneity: From Identity to Alliance Studies," *ESEM* 12 (2007): 184; see also Diamond, "'Allowing the Listener to Fly,'" 27.

97. Greene, "Wired Sound and Sonic Cultures," 9.

98. Landzelius, "Introduction," 3.

99. Ian Hutchby, "Technologies, Texts and Affordances," *Sociology* 35, no. 2 (2001): 441–56.

100. The term "repatriation" itself has certain ideological and legal connotations that might not fit comfortably with indigenous philosophies and experiences,

as Perea notes in this volume. Carolyn Landau and Janet Topp Fargion, "We're All Archivists Now: Towards a More Equitable Ethnomusicology," *Ethnomusicology Forum* 21, no. 2 (2012): 134.

101. This project is also documented in Linda Barwick, Nicholas Reid, and Lysbeth Ford, "Communities of Interest: Issues in Establishing a Digital Resource on Murrinh-Patha Song at Wadeye (Port Keats), NT," *Literary and Linguistic Computing* 20, no. 4 (2005): 383–97.

102. Greene, "Wired Sound and Sonic Cultures," 6–7; Taylor, *Strange Sounds,* 19.

103. Landzelius, "Introduction," 5; Dyson, Hendriks, and Grant, "Preface," xiii.

104. Diana Taylor, *Performing Cultural Memory in the Americas* (Durham, NC: Duke University Press, 2003).

105. Thomas R. Hilder, "Repatriation, Revival and Transmission: The Politics of a Sámi Cultural Heritage," *Ethnomusicology Forum* 21, no. 2 (2012): 161–79.

106. Hugo Zemp, "The/an Ethnomusicologist and the Record Business," *Yearbook for Traditional Music* 28 (1996): 36–56.

107. Simon Frith, "Music and Morality," in *Music and Copyright,* ed. Simon Frith (Edinburgh: Edinburgh University Press, 1993); Sherylle Mills, "Indigenous Music and the Law: An Analysis of National and International Legislation," *Yearbook of Traditional Music* 28 (1996).

108. Tan, *Beyond "Innocence,"* 1–6.

109. Scales, *Recording Culture,* 281.

110. Henry Stobart, "Rampant Reproduction and Digital Democracy: Shifting Landscapes of Music Production and 'Piracy' in Bolivia," *Ethnomusicology Forum* 19, no. 1 (2010): 27–56.

111. Ibid., 50–51.

112. Sterne, *MP3: The Meaning of a Format,* 28.

113. See, for example, Thomas R. Hilder, *Sámi Musical Performance and the Politics of Indigeneity in Northern Europe* (Lanham, MD: Rowman & Littlefield, 2015), 149–86.

114. Baudrillard, *Simulacra and Simulation,* 1–42.

115. Rob Shields, *The Virtual,* 37, 44.

116. Ramnarine, "Acoustemology, Indigeneity, and Joik," 187–217.

117. Haraway, "The Cyborg Manifesto," 178.

118. Teimouri, "On the Question of Overlap," 1–12.

119. Helen Gilbert, web page for *Indigeneity in the Contemporary World: Performance, Politics, Belonging,* accessed September 1, 2016, http://www.indigeneity.net/.

120. Ginsburg, "Rethinking the Digital Age," 304.

121. I am very grateful to Shzr Ee Tan and Henry Stobart as well as the anonymous reviewers for feedback on this chapter.

Chapter One

Taiwan's Aboriginal Music on the Internet

Shzr Ee Tan

More than a decade since the settling of a controversial lawsuit involving pop group Enigma's use of Amis song in the 1993 hit "Return To Innocence," aboriginal musicians in Taiwan are grappling with new ideas about mediation, self-representation, cultural ownership, and musical stewardship. Emerging issues in today's diversified networks of music production and consumption extend beyond old debates about copyright; a newer line of inquiry traces the interacting pathways old and new media platforms have carved out in recent years. This article examines how regionally oriented rural routes established through cassette cultures of the 1980s, still prevalent, are being tapped into by more modern (and superficially "urban") channels of CD distribution. Internet and mobile technology have also remapped old configurations of cultural flow. This is observable not only in the development of parallel online and offline musical communities but also in the widening, global reach of music-inter-faced aboriginal transnationalism. At the same time, these routes have also paved the way for emerging cultural disjunctures. In particular, I investigate how the digital divide can be articulated not as a "Han-vs.-aboriginal" or even a "rural-vs.-urban" pattern, but as a generation gap. I study how this gap is itself bridged through mediated musical practices that integrate live and physical dimensions. I look at how feedback between new and existing communities impacts aboriginal musical ecosystems, and study how cultural identities are deliberately or incidentally represented.

The sections to follow first challenge the idea of "newness" in new media, reexamining old tropes of recontextualization understood through differen-tiated aboriginal experiences of twenty-first century digitality. Here, unequal access to digital resources, information, and power privilege as well as disadvantage intersecting categories of cultural insiders and outsiders and the technologically savvy. Often, the digital quest for a musical connection requires the querent to know exactly what he or she is looking for, even before multiple hidden pathways to the holy grail can show themselves: thus, even slight alterations of Internet music video search parameters lead to dramatically different results. Next, I study how specific parties—from national institutions to commercial players, from local communities to cyberactivists—hold different digital stakes in the game of information representation and music exchange. Frequently, conflicting and situational identities, as well as objectives, cloud the negotiations: do aboriginal musicians in Taiwan want to be represented primarily as aborigines, or as musicians? Do they care about Han or overseas audiences as much as we think they do? How does Internet technology bolster or undermine these different positions? Finally, I consider new media as a particular Appaduraian "scape," making cross-sections within and beyond other ecosystems of activity—determined by politics in Taiwan, for example, or by global indigenous nationalism. Indeed, one must be wary of fetishizing the novelty and uneven impact of new media. It must be asserted that considerations of the integrated ways in which technology has carved inroads into humanity are crucial: the ubiquity of the digital world is taken for granted in contemporary life in a way that indigeneity is not.

Introduction: What's So "New" about New Media to Aborigines in Taiwan?

The term "new media" has been used since the mid-2000s in reference to Internet-enabled technologies ranging from e-mail, interactive websites, blogs, and social networks to platforms such as Skype, YouTube, Wikipedia, and Facebook.[1] More recently, streaming music, mobile technology and augmented reality have joined the list. Much of the discourse has emphasized the notion of "Version 2.0," which implies the existence of a superior generation of technology and corresponding users who have become content-collaborators. Within this trope of newness, Lawrence Lessig's theories on convergence culture[2] and Bolter and Grusin's take on remediation[3] are useful. Instead of supporting the modernist and deterministic idea that newer technologies necessarily replace older technologies, the writers argue that cultures are always refashioned in relation to (and often in extension of) the past and present.

In the world of digital indigeneity, I argue for a similar approach toward understanding musical production, consumption, and negotiation. This can be seen in changing dynamics of the power to represent. Back in 2000, over my first months of fieldwork as a young, "technologically privileged ethnomusicologist"[4] living among the Amis of Eastern Taiwan, researchers were only just weaning off DAT machines in favor of the short-lived minidisc recorder. My indigenous informants-turned-friends were dancing to cassette tracks blasting from portable boomboxes. Today, field recordings-turned-home-videos are made by young aborigines and researchers on devices ranging from mobile phones to Zoom H2s, even as all generations within the proverbial village continue to sing and dance to a portable CD player or, more recently, an iPod. Where do the technological privileges realign in the corresponding—if asymmetrical—shifts in formats? Kyra Landzelius asks important questions: "Can the info-superhighway be a fast track to greater empowerment for the historically disenfranchised? Or do they risk becoming "roadkill": casualties of hyper-media and the drive to electronically map everything?"[5]

New media has restratified notions of musical marginality among Taiwan's aborigines, making new articulations of frontier, regional identity, and national difference. However, these changes reflect ethics of adaptation rather than obsolescence. They hinge on constant feedback between existing and emerging logics, practices, and the musical communities themselves. Often, these processes work within dynamic ecosystems of song, culture, and technology, as acts of constant rebalancing between human agents, sonic cultures, institutions and technoscapes that are often themselves objects of attainment even as they work as the tools of indigenous musicians and listeners. On the one hand, the websites and search-result rankings singled out as examples in this article will likely expire or become archived in a matter of time—months rather than years. On the other hand, they will—in time-lapsed fashion or remediation—continue to play a part in remaking yet newer musical articulations and hierarchies. On account of the constantly moving terrain of this research, there is value in documenting their states of change. At the same time, one must also remember that even as these technoscapes morph, their widespread presence in the lives of aborigines is taken for granted as a co-presence in the general march beyond modern—indeed postdigital—life.

A wider context can be given to Taiwan's aborigines and technology in Taiwan. Numbering some 400,000 in population, indigenous peoples are depicted by government authorities as living in 14 ethnically mapped-out "tribal" territories on the island. Currently, individuals and groups prefer to call themselves "aborigines" in English, although the commonly used Chinese word *yuanzhumin* is occasionally translated as "indigenous." This essentialist mapping of aboriginal culture, however, has to be tempered by an appreciation that while elder generations live and work the land in rural areas, younger aborigines have migrated to Taiwan's cities for education and work. In the 1980s, aboriginal males also ventured overseas, serving as crew on container ships and fishing boats. There has been considerable intermarriage between aboriginal ethnic groups and also with the dominant Han population, which makes up 96% of Taiwan's population. Finally, the notion of farming or fishing villages as isolated enclaves needs to be reappraised against the fact that such communities often network into a transport system that boasts one of the highest-speed rail technologies in Asia. Taiwan, meanwhile, enjoys one of the world's highest Internet penetration rates, at 75.4%.[6]

Today, Facebook, YouTube, and the Taiwanese equivalents of Google (Yam) and Wikipedia (Chinese Wiki) are household brands, if not utilized evenly by every demographic. My own experience in the field suggests that the digital divide in Taiwan occurs less along the fault line of ethnicity than that of age. Communication trends specific to Taiwan show a general preference for chat interfaces and blog interaction (accessed mainly via mobile phones) over e-mail exchange, while music consumption over the Internet in Taiwan appears to be shifting—as in the rest of the world—from downloading to streaming.

How do these emerging trends reflect on aboriginal music in Taiwan? Scholars have investigated this subject over the past decades, with research ranging from old-school nomenclatural accounts of ritual and folksong ascribed to specific "tribes"[7] to indictments of first-world media practices in reference to the sampling of aboriginal song in pop tracks.[8] Yet others have pointed out that far from being untouched by technology, Taiwan's aboriginal music has, under the influence of Japanese *enka* and Taiwanese *taiyu* popular song, manifested itself in an active cottage record industry.[9] This peaked during the 1950s to 1980s, but still retains a major presence in village gatherings, regional aboriginal networks, and diaspora soundscapes. My own research specifically posits Amis song as an ecosystem, symbiotic components of which interact and feedback upon one another in intersecting platforms of village life, festival celebration, tourist performance, popular song, art music, Christian hymnody, and more recently, new media.[10] Elsewhere, Futuru Tsai has investigated media-enabled Amis musical articulations that juxtapose ethnically marked content with selective borrowings outside imagined traditions, arguing that they form mosaics of distinctively indigenous modernity.[11]

Content, Context, and Transference: Knowing What to Look for First

The issue of how content is changed and context lost in the transference of musical culture across formats, modes of performance, and geography is an old debate. While speed, accessibility and low cost have revolutionized musical practices, the introduction of digital technology to aboriginal music raises questions that to some extent have already been explored with the earlier rise of recording and broadcast technology.[12]

How is musical activity turned into an object—and in the case of a YouTube video, ten minutes of audiovisual footage? Recording and music production—via digital and analog technologies—have no doubt had an impact on the oral transmission of song cultures. Correspondingly, new audiences—casually browsing world-music sites or accidentally clicking on a friend-of-a-friend's hyperlink on Facebook—have come to appreciate the nuances of ritual and performance in the proverbial field, now accessed through amateur tourist videos. Now that performances of indigenous music are available to anyone with an Internet connection—including many aborigines living in Taiwan's urban areas—the implications for copyright and cultural ownership of folk material are many, including how the aesthetics of aboriginal song may be altered by the pop industry.

As far as new media can be understood as separate from (but not replacing) older media, perhaps the most scene-changing developments are increased accessibility and representation. One might argue, quoting Marshall McLuhan, that "the medium is the message"—context is effectively content.[13] A demonstration of this can be found in examining how different kinds of aboriginal music are accessed on one of the world's most ubiquitous video-sharing platforms, YouTube.

Entering the English search terms "aboriginal music Taiwan" for example, yields as among its top results a home video based on a tourist's motorcycle road trip in Eastern Taiwan. It features an ambient track by Puyuma pop singer Samingad, who is credited not in the footage itself but in notes appended to the clip.[14] On the other hand, replacing the keyword "music" with "song" leads to an ethnographic track, "Elder's Drinking Song," by Amis singer Difang. It plays against the static cover of his pop-inspired album *Circle of Life*.[15] Altering the search framework a third time using the Chinese characters *yuanzhumin yinyue* (aboriginal/ indigenous music) brings a new-age music-fronted slideshow of Paiwan musician Sedar Chin collaborating with mixed Chinese orchestral and Western chamber ensembles.[16] And why stop at searches in Chinese—the language of the colonizer? Yet finding appropriate indigenous terms to feed Google's all-knowing engines would be problematic. Questions arise: How would Internet users have the specialist knowledge of spelling variations in romanized Amis for a range of indigenous genres, rituals, and festivals across all of Taiwan's fourteen officially recognized groups? Would (and why would) the budding anthropologist or ethnomusicologist—or indeed an aborigine of X ethnicity in Taiwan—be using YouTube (or Google, as opposed to Yam) in the first place?

Such questions do not simply show up the fallibility of mechanisms such as Internet tags, keyword searches in different languages, translations, or logarithms. They address larger asymmetries of information organization, power, access to technology, music production, and processes of recontextualization, remediation and representation. Inherent meanings will be experienced in different ways by intended and unintended audiences—aboriginal, Han, and global. Just as it is erroneous to assume that Taiwan's aborigines have less access to digital technologies than people in more industrialized areas of the world, one cannot presume that aborigines use these technologies in the same ways, or indeed in only one way. In postdigital terms, it is also important to think about aboriginal communities who see (or fetishize) technology as a means of rehumanizing themselves and reclaiming political status as contemporary equals in Han-dominated Taiwan. In this respect, digital indigeneity enables less a construction of a new identity for aborigines than a relegitimization of their egalitarian existence. Yet even this process of relegitimization is dependent upon access to digital data—access that is not always equal.

Separate streams of musical information privileging different audiences show that the savvy searcher has to *know exactly* what he or she is searching for; that there are specific keywords which can unlock doors to niche websites. These feed back into "old" media, even as they network across hyperlinks, video recommendation lists, Facebook tags, newsfeeds, and Twitter posts; they also surface in the old-school format of e-mails, circulated by record companies, artists, bloggers, activists and music lovers.

Returning to my first demonstration of a YouTube inquiry, it can be shown that the video featuring music by a faceless Samingad accompanying a motorcycle ride is only five clicks and several scrolls away from footage of Bunun ritual declamations in Nantou.[17] On YouTube, pages expand into bigger menus, exponentially expanding the initial material. Clicking on usernames or particular channels, or copying and pasting search terms found in comments would also lead one beyond YouTube into aboriginal music blogs, artist pages, and chatrooms.

The bigger picture does not only concern "the search" itself, of course. Indeed, one might look at the quest in reverse and consider the originators of content. How do these individuals, communities, or institutions choose to represent aboriginal music on the Internet? What are their preferred platforms? What are their aims and who are their audiences? The next sections in this chapter consider specific processes of recontextualization, and investigate how different producers of content network with each other and media institutions within and outside Taiwan.

Faye Ginsburg sees indigenous digital media as having

> raised important questions about the politics and circulation of knowledge at a number of levels; within communities this may be about who has had access to and understanding of media technologies, and who has the rights to know, tell, and circulate certain stories and images. Within nation-states, media are linked to larger battles over cultural citizenship, racism, sovereignty, and land rights, as well as struggles over funding, airspace, and satellites, networks of

broadcasting and distribution, and digital broadband that may or may not be available to indigenous work. The impact of these fluctuations can be tracked in a variety of places—in fieldwork, in policy documents, and in the dramas of everyday life in cultural institutions.[18]

Here, one could argue that YouTube was only a particular "slice" of the new media pie, even if it remains a preferred site of younger aborigines. In reality, the larger representation, mediation and creation of Taiwan aboriginal music is co-negotiated by many institutions, groups and individuals, from government-backed agencies to community blogs, artist Facebook pages, and record company websites. As Lysloff and Gay expound on the concept of "technoculture," such virtual musical utterances should not be seen as entities divorced from culture but rather as proboscis extensions of existing and changing power structures, much in the same way that "technologies become imbedded in cultural systems and social institutions, which, in turn, are reconfigured by those same technologies."[19] It goes without saying that among Taiwan's aboriginal communities, significant musical content created for the Internet originates from institutions with already active pre-Internet profiles.

Institutional Sites, Tourism, and Representing National Discourses on Aborigines via Music

A few categories of content producers come to mind. The first comprises institutional and educational websites, funded by the government or private foundations that provide an official staging of identity on behalf of aborigines. These include the website for the Council of Indigenous Peoples, which hosts generic information on the state-recognized fourteen aboriginal groups. Its English site houses several introductory videos with musical components. These are celebratory in nature, aimed at nonaborigines and presented in Mandarin and American-accented English, with shifting images of the aboriginal countryside and costumed performers set to musical collages of ethnographic recordings, diegetic sounds, and New Age–style pop. On the site's Chinese portal, however, there is a small selection of original cartoon videos in several indigenous languages, targeted at the separate demographic of aboriginal children. The videos feature myth-based adventure stories and are set to action-movie-styled soundtracks.[20]

Another institutional site, the Digital Museum of Taiwan's Indigenous Peoples, hosts downloadable video files of news reports, stage shows, and festivals, and gives brief descriptions of the songs and dances of officially designated "tribes" in Chinese text.[21] Here, music and dance numbers are performed by troupes and trained singers belonging to organizations such as the Formosan

Aboriginal Song and Dance Troupe and church-linked choirs. A third institution, the National Museum of Prehistory has created for its site shorter computer simulations with story lines about early aboriginal life.[22] Made for purposes of both outreach and "inreach,"[23] the clips are scored to video-game music integrating aboriginal percussive and musical accents.

A second category of semi-institutional platforms showcasing aboriginal music includes the websites of cultural troupes, primarily aimed at Han tourists. In Landzelius's terms, these serve as "virtual gatekeepers in the field of impression-management," often in "first-encounter" scenarios.[24] An introductory video embedded in the Taiwan Indigenous People Culture Park's home page features a collaged soundtrack of ethnographic sounds, popular songs, and voice-overs, playing against images of dramatic natural scenery and aborigines in costume.[25] Elsewhere, the Formosan Aborigine Cultural Village in central Taiwan, a theme park for indigenous culture showcasing daily performances by resident troupes, features a timetable of concerts and a virtual listening booth on a graphics-heavy website. Streaming tracks of 1980s-style aboriginal pop known as *shandige*, with electronic beats and basic synthesizer accompaniment, can be appreciated.[26]

In a third category, several other organizations have focused on aboriginal ethnographic recordings. *Yuanyin zhimei*, a site hosted by the National Taiwan Normal University is an extensive digital archive of sound and video recordings largely made in the field and recontextualized in a virtual library alongside transcriptions, photographs, and academic notes.[27] Access is checkpointed through a terms-of-agreement form that nominally safeguards copyrighted material. Target audiences are researchers, classroom teachers, and general enthusiasts of aboriginal culture.

Beyond *Yuanyin*, slightly less extensive documentary operations include the Digital Archives of the Formosan Aborigines and the Taiwan aboriginal e-learning portal.[28] Both are electronic data repositories with music components, requiring user registration passwords. Finally, Taiwanese record company Wind Music can be mentioned here as a separate commercial player in a scene otherwise helmed by national organizations. One of the first ports of call on Google searches for "Taiwan aboriginal music" and "*yuanzhumin yinyue*," its nested web pages offer information and listening excerpts for an entire series of albums produced by French-trained ethnomusicologist Wu Rong-shun, dedicated to at least eight different "tribes."[29]

Brief notes can be made about such institutional platforms. With the exception of *Yuanyin* and Wind, music, where featured, is usually contextualized within videos. These in turn work within the larger trope of multiculturalism underscored by Taiwan's national agenda: that the aborigines are a marginal people formed of fourteen official "tribes"; that each tribe has its designated space; and that different peoples exhibit particular customs, costumes, and handicrafts. Such presentations are in keeping with pre-Internet representations of Taiwan aboriginal culture on official platforms, as critiqued by writers such as Hsieh[30] and Tan.[31] Interestingly, most sites (except *Yuanyin*) use several styles of music—not always aboriginal—to reach Internet audiences divided along ethnic, national, and generational fault lines. Institutional sites also link to noninstitutional content such as the home pages of aboriginal music artists. Conspicuously absent in terms of musical genre, however, is *shandige* (mountain song), or a Japanese *enka*-inspired popular song style featuring trembly vocals set to synthesizer beats. Often heard across Eastern Taiwan in rural aboriginal locales, the remediation of this genre will be discussed later.

Artist Platforms and Virtual Communities: Outreach or Inreach?

Unlike the slick multimedia showcases of institutional sites, virtual aboriginal communities share music in a more haphazard if organic way. Designed less to educate than to share news and opinions, sites like the Taiwan Indigenous People's Portal,[32] Wawanet,[33] Millet Garden,[34] Hohayannet,[35] the Aboriginal Science Education site,[36] Piyouma blog,[37] and Shanhai Culture Magazine[38] specifically target aboriginal Internet users through "community inreach."[39] They do not host musical content so much as provide space for the discussion of it, alongside the notification of festivals and performances.

Wawanet, designed for aboriginal children, regularly reviews aboriginal musical albums and books. It links to similar forums, allowing for the emergence of hopscotch-like Internet pathways that lead commentators and readers through various tangents to a range of performances and recording artists. Many of these community sites also redirect to documents from indigenous interest groups around the world such as Nativeweb and the Fourth World Institute, reflecting indigenous Taiwan's integration into global networks of aboriginal transnationalism.

The recording artists' blogs are perhaps the best portals to indigenous music. Some of these are supported by record companies: they include the blogs of relatively well-known acts such as Puyuma blues man Kimbo (Wildfire), Bunun singer Biung (Linfair Records), reggae band Matzka, Atayal singer Inka Mbing (Trees Music), Amis singer Suming (Wonder Music) Puyuma singer-songwriter Pau-dull (Taiwan Colors Music), and Amis songstress Ilid Kaolo (Wind Music). Professionally designed and commercially oriented, these pages host parallel Chinese and English language interfaces and link to store menus where albums can be sampled and bought, and where gigs are advertised. Ranging from glossy multimedia tableaux to text-only pages, these sites are geared toward a youth-centered public reading in Chinese or English.[40] Offline, the members of these publics are young aborigines, world music fans, university students, and expats who head to bars and clubs to listen to live performances.

While a full analysis of aboriginal pop and its politics has been covered elsewhere,[41] it has to be said that the virtual existence of this popular music is both influenced by and contributory to its offline existence. Web links to Facebook pages, artist blogs, fan articles, embedded YouTube videos, outdated MySpace sites, and Chinese Wiki entries, plus equivalents on its China-originated version, Baidu, intersect liberally, where current updates exist alongside expired or dormant pages. Samingad, whose voice is the first heard by most YouTube users new to the world of Taiwan aborigines, maintains a very basic website, courtesy of her record company, WildFire Music. However, she has recently been maintaining a quiet profile; she has not been updating her own site or her hyperlinked blog on the Taiwanese interface wretch.cc. Both of these spaces link to active artists such as Kimbo and sister marketing campaigns of her record company. Not content with the one record company profile on WildFire, Kimbo has three portals catering to separate needs: news, the selling of records, and the discoursing of his personal politics. Collectively, they cater to an audience beyond Taiwan, hinting at the global dynamics of indigenous nationalism. Yet another indigenous activist-singer, Panai, has moved off the record company grid, hosting content on her wretch.cc blog Panaipa[42] and on SoundCloud.[43] YouTube has also begun meeting the personal needs of singers and performers. Aboriginal artists Pau-dull and Suming have set up channels subscribed to by thousands of fans. Not restricting their private accounts to musical content of their own making, both artists share and repost videos from the comic to what they deem as general news.

Indeed, the record company is far from the sole mediator of aboriginal pop in Taiwan. Artists who attempt self-production—for more direct control or to simply keep up with the ubiquity of social media—include veteran singer and activist Kao Tzu-yang. His do-it-yourself ethic led him early in the game to build his own recording studio and Internet site. His distribution mechanism relies partly on videos that he uploads to YouTube and partly on the existing regional cassette/ CD industry.[44] In an interview in Taipei in 2011, Kao admitted to not updating his site for lack of money. He also maintained that "somehow, my music will get out because there are so many websites; everything links to everything else. . . . Those who know me or about me will know how to find me."

Another advocate of multimedia representation and marketing is the twenty-something Amis singer and "alternative cultural activist" Suming, who, until his recent association with the Taiwanese label Wonder Music, was an unsigned artist operating between Taipei, Taitung, and his home village of A'tolan.[45] In an interview in Taipei in 2011, he whipped out a shiny MacBook to show his wares, opening multiple windows and scrolling through images, music, and bookmarks. Suming waxed lyrical in Mandarin over the importance of

doing everything you can to reach people . . . I never thought too much; I
just did it. We were going to make a music video in my hometown A'tolan. So
we rounded up friends and relatives there, and did it—all by ourselves with a
cheap camera! We edited everything; put it up on the web. We told friends,
parents, and grandparents. A lot of the villagers are in the video, so they'll go
to YouTube and see it, show others. I'm on Facebook too, and use it to communicate with many people. These people also help me spread the word further, as you will also—beyond the Internet, beyond Taiwan. (Interview with
author, June 28 2011, Taipei)

Suming's story is not unique. His words speak for a growing number of
young aboriginal artists who have embraced many aspects of Internet technology as a proactive stance in outreach and inreach. This is sometimes under-
lined as a matter of necessity rather than creativity—a means of staking a place
in world where digitality is a prosthetic extension of human agency. Musicians'
wares are not only promoted by record company websites and featured on official government platforms, but are remediated into new contexts haphazardly
carved out in intersecting online and offline pathways, finding life in ecosystems co-created by fans, generic music consumers, random browsers, music
industry professionals, handicraft shops, advertising industry executives, cultural and tourist industry workers, indigenous nationalist groups, and even
politicians. These remediations are also uploaded onto networks turned de
facto hosting archives such as YouTube, FaceBook, SoundCloud, the Chinese
mp3 library Sogou, Chinese Wiki, and Baidu. Such sprawling, secondary interfaces enjoy broad coverage while retaining the ability to be uniquely connected
to any individual listener's specific taste upon the application of carefully cali-
brated search terms, or the simple posting of a clip onto a personal channel or
Twitter update.

For the Internet surfer, the question becomes not just one of whether the
"correct" search terms have been applied but where the quest should begin.
Entering the Sinicized name of Puyuma singer Chen Chien-nien, for example,
on the commercial Han-friendly online music providers Sogou, Douban, and
Xiami, or on iTunes, will bring up a more systematic list of downloadable mp3s
than the politically correct, Romanized name "Pau-dull" on YouTube, even
though the singer's personal music and Flickr photography sites may employ
both handles. Indeed, the winner of this game is the insider or educated
searcher who has demystified the politics of representation, or who persists in
following tangents.

In many ways, fans and listening communities play an important part in
remediating aboriginal music on mainstream and substream circuits. This
is seen in emerging YouTube channels maintained by young aborigines or
enthusiasts of aboriginal and alternative music. Again, these platforms integrate into larger virtual networks, if geared to different taste profiles. Users

<laucudrulaun1>, <leohualien1>, <fancahlay>, <joannachiang515>, <guanyuu> and <kakeng1999>, for example have put together playlists focusing on different aspects of aboriginal contemporary pop recordings, interspersed among home videos of village life and the odd TV report or variety show; <ckelly1115>, <toutou530> and anthropologist <futuru tsai> bring together ethnographic videos of song and dance troupes in rehearsal, public performances, and village ritual festivals. Commentators post frequently on their pages, interacting in time-lapse chats on topics ranging from information around the recordings to random remarks about gigs, celebrity gossip, and world news.

The game is also played beyond websites or indeed computers; chat programs such as QQ, which account for more communication traffic than e-mail in East Asia, encourage young users to surf and share music "in the moment" as they talk about aboriginal artists on their iPads and smartphones. The rise of mobile media has also broadened the physical scope of music sharing beyond desk-bound machines, even as aboriginal pop tunes can be downloaded as ringtones or call-waiting music, a popular feature widespread in Taiwan.

Copyright, Cultural Rights and New Media: Sharing is Good

With constant reproduction and remediation of music, the long-debated issue of copyright is slowly becoming a moot point, at least for some younger aboriginal artists. Here, Lessig's stand on the notion of digital culture as inevitably remixed by end users-turned-creators in a hybrid economy holds, to some extent.[46] In the relatively niche world of aboriginal pop, artists would rather their creations be circulated through as many platforms as possible than restricted by copyright. As Suming explained in an interview:

> People have asked about what has happened after Difang and the "Return To Innocence" court case, and piracy. But I'm not worried about copyright, I'd rather people get to listen to my music. I'm active myself on the Internet; everyone who's worth knowing who gets to my music will eventually know it's me. They get to understand my cause, and they actually buy more of my CDs for themselves, to give to friends.
>
> But even that's not so important. I'm more interested in passing down my culture in as many different ways as possible. It can be fashionable like pop music on the Internet, or it can be something more traditional like our festivals. Anyway, I alone don't own my culture. It's a culture that belongs to everyone; the world. I'm just keeping it alive and relevant to other people and generations. So because of this I'm not just on the Internet, or doing live gigs in clubs. I'm a painter, a basket weaver, a storyteller; I go back to the village. I'm an educator too, I run summer camps for Amis boys during our annual festivals in A'tolan, where I teach them songs, and about

botany, about fishing and hunting. And then I write about all of this again on the Internet. And then people discover all this and come to find out more. (Interview, June 28 2011, Taipei)

Suming's social-enterprise approach to making music and networking can be thought of as part of a second wave of indigenous musical activism, built upon a history of aboriginal nationalism shaped by 1990s artists such as Kao Tzu-yang and the now inactive aboriginal collective Beiyuan Shanmao. Themes concerning land and hunting rights, the dumping of waste and sociopolitical marginalization continue to be explored by other contemporary aboriginal musicians directly in song or via new soapboxes emerging alongside musical spotlighting.

Faye Ginsburg points out that "the term *the digital age* stratifies media hierarchies for those who are out of power and are struggling to become producers of media representations of their lives. It is an issue that is particularly salient for indigenous people who, until recently, have been the object of other peoples' image-making practices."[47]

Often, digital remediation is key to reclaiming aboriginal artists' multiple identities as musicians consciously plugged into technological developments, urban life and politics. Kimbo, for example, has presented on "simple living" at the international Internet-hosted TedEx conference in Taiwan, taking control of his own image as an urbanite, tech-savvy naïf.[48] Panai, Samingad, Ilid Kaolo, Suming, Leo Chen, and Chen Chien-nien, among others, have spoken to newspapers, TV crews, and websites on behalf of their musical contributions while segueing into talk about politics, even as they sing about aboriginal issues. Their mainstream media appearances cross-reference web platforms. Aborigines rally to the cries of potent pan-aboriginal vocables such as "Hohayan!" in song.[49] Over the Internet, such musical utterances have also been directly incorporated into web domain names, as in the aboriginal community site hohayan.com.

A note on the issue of copyright can be made of this embracing of new media, otherwise in line with the ethics of Web 2.0's crowd-harnessing capabilities.[50] What is interesting is that two constructions of the "public" have emerged among different generations of aboriginal musicians. The first "public"—or rather, "people"—can be understood in Habermas' terms of the "public sphere," and constitute the anonymous masses of Internet users in Taiwan—and those beyond—working, playing and making connections over the web; they are the "everyone" and the "world" that Suming speaks of. A second "public" comprises government institutions and big record companies who play gatekeeper to funds behind social or cultural initiatives implemented in the name of good aboriginal policy-making. These include institutionally backed academic researchers who have attempted to negotiate with rights-conscious individuals over collecting songs for ethnographic archiving. Increasing wariness of the second kind of "public" among older aborigines can in part be traced to fallout from the well-known copyright infringement lawsuit involving the 1993 dance hit "Return To Innocence," which featured, allegedly without authorization, the sampled voice of Amis aboriginal singer Difang. The original recording had been made by Han Taiwanese ethnomusicologist Hsu Tsang-hoei.[51] Fast-forwarding to 2013, increased safeguarding of cultural ownership from misappropriation has led to a rise in financial recompense for singers, complex legal transfers of intellectual property and the creation of limited-access Internet sites protected by passwords.

A second force behind this new vigilance has also been galvanized by larger, global movements which frame power shifts in national or international politics as the result of the technological enablement of the rising "anonymous" masses.[52] Through new media and networked infrastructures, these masses have come to possess louder political voices and the ability to self-organize on instant and large scales. Younger indigenous communities have been quick to harness this aspect of the Internet, turning to cyberactivism, which—as Ginsburg writes—offers "some other coordinates for understanding what such an interconnected world might be like outside a hegemonic order."[53] While the orchestrated robustness of web campaigns remain to be evaluated, pro-aboriginal discoursing of news and ideas is prevalent among subscribers of aboriginal news and music sites, as seen for example in the nearly 5,000 "friends" who post regularly on Suming's Facebook and YouTube profiles, leaving thoughtful comments on politics.

Returning to young Amis singers again, a final remark can be made on their digital musical indigeneities, which ultimately have to be understood as only one, postdigital aspect of their varied lifestyles. Pau-dull's YouTube channel, for example, features more than his own music; footage ranges from diving expeditions set to Keith Jarrett's music to scenes of flora and fauna. Suming takes new media for granted; they function as prosthetics for life at large. He also explains that his interaction with media is none too different from that any other contemporary urban Han person. Suming's stance echoes the larger concerns of postdigital thinkers in their consideration of technology's inroads into humanity.[54] On and off the Internet, he has been vocal about his duties to larger society via his loyalties to different communities, negotiating the multiple identities of son, brother, friend, teacher, client, employer, villager, and urbanite. His indigeneity exists within a larger ecosystem of culture and politics. Thus, his Facebook page and YouTube channel project diverse sounds and images from these different aspects of contemporary life, ranging from gig reviews to photos of friends' babies to articles on Pride marches in Taiwan and recipes for making rice wine. Collectively, these presentations reference symbols of stereotyped Amis "traditionality" but also offer a holistic picture of a contemporary, networked aboriginal musician's life beyond the notion of any "authentic" or "ethnic" Amis-ness. The same can be argued for fans of Suming and aboriginal music communities at large. A casual glance at the playlists of some of the aboriginal-authored YouTube channels named above will showcase content beyond indigenous culture, reflecting the aboriginal music fan's wider contemporary lifestyle, tastes, pursuits, and responsibilities.

New Media, Old Media, Time Warps, and the Generation Gap

If the discussion so far has privileged the demographic of an under-50 Internet user, then a closer examination of the generation gap might be useful. The singer Suming might write about learning songs from his grandmother in his home village, but how has new media impacted his grandmother's generation?

My field experiences have shown that aborigines of a senior demographic, largely resident in outlying villages and pursuing semi-subsistence lifestyles while also dependent on income from offspring, do not (for now) seem greatly impacted by the Internet. To be sure, aboriginal communities have created multiple and symbiotic contexts for singing what they idealize as "traditional" or "folk" song, turning work songs which would have otherwise died out with the advent of farming technology into generic "leisure songs." Disappearing melodies are preserved through indigenized church hymnody and enter the electronic repertoire of communal karaoke sessions.[55] Aborigines of all ages continue to engage enthusiastically in seasonal festivities involving song and dance, keeping recontextualized rituals alive less for purely cosmological reasons than as acts of identity assertion.[56] However, many village-based aborigines over fifty do not seem particularly concerned if these examples of musical activity do not feature as popularly on YouTube, Facebook, and wretch.cc, etc.

Indeed, senior aborigines remain seemingly ambivalent about debates over Internet representation of their music and their own general access to the web. Unlike some younger, vocal members of the community, they also appear relatively phlegmatic about the loss of context and content when five-day-long festivals are reduced to a ten-minute collage of highlights on YouTube. For many, the format is far too much of an occasional novelty to be taken seriously as an instrument of practical value. To be sure, the Internet and wireless networks are widely available across the whole of Taiwan, including aboriginal villages. However, in the more remote villages, the senior aboriginal demographic rarely uses computers or smartphones. Instead, they communicate with friends and relatives through the simple act of walking across the street to talk in person, or using landlines or simple mobile phones. In a way, one could argue that this sector of the aboriginal population is practicing self-exclusion from certain processes of empowerment—particularly of interaboriginal and global indigenous nationalist movements networked through new media platforms.

This is not to say that elder generations are not technologically enabled. As in rural India, where Peter Manuel has found that cassettes served as a form of local cultural resistance,[57] an industry of regionally distributed CDs (and until recently also cassettes) has been in existence for a few decades. Pre-Suming aboriginal artists in their fifties and sixties have been releasing new albums based on popular song styles of the 1950s and 1960s. Featuring a trembly vocal style and wide vibrato, this time-warped genre of early aboriginal pop is inspired by the Japanese genre of *enka* and finds its origins in nostalgia for to the historical Japanese colonization of Taiwan from 1895—1945. Referred to as *shandige* (mountain songs) or *wuqu* (dancing songs), such aboriginal-language and Mandarin offerings are set to pentatonic melodies and layered over with electronic beats and synthesized accompaniments. However, due to the new media divide across the generation gap, the genre is primarily circulated through hard copies of individual CDs purchased in regional and niche shops and played on portable boomboxes, rather than as YouTube videos or streaming files. *Shandige* and *wuqu* are the staple musical diet of karaoke sessions, wedding banquets, village socials, and special performance items in ritual festivals. The covers of the CDs, featuring artists festooned in colorful ceremonial gear, are the mainstay of bus, truck, and taxi circuits between aboriginal villages.

Disjunctures emerging through this asymmetry between format, consumption, and listener demographics are interesting to consider. A case in point is veteran singer Hoceko Lu Jingzi, one of Taiwan's first aboriginal pop stars to achieve fame in the 1950s. Lu, who is in her seventies today, has become canonized as one of the founders of *shandige* aboriginal pop.[58] Her early albums first produced on crackling records and now remastered as CDs continue to be sung and danced to at karaoke and wedding celebrations, while album covers showcase her in time-warped glory as an eternally svelte seventeen-year-old. Lu took a break from singing and recording during the 1980s and married a Han businessman, eventually starting a family of her own. In recent years she has made small comeback as a guest star at contemporary aboriginal pop concerts and on aboriginal variety TV shows. Recordings of some of these later performances have found their way onto YouTube through younger singers rebroadcasting their shared platforms. In such contexts, Lu is usually presented next to her younger counterparts, shown in streetwear, wearing colorful aboriginal gear. Holding on to her doyenne status via a microphone, her thrice-remediated voice—on YouTube, on television, via a PA system—is today husky, matronly, and deep, in comparison to the high-pitched stridence of her youth, preserved on vinyls remade as CDs.

The two parallel presentations of Lu on different media present dissonances of time, production values, musical style, vocal quality, star image, and audience consumption. On the YouTube clip, cloned off an aboriginal TV variety show, Lu interacts with younger Amis singer and TV show host, Ado

Kaliting, who has interpreted the older singer's original song in the style of a blues improviser. The elder Lu is reintroduced to younger audiences as a "classic" and featured in juxtaposition with the sassy Ado as an "older" voice. However, outside of the TV show and Internet, an earlier version of Lu as a seventeen-year-old singer is remembered on CD by her earliest fans, who access an entirely different aspect of this same "classic" voice. The former situation is a performance of age; the latter is of time.

Lu's temporally phased representations on YouTube and CD reflect a particular kind of technological determinism at work. This in turn has to be understood in an environment where concepts such as "technological catchup," "backward," or "up-to-date" cannot be ruled only by the linear progression of time. If anything, there is a constant shifting, exchange, adaptation, and remaking of content and style across coexisting platforms. The delineations are never clear-cut: separate versions of Lu's mediated artistry coexist not only on the Internet and in regional CD distribution circuits, but also on the broad-capture medium of television, attesting to overlapping consumer habits. This crossover is achieved with different media formats telescoping into each other. Lu's original TV appearance itself incorporates film footage from a separate occasion when she is shown semi-improvising in folksong style without instrumental or electronic accompaniment. The same show further integrates historic excerpts from her early recordings, aptly demonstrating Jenkins's notion that different forms of media converge rather than replace or overtake each other.[59]

Not all the work is accomplished within the mediated world, however: alongside the possibilities of time-phasing, person-to-person contact and family ties play important roles in addressing the digital divide itself. Back to Lu again: while she maintains that she is far from a regular Internet user, she did own a blog during the late 2000s. The site was first set up by a young fan who was also a web designer, and later handed over to Lu's daughter. In an interview at her home in Taipei in 2011, Lu described organizing face-to-face meetings for the sole purpose of initiating online communications:

> It's not much of a site, I just wanted to have a presence on the Internet I could control. Everybody seems to have a website these days. It's helped me publicize and sell my rereleased albums. Occasionally fans write in. My daughter, who would come round and visit me anyway, would sit down with me in front of her laptop and I'd ask her to put up what I want to say, or change the pictures. She'd also advise me on how to blog. But then my daughter got busy with her own kids, and I didn't know what to do. It's gone dormant. (Interview, Taipei, June 27, 2011)

Lu is by no means a technophobe; her early experience in the record industry and her familiarity with studio work stand her in good stead handling microphones and mixing desks when she sings and presents programs at radio stations. Like many Taipei residents of her age, she has also become proficient with mobile phones. She has configured her current ringtones and caller playback tunes to broadcast her own hit songs from the 1960s in addition to her favorite Mandopop tunes. More interestingly, Lu engages with the Internet in her own roundabout way, vicariously watching content downloaded by her daughter and her friends' children; calling on Internet-monitoring favors from visiting academics (including myself); and leaning on fans who bring their laptops into her home to show her streaming footage of herself on YouTube.

While Lu has not professed interest in listening to performers other than herself and a few friends on YouTube, nor shown the urge to engage in more adventurous surfing, my own field experiences have shown the elder generation of aborigines coming to treat computers and wide-screen smartphones as de facto television sets. Often, intergenerational groups of aborigines sit around a computer screen or a smartphone screen. These devices are often operated by visiting children and grandchildren, who provide ongoing commentaries on the videos. Most of these shared viewing sessions feature home footage or TV shows involving friends or relatives, sometimes in musical performance.

On one occasion in the village of Fafokod in Southeastern Taitung, I came across a fifty-something aboriginal man singing songs and sharing musical insights with his amateur musician son through Skype. Over the course of this conversation, the man also received a tutorial on how to use the Internet itself, with his son sending YouTube hyperlinks via Skype's chat function, and giving verbal instructions on how to type keyword searches into Google. The elder aborigine was clearly struggling to deal with both channels of video and chat communication. In the end, the preferred format of Internet messaging in Taiwan proved too much of a challenge for the new user, and wherever possible the older man would adopt the—ironically—even newer technology of voice-over Internet protocol. While such occasions of web-based bonding are relatively uncommon, cross-generational contact through new media itself has contributed interesting ways of sharing and experiencing music among aboriginal communities. Even as technology has polarized the generations, newer generations of technology have come to bridge some of the resulting schisms.

Postdigital Integrations into Aboriginal Ecosystems: "We're not *Just* Aborigines but All Human"

A caveat has to be made with regard to the generation gap I have so far identified in the musical practice of digital indigeneity: this "gap" is also a function of intersectional factors. These include the relative willingness to adapt; varying access to different languages and input formats; the availability of Internet facilities in public and private spaces of city centers and rural-urban fringes such as village community centers; and itinerant and dynamic migration.

A better modeling of the situation places digital musicking within a larger ecosystem of Amis song, nested within or intersecting with sister ecosystems of aboriginal culture and Taiwanese society at large. Here, the relationships between realms of practice are never linear. As shown in the asynchronicities of Lu Jingzi's multiple musical presences on- and offline, or in overlapped new media-based appropriations of aboriginal pop, ethnographic content and incidental home videos, there is constant blurring of boundaries in nonstop re-creation of music. In this sense, new media exhibit a more humanistic, postdigital paradigm through deep integration into many aspects of life: a tourist video on Youtube made by a Han visitor during the *kiloma'an* festival season, for example, links to and becomes eventual inspiration for larger self-documentary projects by local Amis youth who use the same kinds of technology with a slightly different gaze to depict the same ritual celebrations. Nestled within the resulting videographies are other kinds of mediated aboriginal musics performed within official festival contexts, featuring, for example, physical song-and-dance reinterpretations of *shandige* sung not by their original aboriginal recording artists, but by a team of seniors who feel more at home with karaoke machines than with the mobile-phone video platforms on which they have been recorded by their grandchildren. Meanwhile, aboriginal TV producers scout these videos for story ideas to feature on variety shows that reach older audiences on television but later are rebroadcast on Youtube and then embedded in Facebook. The shows bring together local singers, recording artists, and state cultural troupes, on and offline. Many of them also individually consult for state organizations and institutions that borrow from, appropriate, and recreate yet other kinds of musical articulations, feeding back into educational, Han, scholarly, and tourist markets on and off the Internet.

A final case in point can again be found in Suming, who points out that today's media landscapes have moved on from the time of "Return to Innocence." As he understands, digital enabled-ness and the ability to manipulate—instead of simply reproducing—have become powerful tools of Alvin Toffler's "prosumer."[60] He also believes that his primary business model relies as much on selling mp3s as on selling CDs, and he uses his recordings as leverage to set up performing engagements. He says: "I want people to use my music and take it to further places, even if it means they make it into something else. Sometimes I get to see how people reuse my music when they repost it on the Internet. All this comes back to me. I get invitations to perform. It leads to different kinds of opportunities." (Interview, June 28 2011, Taipei)

Suming acknowledges that CDs still play an important part in circulating aboriginal *shandige* among senior aborigines living in rural-urban fringes. However, he has also worked to bring new media into the same networks with his brand of music, strategically styled to address generational divides and the tastes of aboriginal and nonaboriginal listeners. The track "Kasaopoan A Radiw No Etolan A Kapah" on his album *Suming* is an unaccompanied, ethnographic recording of youths gathering in the village of A'tolan. It is interpolated into the urban and contemporary feel of a parent album focusing on hip-hop. On the same album, another rap and techno-inspired number, "Kayoing" (Young girl), is heavily promoted via YouTube and weaves in ethnographic images of elderly men and women from his home village of A'tolan. Rather than wearing stereotypically colorful aboriginal dress, they are in everyday clothes. They laugh at and look with amusement, curiosity, and affection directly into Suming's camera and at his antics. They are unlikely stars of a pop video, a format whose superficial incongruity with imagined everyday village lives becomes a feature of the performance itself. Where costumes are concerned, it is a troupe of young female dancers—donning adapted versions of festival wear with short skirts—who, instead, play the self-essentializing card. In "Kayoing," the girls exhibit moves that hark back to both Amis circle-dance gestures and hip-hop, juxtaposing the modern and the imagined traditional. Writing on Amis bodily expressions, anthropologist Futuru Tsai describes such displays as "the performance of subjectivity and identities blended with the global flows of music and dance movements under the specific sociocultural environment of the A'tolan Amis."[61]

To the nonaboriginal audience, such interpolations insert a slice of the imagined "authentic" village experience within a modern, slick album. But the interpolation also works both ways. Suming speaks of how he and younger generations bring their computers back to ancestral villages to showcase music videos in which elder folk have been featured. In turn, elder folk come to their own terms with this new technology: YouTube videos become interfaces that bridge and bond generational and digital divides, even as they have once been cause of schisms.

Suming's promotion of intergenerational communication comes from his championing of aboriginal nationalism and a longer-range stance on cultural stewardship. His nationalism taps into larger tropes about humanity at large. He is forthright about his multiple identities, refusing to be categorized as only a musician or an indigenous person: he sees himself as also being a craftsman, farmer, fisherman, filmmaker, political activist, and educator. He sees his diverse profiles as feeding into the larger ecosystem of aboriginal modernity, into which digitality closely integrates. He envisions himself as an instrumental agent in co-creating this modernity, blogging about old and new songs prescribing Amis lifestyles to younger aborigines at summer camps. He revives rituals, discussing their specificities beyond the village and across history. He speaks at island-wide meets, postconcert talks and panel discussions—many of which are captured on social networks via embedded YouTube broadcasts.

His upbeat songs are set to his native Amis language. Their multifaceted elements reach out to Amis, non-Amis, aboriginal, and nonaboriginal audiences. His urbanite fluency with manipulating media and ability to traverse multiple digital formats is part of his complex aboriginal identity, as it also serves to promote aboriginal awareness and causes beyond official discourses.

That the pathways through Taiwan aboriginal music created by new media developments are criss-crossed, layered, and messy is patently obvious—as is true, perhaps, with the advent of new media anywhere else in the world. To an extent, the issues brought about by the integration of the Internet into aboriginal life and society are symptomatic of developments understood as par for the course in twenty-first-century communities. For a growing number of young aboriginal musicians, the increasing ubiquity of technology has also lessened its novelty and life-altering values.

Postdigital scholar Maurice Benayoun writes: "One of the important impacts of technology on art will probably be the absolute refusal by the world of art to accept it, and there are already a large number of projects flourishing that are low tech and unplugged and for which it is difficult to ignore the fact that technology is too visibly rejected for it not to be the true subject matter."[62]

In other words, digitality has become such a common phenomenon that human creativity, even through its express harnessing of technology, is often defined separately and exclusively from its very reliance on technology. Suming, for example, takes his digitally networked existence—through music, on the Internet, via his mobile phone—for granted in ways that he would not his indigeneity.

Indeed, the specific marginality of aboriginal existence in Taiwan has played out in unique ways across particular types of connectivity. This has happened not only in the unsurprising co-option of music platformed on new media for aboriginal cyberactivism, but also in the remaking of submarginalities and new disjunctures—in age gaps and geographical spread; in time-warped musical identity articulations. Related to the marginality of aboriginal existence in Taiwan is the issue of capacity and size. One could also argue that these networks—of which new media in an Appadurian sense has become a crucial "scape"—have grown to be as interlocked as they are only because of their relatively small size. The ascent of new media has created interaboriginal links that have brought degrees of separation considerably closer.

Here it might be useful to revisit the ideas behind my exercise of conducting a search for aboriginal song on the Internet according to specific parameters. The relative and mediated "authenticities" of corresponding results can, at the end of the day, be understood as equally valid to each of their specific contexts; to the circumstances of the quest; to the backgrounds of the questioner; to the needs of specific information providers; and to the longer back-stories of the development of convoluted pathways bringing producer of content to seeker of information. Thus, a recording of aboriginal music posted by a tourist on YouTube may hold as much cultural value as a cartoon synchronized to music promoted by a government agency. An ethnographic-aspiring home video of a ritual dance shared on Facebook is as relevant as the broader making of musical indigeneity in a pop track automatically played upon visiting a commercial record company's website. The old issues of reduction of content through the introduction of different as opposed to successive media do not have either/or solutions, but rather, multiple solutions.

Meanwhile, in the making of this dynamic equilibrium, change continues to be the constant as more disjunctures emerge. Musical communities continue to be restratified through newer submarginalities. At the same time, through shifting new media networks, they carry on negotiating scaled concepts of village identity, pan-aboriginality and global indigeneity. Ideas of musical heritage and cultural ownership are remade with the rise of more egalitarian access to reproduction technology, even as generational and geographical gaps form and close around technological fault lines. National discourses on aboriginal matters fluctuate alongside the political empowerment of rising cross-sections of aboriginal society in Taiwan, rallied in part through Internet musical campaigns. One could say that the evolving state of music and indigeneity—certainly in aboriginal Taiwan—is less a digital than postdigital issue, where new media have become a large part of an ecosystem interrogating what it means to be a human. Kim Cascone writes of how digitality has become taken for granted and fully integrated into commercial modernity;[63] Mel Alexenberg describes how cutting-edge technologies function less through the fetishization of newness than through their humanized dimensions.[64] Taiwan's aborigines continue to remake their music in holistic—if not always clearly defined— engagement with newer technologies.

Notes

1. Henry Jenkins, *Convergence Culture: Where Old and New Media Collide* (New York: New York University Press, 2006), 1–24. Jay Bolter and Richard Grusin, *Remediation: Understanding New Media* (Cambridge: MIT Press, 1999), 20–51; Lev Manovich, *The Language of New Media* (New York: Leonardo, 1999), 18–45.
2. Lawrence Lessig, *Remix: Making Art and Commerce Thrive in the Hybrid Economy* (London: Penguin Press, 2008), 1–22.
3. Bolter and Grusin, *Remediation*, 20–51.
4. Rene T. A. Lysloff and Leslie Gay, *Music and Technoculture* (Middletown CT: Wesleyan University Press, 2003), 3–5.
5. Kyra Landzelius, 2006. "Introduction: Native on the Net." In *Native on the Net: Indigenous and Diasporic Peoples in the Virtual Age*, ed. Kyra Landzelius (London: Routledge, 2006), 1.

6. This figure was obtained June 2012 from the internetworldstats.com website, http://www.internetworldstats.com/stats3.htm.

7. I-to Loh, "Tribal Music of Taiwan: With Special Reference to Amis and Puyuma Styles" (PhD diss., UCLA, 1982); Tsang-houei Hsu, *Minzu Yinyue lunshugao* [Ethnomusicological essays] (Taipei, 1987–92); Tsang-houei Hsu and Shui-Cheng Cheng *Musique de Taiwan* (Paris: Guy Tredaniel, 1992).

8. Nancy Guy, "Trafficking in Taiwan Aboriginal Voices," in *Handle with Care: Ownership and Control of Ethnographic Materials*, ed. Sjoerd R. Jaarsma (Pittsburgh, PA: University of Pittsburgh Press, 2002), 195–209; Timothy Taylor, *Strange Sounds: Music, Technology and Culture* (New York: Routledge, 2001), 128–31.

9. Chun-bin Chen, "Voices of Double Marginality: Music, Body, and Mind of Taiwanese Aborigines in the Post-modern Era" (PhD diss., University of Chicago, 2007); Chun-bin Chen, "Shandige: Yinyue tazhe de jiangou, yi Taiwan Yuanzhumin wei li" [Shandige: Construction of the musical other using the example of Taiwan aborigines], a paper given at a conference on musicology in Taiwan, National Taiwan University of the Arts, 2007; Kuan-ming Chiang, *Xiandai Houshan Chuangzuo Geyao Takan* [Establishing contemporary creative songs of Houshan] (Taitung: Taidong Xianli Wenhua Zhongxin, 1999).

10. Shzr Ee Tan, *Beyond "Innocence": Amis Aboriginal Song in Taiwan as an Ecosystem* (Aldershot, UK: Ashgate, 2012), 19–44.

11. Futuru Tsai, "Kapah (Young Men): Alternative Cultural Activism in Taiwan," *Savage Minds* blog, August 4, 2010, http://archive.feedblitz.com/42193/~3872736.

12. Michael Chanan, *Repeated Takes: A Short History of Recording and its Effects on Music* (London: Verso, 1997), Mark Katz, *Capturing Sound: How Technology Has Changed Music* (Berkeley: University of California Press, 2004).

13. Marshall McLuhan, *Understanding Media: The Extensions of Man* (Cambridge, MA: MIT Press, 1994).

14. "Taiwanese Aboriginal Music," YouTube video, 4:27, posted by "M13," March 16, 2007, http://www.youtube.com/watch?v=0okzIV9jCtw.

15. "Difang—Elders Drinking Song," YouTube video, 3:57, posted by "bafagu2," September 19, 2008, https://www.youtube.com/watch?v=6oHGUr6HEow.

16. "Flying Fish Cloud Leopard—100-year return of the Paiwan," track 11, "Rebirth," YouTube video, 7:29, posted by "abomusicabo," January 3, 2011, http://www.youtube.com/watch?v=DHIIZVS-7Js&list=PL4D6CA4423E99E94B.

17. Nantou County: First communal reportage of exploits by different Bunun groups, YouTube video, 2:14, posted by "Madu Bunun," May 17, 2012, http://www.youtube.com/watch?v=mKvMV_GlnbY.

18. Faye Ginsburg, "Rethinking the Digital Age," in *Global Indigenous Media: Cultures, Poetics, and Politics*, ed. Pamela Wilson and Michelle Stewart (Durham, NC: Duke University Press, 2008), 303.

19. Lysloff and Gay, *Music and Technoculture*, 8.

20. Council of Indigenous Peoples, Executive Yuan, http://www.apc.gov.tw/portal/?lang=en_US. CIP Mandarin site, http://www.apc.gov.tw/portal/docDetail.html?CID=176B89C52746BB64&DID=0C3331F0EBD318C27FDD4B1

AE31B1050. Cartoon in Amis language, http://www.apc.gov.tw/portal/doc Detail.html?CID=30E0B3A43B549A48&DID=0C3331F0EBD318C253E4C2DD 51FF3887. All accessed September 1, 2013.

21. Digital Musuem of Taiwan's Indigenous Peoples web page, accessed September 1, 2013, http://www.dmtip.gov.tw/Aborigines/Article.aspx?CategoryID=5&Cl assID=17&TypeID=37&RaceID=1.

22. National Museum of Prehistory web page, accessed September 1, 2013, http://www.nmp.gov.tw/index.php.

23. Landzelius, "Introduction," 9.

24. Ibid., 11.

25. Taiwan Indigenous Peoples' Culture Park web page, accessed September 1, 2013, http://www.tacp.gov.tw/home01.aspx?ID=1.

26. Formosan Aborigine Cultural Village web page, accessed September 1, 2013, http://www.nine.com.tw/buy_02.htm.

27. *Yuanyin Zhimei*, accessed September 1, 2013, http://archive.music.ntnu.edu. tw/abmusic/index.html.

28. The Digital Archives of the Formosan Aborigines, accessed September 1, 2013, http://www.aborigines.sinica.edu.tw/english/; Taiwan aboriginal e-learning portal, http://www.apc.gov.tw/portal/?lang=en_US.

29. Wind Music online store, accessed September 1, 2013, http://www.wind music.com.tw/en/pro_list.asp?LIB_ID=C&SET_NO=CX01&id=03; http://music. sogou.com/singer/65/detailSinger_%CC%A8%CD%E5%D4%AD%D7%A1%C 3%F1%D2%F4%C0%D6%BC%C7%CA%B5.html.

30. Shih-Chung Hsieh, *Shanbao Guanguang: Dangdai Shandi Wenhua Zhanxiande Renleixue Quanshi* [Mountain peoples and tourism: The anthropology of contemporary cultural representations of mountain peoples] (Taiwan: Ren yu Sisiang Silie, 1994).

31. Tan, *Beyond "Innocence,"* 121–74.

32. Taiwan Indigenous Peoples' Portal, accessed September 1, 2013, http://www. tipp.org.tw/.

33. Wawanet, accessed September 1, 2013, http://wawa.pts.org.tw/index.php.

34. Millet Garden, accessed September 1, 2013, http://www.tacocity.com.tw/aliyan.

35. Hohayannet, accessed September 1, 2013, http://citing.hohayan.net.tw/.

36. Aboriginal Science Education, accessed September 1, 2013, http://www.yabit. org.tw/index.php.

37. Piyouma, accessed September 1, 2013, http://paiwan.tacocity.com.tw/.

38. Shanhai Culture Magazine, accessed September 1, 2013, http://tivb.pixnet. net/blog.

39. Landzelius, "Introduction," 9.

40. Matzka, http://www.matzka.com.tw/m4.htm/; Pau-dull, http://www.tcmusic .com.tw/artist/paudull/Index.htm; Kimbo, http://www.arakimbo.com/main .htm; Trees MusicL, http://www.treesmusic.com/artist/inkambing/about. htm; Linfair Records, http://www.linfairrecords.com/artists/profile.php?id= 539; WindMusic, http://www.windmusic.com.tw/en/pro_detail.asp?PDT_NO= TCD-5614; Taiwan Colors Music, http://www.tcmusic.com.tw/artist/samingad/ Index.htm. All accessed September 1, 2013.

41. Tan, *Beyond "Innocence"*; Chen, "Voices of Double Marginality"; Chiang, *Establishing Contemporary Creative Songs.*

42. Panai's blog, accessed September 1, 2013, http://www.wretch.cc/blog/panaipah.

43. Panai's profile on SoundCloud, https://soundcloud.com/zamulee, accessed September 1, 2013.

44. Kao Tzu-Yang's site, http://we-168su.myweb.hinet.net/my01.htm, accessed September 1, 2013.

45. Tsai, "Kapah (Young Men)."

46. Lawrence Lessig, *Remix: Making Art and Commerce Thrive in the Hybrid Economy* (London, Penguin, 2008), 1–24.

47. Ginsburg, "Rethinking the Digital Age," 301.

48. "TedxTaipei Hu Defu—Inspiration for a Simple Life," accessed September 1, 2013, http://tedxtaipei.com/2012/03/defuhu-simplelifeidea/.

49. Chen, "Voices of Double Marginality."

50. Jeff Howe, "The Rise of Crowdsourcing," *Wired Magazine* 14, no. 6 (2006), http://www.wired.com/wired/archive/14.06/crowds.html; Lessig, *Remix,* 68–75.

51. Tan, *Beyond "Innocence,"* 1–11; Taylor *Strange Sounds;* 128–31 Guy, "Trafficking," 195–209.

52. Cory Doctorow, *Content: Selected Essays on Technology, Creativity, Copyright, and the Future of the Future* (San Francisco, CA: Tachyon, 2008), 101. Lessig, *Remix,* 68–69.

53. Ginsburg, "Rethinking the Digital Age," 304.

54. Mel Alexenberg, *The Future of Art in a Postdigital Age: From Hellenistic to Hebraic Consciousness* (Chicago: Intellect, 2011).

55. Tan, *Beyond "Innocence,"* 175–230.

56. Ibid., 81–120.

57. Peter Manuel, *Cassette Culture: Popular Music and Technology in North India* (Chicago: University of Chicago Press, 1993), 21.

58. Chun Yen Sun. "A Mountain Love Song between Cross-Cultural Couples: A Study of the Origin and Imagined Identity of 'The Maiden of Malan,'" *Minsu Quyi* 181 (2013): 265–319.

59. Jenkins, *Convergence Culture,* 1–22.

60. Alvin Toffler, *The Third Wave* New York: Harper Collins, 1980), 20.

61. Tsai, "Kapah (Young Men)," 175.

62. Maurice Benayoun, "Art after Technology," *MIT Technology Review* 7 (2008) *French Edition.*

63. Kim Cascone, "The Aesthetics of Failure: 'Post-digital' Tendencies in Contemporary Computer Music," *Computer Music Journal:* 24, no. 4 (2000): 12–18.

64. Alexenberg, *The Future of Art,* 9.

Chapter Two

Recording Technology, Traditioning, and Urban American Indian Powwow Performance

John-Carlos Perea

Introduction

The activity of music has always played a crucial role in my life as a teacher, scholar, musician, and human being. While changes in the technologies used to listen to music are often phrased in terms of "replacing" what came before for the sake of convenience, superior sound quality, or some other benefit, I find that my music collection at home still contains fairly equal parts vinyl, cassette, compact disc, and mp3. As a professional musician and scholar of American Indian musics,[1] I have found that no single recording medium can serve all my needs. This is especially visible and audible when I look and listen to my collection of powwow music, in which homemade and commercially produced cassettes outnumber other formats.[2]

This paper will reflect upon my lived experiences using both analog and digital recording technologies as a means to learn, archive, and disseminate powwow music. In this way the present work is broadly inspired by my correspondence with Professor David McAllester, in in which Professor McAllester once remarked that "much of the future of American Indian ethnomusicology will be 'homework' rather than 'fieldwork' and in the hands of Native musicologists."[3] As an urban Native (ethno)musicologist of Mescalero Apache, Irish, German, and Chicano descent, my homework for this chapter begins by situating myself more specifically in relation to relevant studies in ethnomusicology and American Indian Studies. I then discuss my formative period utilizing analog technology to learn Northern Plains powwow singing under the tutelage of Dr. Bernard Hoehner (Lakȟóta) as an undergraduate student at San Francisco State University (SFSU) in the mid-1990s.[4] I then turn to my experiences utilizing analog and digital technologies while co-leading the Sweetwater Singers and teaching American Indian music at universities in the San Francisco Bay Area from the early 2000s to the present.

In the context of this volume, the practices and experiences discussed in this chapter address "the ways in which Indigenous people have utilized digital technologies to revive . . . and transmit musical traditions in complex articulations of Indigeneity."[5] The articulation of Indigeneity emerging from my own classroom is perhaps better qualified as "urban Indigeneity"[6] due to our location at San Francisco State University and our proximity to the living histories of the Federal Relocation Program in the San Francisco Bay Area as well as local and national histories of American Indian activism such as the 1969 Occupation of Alcatraz Island by Indians of All Tribes.[7] It is my desire "to explore the opportunities and challenges presented by a range of digital media"[8] for musical performance within the overlapping intertribal and intercultural contexts of my urban classroom in order to better understand their implications for other Indigenous communities.[9] In that process, my students and I must necessarily confront the "ambivalent relationship"[10] between Indigenous communities and mass media while also considering the ways in which our individual and collective usage of digital and analog media in an American Indian Studies music classroom can intersect with and support local and national struggles toward Indigenous sovereignty and intellectual self-determination.[11] Over time, these technological practices and the media archives created from them have transformative potential, similar to that described by Faye Ginsburg, by providing students, teachers, staff and community with "a means of revivifying relationships to their lands, local languages, traditions, and histories, and of articulating community concerns."[12]

Ethnomusicologist Deborah Wong has written that "technology is a cultural practice. . . . An examination of technological practices in context is the only way to get at what technology 'does.'"[13] Following Wong, my goal is to better understand the ways in which my experience of different recording technologies and media have "traditioned" my experience of powwow music and in doing so how I transmit that sense of traditioning to my students. When I bring cassettes of American Indian music and cassette players into my classroom, my younger students and I always joke about my age relative to the recording being played and the technology being used to play it. Cassette recordings that I have digitized for academic archival purposes often elicit a similar response, as they carry the sonic markers of their analog origin in the form of scratches or variations in tape speed.

Jokes about my age or my students' age aside, since beginning my assistant professorship at SFSU in 2010 I have come to a new appreciation of the generational perspectives made audible by my lived experience and those of my students who, in some cases, have grown up in an almost totally digital world. My first experiences learning powwow music were made possible through the use of analog recording technology in the form of audiocassette recorders and commercially produced cassettes by Native American record labels such as Canyon Records and Indian House.[14] While the social experience of that technology may no longer be relevant to younger generations, the medium still provides a foundation for my teaching and musical practice. My archive of cassette recordings does not simply represent the journey of my musicking or my class music curriculum over ten years; it also stands as an aural history archive with implications for understanding aspects of urban American Indian powwow performance in the San Francisco Bay Area as they have emerged from SFSU.

In order to mediate my perspective with those of my students, I use the humor my students find in the visual of a tape recorder or the sonic imagery elicited by a cassette recording as a teachable moment through which to also discuss the social experience of different media and how they contribute to our shared understanding of, in this case, powwow musicking. Further development of this project will provide a foundational archive of recordings and writings through which to hear and read past voices and experiences in the present and, in doing so, to make those pasts and presents available to fill the needs of future generations, who will make these songs and technologies relevant for themselves.

Theoretical Foundations

My interest in exploring the relationship between technology and my personal powwow musical practices is inspired by previous studies relating to technology and First Nations musical practices by ethnomusicologists Beverley Diamond, Anna Hoefnagels, and Christopher Scales.[15] Both Diamond and Scales examine the ways in which Native musicians redefine the social activity of musicking in order to indigenize the environment of a recording studio and the products created therein. Diamond and Scales thus provide a point from which to consider questions of agency and technological mediation. Hoefnagels illuminates issues pertaining to powwow song protocols and highlights the ways in which the use of portable recording technology has made it easier to transmit songs and more difficult, is some cases, to transmit contextual information necessary to their understanding.

I employ the term *traditioning* as a means through which to understand the ways in which my conception of powwow music has been informed by my use of and relationship to particular forms of technology. My use of *tradition-ing* draws from the work of musicologist and pianist David Ake.[16] Focusing on jazz in particular, Ake employs the term as a lens through which to interpret the ways in which choices relating to repertoire, liner notes, instrumentation, arrangement, and album art may "configure jazz identities"[17] and communicate an artist's relationship to aspects of jazz "tradition." Listeners come to identify with these unique sonic markers and as such they potentially carry great weight in terms of their role in formulating knowledge about what does or does not constitute part of a given musical "tradition." If recordings can be analyzed as configuring elements of jazz identity, then I wish to import Ake's thinking into my own work and ask how recording technologies might configure powwow identities.

As I will show, developments in recording technology over the years during which I have been a powwow singer have allowed me to carry a portable recording studio with me. How have my lived experiences using analog and digital recording technologies traditioned the ways in which I hear, understand, and reproduce powwow music? How are those senses of tradition communicated and interpreted through making and sharing powwow drum rehearsal recordings? How has my traditioning changed over time, and how is this process shared with students and fellow powwow singers? These kinds of questions intersect not only with Ake's scholarship but also with that of earlier writers who have explored the "audible entanglements"[18] between the social uses of cassette media in relation to various aspects of identity formation.[19]

Finally, my intention to conduct autoethnography must be situated before proceeding. I have been fortunate enough to maintain a career as a performing musician since the mid-1990s. As much as I may have once wished to devote myself fully to performance, in the process of my undergraduate studies I came to realize that the role of a musician may productively involve equal parts teaching, study, and performance. It is through a balanced perspective between the identities of professor, scholar, and musician that I am able to contribute a unique critical perspective to ethnomusicological and American Indian Studies discourses and, for the purposes of this work, I have chosen to engage this effort in a self-reflexive fashion by conducting autoethnographic analysis and reflection on my changing musical practices over time.

My first exposure to this type of analysis was through the work of Deborah Wong.[20] Citing ethnomusicologist Michelle Kisliuk and sociologist Norman Denzin as influences, Wong examines her own taiko musical performance practice through the lens of performative ethnography: "I want to try to convey the vibrancy and the critical effects of taiko in all its particularities, and to reflect on my own process of telling, testimony, and cultural critique."[21] Wong's mention of Denzin's work on performative ethnography[22] led me to the term autoethnography, defined by Carolyn Ellis and Arthur P. Bochner as "an autobiographical genre of writing and research that displays multiple layers of consciousness, connecting the personal to the cultural."[23] Mary Louise Pratt speaks to a political "layer of consciousness" in her definition of autoethnography: "This term . . . refers to instances in which colonized subjects undertake to represent themselves in ways that *engage with* the colonizer's terms. If ethnographic texts are a means by which Europeans represent to themselves their (usually subjugated) others, autoethnographic texts are texts the others construct in response to or in dialogue with those metropolitan representations."[24] I find each of these conceptions useful for the project and am therefore reticent to classify the present work as "performative ethnography" or "autoethnography" alone. Like Wong, I want to try and convey my process of learning, archiving, and transmitting powwow music to you in all of its complexity and, in doing so, to reflect upon my own role in that process. That process must necessarily take place through the "multiple layers of consciousness" referred to by Ellis and Bochner, in my case reflecting the aforementioned balance I wish to foreground between teaching, scholarship, and performance. I also want to recognize and interrogate the politicized nature of these activities emanating from an urban American Indian community in a department of American Indian Studies in a college of Ethnic Studies.

Given these many entanglements, I want to situate myself in relation to these ideas and allow the progression of the study to suggest further implications and areas for continued development. I am aware that this type of analysis potentially triggers questions of "insider/outsider" status and the perceived effect of that binary on the present work. For myself, I do not subscribe to the idea that I must study music other than my own in order to produce results that can be considered "valid" or "truthful." Texts such as Barz and Cooley's *Shadows in the Field: New Perspectives for Fieldwork in Ethnomusicology* have provided insight into different fieldwork experiences on the part of researchers who perform and conduct research on music from their home communities.[25] These investigations illuminate the idea that the complexity of ethnomusicological discourse cannot simply be known by tracing moments of similarity between scholars and the people whose music they study. In fact, it is equally if not more important to come to an understanding of the differences between music-cultures—and the diverse approaches of the many ethnomusicologists who study them—in order to become critically aware of one's place within the world of musicking.

Here I find it useful to recall the words of author Thomas King (Cherokee): "The truth about stories is that's all we are."[26] Research findings, whether they are obtained through scientific, autoethnographic, or other means, are stories through which we understand our place in the world and its changes over time. My interest is not to present a scientific account of one powwow singer's experiences with analog and digital technologies but rather to relate the intersections between my own lived experiences and the lived experiences of the many individuals whose combined efforts contribute to a global ethnomusicological discourse. This is not to say that different methods cannot coexist within that discourse. In fact, I believe that it is only through greater attention to these types of differences that a state of equilibrium will ever be achieved. To paraphrase artist Jimmie Durham (Cherokee), that process cannot begin with a longer list of facts.[27] Instead, I follow curator and author Paul Chaat Smith (Comanche), whose comments on art practice I find similarly applicable to ethnomusicological method and the present study: "At best, this is what serious art practice is about: choosing the right questions and finding ways—visually, intellectually, emotionally—to explore them with viewers. It is not really about answering them. Often a successful investigation will not answer a single one, and instead raise new questions."[28] It is hoped that by mobilizing the aforementioned concepts under the theoretical framing of "homework" gifted by Professor McAllester, other performers and scholars will consider the applicability of these ideas as a way of thinking about their own works in order to understand points of intersection and divergence between different cultures and their musical and media practices. The purpose of this work then is not to answer questions as much as it is to pose questions that will continue a long-lasting conversation as fluid as the practices under consideration.

Early Experiences

I was first introduced to powwows and powwow singing as a child, while attending local San Francisco Bay Area events with my mother and father. I did not have an opportunity to begin singing, however, until I began my undergraduate studies at SFSU, where I met Dr. Bernard Hoehner. Dr. Hoehner was a Lakȟóta (Húŋkpap'a and Sihásapa) powwow singer, Northern Traditional powwow dancer, powwow emcee, World War II veteran, and one of the first American Indians to graduate with a degree in veterinary medicine. By the time I met him in the early 1990s, Dr. Hoehner had been lecturing in American Indian Studies at San Francisco State for almost twenty years while maintaining a successful veterinary practice. He taught classes on religion and philosophy, science, the Lakȟóta language, and powwow music and dance. Dr. Hoehner and I met and began our relationship in the context of his AIS 220 American Indian Music class.

AIS 220 focused on the music and dance of the intertribal powwow. The class began by providing students with an introduction to the many histories informing contemporary powwow music and dance. With that foundation, Dr. Hoehner would then teach students how to make their own powwow drumsticks. At that point, in order to begin teaching the section of the class devoted to powwow music, students were invited to sit at Dr. Hoehner's powwow drum, a bass drum adapted from a Slingerland drum kit. The unique opportunity to learn to drum and sing made AIS 220 a very popular class with both Native and non-Native students.

The powwow songs learned in AIS 220 came from a variety of sources. In some cases we learned songs that Dr. Hoehner had acquired through his many years attending, emceeing, dancing, and singing at powwows. In other cases the songs were originals made by Dr. Hoehner.[29] Dr. Hoehner stipulated that we would learn the songs aurally; we were not allowed to use Western musical notation to write them out. Lakȟóta lyrics were provided by Dr. Hoehner where appropriate but, due to the mechanics of powwow singing, it is fairly difficult to read music and sing at the same time, so those lyrics were only useful in a "homework" study capacity. Dr. Hoehner encouraged students to use their ears in the process of learning and memorizing powwow songs, as this was how he himself had learned to sing. He also allowed students to bring handheld audiocassette recorders to class and to record classes in which drum rehearsals were conducted. One of my earliest memories of singing with Dr. Hoehner involves going with him to the SFSU student store to purchase a handheld cassette recorder to take with me to class. I still have cassettes in my personal archive made during my first class meetings as a student in AIS 220.

In addition to encouraging students to make use of handheld cassette recorders in class, Dr. Hoehner also created tapes of listening examples and made them available to students through the school reserve library. These tapes were made from a variety of LP and other cassette sources, as well as from original recordings of Dr. Hoehner's voice. By the time I took AIS 220 with Dr. Hoehner in the early 1990s and later began serving as his teaching assistant, the listening tapes were primarily live recordings of Dr. Hoehner singing the songs that were to be assigned and learned for that particular term. Dr. Hoehner and I would sit in his office with a cassette tape recorder between us in order to learn, sing, and record the songs for a given semester's class. I have copies of these cassettes in my archive, as well.

These early cassettes form the archival basis of my understanding of powwow music and were/are consumed in a variety of contexts. As a student in AIS 220, I used Dr. Hoehner's listening example tapes to study for listening quizzes that were given as part of the class. These tapes, however, although good for learning to identify a song, were not always the best to use for learning to sing a song. Since the listening example tapes usually contained shortened versions of the powwow songs taught in class, I often made use of in-class rehearsals to record Dr. Hoehner singing a longer version of a particular powwow song I wanted to learn. I would then create mix tapes of my favorite powwow songs. My own powwow practice regimen involved repeatedly singing and drumming along with those mix tapes until I could commit a song to memory. Given the immediate need in class to use listening example and rehearsal tapes as study aids, I recall that most students brought handheld recorders to class meetings and, with Dr. Hoehner's encouragement, shared their tapes when needed as a form of class notes.

My use of analog technology in the early stages of my experiences with pow-wow music traditioned me to favor a particular practice regimen that used the qualities of cassettes to mimic the experience of singing and drumming. I hear myself as socially interacting with the cassette recorder and the musical encounters contained on the tapes I made in class. That interaction is not limited to the activity of practicing, but also includes repeated interactions with the content contained on the cassettes. When I listen back to recordings I made as a student in Dr. Hoehner's class, I am immediately struck by the fact that there is in some cases more discussion and conversation on those recordings than actual singing. Dr. Hoehner constantly drilled his students, myself included, on the importance of singing the right song for the right occasion when at a powwow or other community event.

The listening example tapes I made with Dr. Hoehner as his teaching assistant are similar to the classroom study tapes I made as a student, in that group discussion and conversation are just as prevalent as the actual songs. I recall that in some cases we would use one cassette to record our rehearsing and talking about the songs and another blank cassette to make a clean study copy for class use. The speed and ease of replacing cassettes, as well as the relatively low cost of the media, made it possible for Dr. Hoehner to generate a large amount of material in a short amount of time and to listen back to those songs or stories almost instantaneously.

The fidelity of these tapes is another interesting issue to consider. Sometimes when I recorded, I was standing too close or the recorder was placed too close to the drum while a song was being sung. This resulted in a recording with indecipherable lyrics or vocables but a clear spoken explanation of its purpose and function. In other cases I have recordings where I was standing too far away with my recorder, leading to an unclear explanation but a better overall recording of the song as sung. It is important to realize that no one tape can be considered "good" or "bad," since it is often necessary to use multiple tapes in order to fully learn and attempt to understand a song. My tape archive reflects this in its size, as it is often necessary to keep one tape for the simple fact that it contains a prized recording of a single song.

The learning experiences described here can be contextualized within ethnomusicological literature for the purpose of illuminating tribal specificity and intertribal exchange with regard not just to musical transmission and technology but also to formulations of what constitutes traditional learning and, by extension, traditioning. Frances Densmore and Bruno Nettl are two of the many ethnomusicologists who have written about the religious and philosophical foundations of Native singing traditions in which a particular song might be learned through a dream or through a relationship to a spiritual guide.[30] I do not recall Dr. Hoehner discussing these concepts directly in a classroom setting, but he referenced them indirectly by relating the functionality of powwow singing to the holism of intertribal American Indian worldviews. In *Ethnomusicology of the Flathead Indians*, Alan P. Merriam cites the themes of persistent community participation and imitation as necessary to the development of a Flathead singer.[31] Dr. Hoehner's classroom and listening tapes provided a space for students to practice imitation and in doing so to choose the level of persistence they applied to their studies inside and outside the classroom. Luke Lassiter, writing from his experiences with Kiowa singers, notes the importance of persistent community participation and imitation and also highlights family transmission, relationships with older singers, and learning the functionality of different song types as essential to the development of a singer.[32] Dr. Hoehner's classroom and listening tapes provided a way for students to develop a relationship to Dr. Hoehner as an elder singer and to experience the responsibilities of powwow singing as transmitted through knowledge of their functional use in a given powwow. In retrospect, I recognize how incredibly fortunate I am to have had a relationship with Dr. Hoehner. He passed away in 1995, and as the years pass, I feel the responsibility to provide guidance in a similar and respectful fashion for the students who take my classes.[33]

When I listen to these recordings today in order to teach my classes at SFSU, my students and I socially interact with the past in our present. The elements of tradition imparted by Dr. Hoehner and recorded by students in class can be archived via the use of technology, but the act of traditioning or configuring powwow identities in my case is dependent upon the social experience of having known Dr. Hoehner and having taken AIS 220. When I listen to my recordings of Dr. Hoehner as part of my current classroom preparations, I listen to them through the past filter of my memories of him and the present filter of my current participation in American Indian communities both on- and off-campus. In this way my students enter into a classroom space where simultaneous experiences of traditioning are mediated along technological and generational perspectives as they discuss past experiences of urban powwow culture while seeking to apply that knowledge in ways that are meaningful to the needs of their own individual and community lived experiences. The stories and other contextual information shared by Dr. Hoehner function in the present moment as a sonic text, directing and teaching listeners through his voice and the voice of the other students present. They are as valuable as any other text in marking a particular moment in time, and therefore the continued sounding of those cassettes carries a particular responsibility on the part of those who listen to them.

The Blue Horse Singers

After studying with Dr. Hoehner in the context of AIS 220 and later assisting him in the same class, I was invited by him to sing with the Blue Horse Singers. Dr. Hoehner founded the Blue Horse Singers as an extracurricular vehicle through which to meet the needs of local urban Native students and community members who wished to perform on the local powwow circuit and serve the needs of the local Native community when and where a drum was requested. At the time I joined the Blue Horse Singers the group had a revolving membership of eight to ten singers who met every Tuesday night for rehearsal at a member's home. Handheld cassette recorders were always present at these rehearsals as a way of documenting the repertoire.

Tuesday night rehearsals always began with a group dinner. At some point after everyone had eaten and visited, Dr. Hoehner would indicate that it was time to start singing, and we would move from the dining room into a space that doubled as our drum rehearsal space. Rehearsals often began with a prayer in Lakȟóta given by Dr. Hoehner or another member of the group designated by Dr. Hoehner. It is interesting to note that while many committees strictly prohibit the audio or video recording of sacred moments at powwows, Dr. Hoehner permitted us to record these prayers so they could be learned and repeated by other drum members. Most singers, myself included, either held our recorders in one hand while drumming with the other or set the recorder on the floor or a nearby surface. In this way cassette recorders were a visible and accepted part of our group rehearsal practice.

The Blue Horse Singers drum rehearsal tapes are similar to the AIS 220 classroom rehearsal tapes in that they document both powwow songs and the stories and other contextual information accompanying those songs. These tapes are subject to the same fidelity issues as the classroom rehearsal tapes; but the Tuesday night rehearsal tapes are different from the classroom rehearsal tapes in that we tended to turn on the tape recorder and let it run at the Blue Horse Singers rehearsals, whereas the classroom tapes are more regular in terms of their start and stop points. Dr. Hoehner and other singers were more informal at these evening rehearsals, and I recall that there was always a sense that it was better to leave the recorder on, as you never knew what stories you might miss if you were not paying attention. Bringing one's recorder to catch the unique experience of a given rehearsal was thus an essential part of the social experience of a Tuesday night rehearsal. The tendency to leave the cassette running also led to interesting moments where the songs or stories are abruptly cut off after the tape ran out. I do not recall a preference for one length of tape over the other on the part of students or singers for classroom or Blue Horse Singers rehearsals. It is most likely that the tapes bought were either (a) easily accessible in bulk sizes or (b) quickly available before class or drum rehearsal at the university student store or corner market.

While both the classroom and Blue Horse Singers tapes are important for the songs and histories sounded through their playing, the Blue Horse Singers tapes take on further importance in terms of providing a sonic referent traditioning listeners as to Dr. Hoehner's preferred drum "sound." Since the Blue Horse Singers were expected to perform at powwows and other community events, Dr. Hoehner can be heard on those rehearsal tapes providing in-depth commentary to singers on subjects ranging from proper vocal production to the particular intricacies of powwow song rhythms. If the classroom tapes provide generalized traditioning as to the comportment and background necessary to become a powwow singer, the Blue Horse rehearsal tapes provided very specific information as to what it meant to sound like a singer from Dr. Hoehner's teaching standpoint. I continue to interact with cassettes from this period in order to refresh my memory of particular songs and, in particular, Dr. Hoehner's powwow music aesthetic.

The Sweetwater Singers: From Analog to Digital

Dr. Hoehner passed away on October 12, 1995. Following his passing the decision was made to continue his teaching and musicking by respectfully retiring the Blue Horse Singers and forming a new drum group. That drum group was eventually named the Sweetwater Singers. The Sweetwater Singers are co-led by my father, Dr. Jacob Perea, and myself. Many of the members are either former Blue Horse Singers or, following another tradition set out by Dr. Hoehner, current SFSU students and former students who acquitted themselves with distinction while taking my American Indian Music class.

As opposed to the Blue Horse Singers, the Sweetwater Singers hold rehearsals based on singer availability. Our tendency is to rehearse in preparation for events, something I attribute to personal habits on my part formed while performing in jazz ensembles since the 1990s. While our rehearsals are not as frequent as the Blue Horse rehearsals were, we still attempt to replicate the atmosphere of past experiences by gathering for meals whenever possible and sharing stories relating to song repertoire as a part of our collective rehearsal practice. My recollection is that the early days of the Sweetwater Singers in the late 1990s were characterized primarily by a reliance on audiocassette technology. Our primary texts used by the group as a foundation for our singing were each singer's archive of cassette recordings from time spent with Dr. Hoehner. As such, we assembled mix tapes of favorite songs to exchange with each other as a way of sharing information and teaching each other songs. Thus, many Sweetwater Singers rehearsal tapes are attempts to sound like the singers on the Tuesday night rehearsal tapes. In other words, we used tapes to replicate the sound of other tapes.

Early Sweetwater rehearsals were not recorded, as our emphasis at that time was more on cataloging older cassettes than on making new ones. By the time we began recording our own rehearsals I had purchased a Sharp portable minidisc recorder and used that for a period of time. This change from analog to digital took place in the early 2000s and to my recollection marks the first time I began using digital technology as part of my powwow musicking. Interestingly enough, I stopped using the minidisc recorder because it was too difficult to make duplicate recordings for other drum members unless they also owned minidisc players. At that time, cassette tapes remained the medium of choice for disseminating songs due to ease of use and relative speed of duplication.

During my time as a lecturer at SFSU teaching American Indian Music in the early 2000s, I also continued to make use of cassette technology in order to disseminate listening examples to my classes. I began by using the playlists I had learned from as a student and eventually began recording my own tapes with teaching assistants as Dr. Hoehner had done with me. I remain surprised at the different uses to which students put those cassette recordings. While many would use them to study from and practice with as I had done, other students would listen to them for relaxation while studying or driving. As a teacher I also became aware that many students were not making copies of the listening example tapes because they felt the process of making cassette copies was too time-consuming; many students advocated for the use of compact disc media in class. The social experience of musicking that influenced my powwow traditioning was beginning to change, and those changes were also being felt by my students in ways that would change us all.

The increasing accessibility of compact disc duplication equipment in laptop computers made it possible to begin using CDs more frequently in the context of teaching and also during my graduate studies at UC Berkeley, beginning in 2003. The time necessary to digitize the large archives of commercial and rehearsal cassettes accumulated by myself and other Sweetwater Singers meant that certain titles became inaccessible in this shift unless a cassette player could be found or until that title was released on CD and became available either at a powwow or online for purchase.

At the beginning of 2008 I worked as a Visiting Artist Fellow with the Institute for Diversity in the Arts at Stanford University. I then decided to upgrade from my minidisc recorder and purchased a Boss BR-600 digital recorder. The BR-600 is essentially built to model a four-track recorder, and one of its main features is the ability to record almost unlimited overdubs. In place of a cassette, the BR-600 stores information on an SD card that can be backed up via USB to a hard drive. This purchase led to a significant change in my powwow musicking, facilitated in part by digital technology.

In the days of the Blue Horse Singers, the ability to create listening tapes for class use was always dependent on the availability of two or more singers. This is due to a variety of factors. First, Dr. Hoehner taught that proper powwow vocal technique is dependent upon the ability of singers to "harmonize" with each other. Since powwow singing takes place in unison, harmonizing refers here to the ability of singers to match pitch and vibrato in a consistent fashion. Dr. Hoehner liked to include this facet on listening tapes and I try to continue his practice. Second, the structure of a powwow song, called a "push-up," consists of a lead phrase sung by the lead singer and a response, or "second," sung by the rest of the drum group. In order to represent the lead and the second prior to the accessibility of technology that made vocal overdubbing easy to create, it was necessary to have two or more singers present for recording. My shift from analog to digital recording technology in the late 2000s drastically changed this requirement.

I first experimented with vocal overdubbing in the context of powwow singing while recording with the Paul Winter Consort in 2007.[34] I remember that experience as exciting but disorienting at the same time, as it caused me to rethink my own singing technique in order to reproduce both the lead and second parts in a powwow song. I recalled that experience while at Stanford in 2008; in order to create the powwow listening examples for that class by myself, I used overdubbing with my BR-600 to represent the lead and second part. In this way I digitally traditioned my powwow musicking, and in the process, a musical activity that my previous analog traditioning had taught me was dependent on multiple social relationships became something I could do alone and in my own home. While I did not consider this change deeply at the time, I will reflect in the conclusion on the implications of this change for the Sweetwater Singers and myself.

Current Teaching and Singing Practices

I currently teach AIS 320 American Indian Music at SFSU. In that class I follow the model set out by Dr. Hoehner, teaching students through active participation by inviting them to sit at the same powwow drum I learned to sing with in the early 1990s. I require my students to use only their ears as they learn five to ten powwow songs per semester. Listening examples are provided online using iLearn, SFSU's web-based learning system. Instead of taking tapes out at the library, I upload mp3 files to a class website. The students use a password to either stream the songs or download and study them by creating their own playlists, as I once created my own mix tapes. I only upload songs that are part of the Blue Horse and Sweetwater repertoire, as those have been publicly shared via analog and digital means since Dr. Hoehner first taught AIS

Figure 2.1. The Sweetwater Singers performing at the Forty-Fifth Anniversary of the College of Ethnic Studies at San Francisco State University, October 26, 2014. *Left to right:* Dr. John-Carlos Perea, Dr. Jessica Bissett Perea, Josephine Perea, Dirk Alphin, Jacqueline Corona, Tonya Joe Dollente, Dr. Jacob Perea, C. S. Gomora. Photo by Luigino De Grandis. Courtesy of the College of Ethnic Studies at San Francisco State University.

220. In order to respect contemporary concerns in relation to copyright and Indigenous intellectual property, I encourage students who are interested in expanding their recording collections to buy directly from Native musicians and recording labels or to purchase texts with listening CDs created in collaboration with Native musicians and recording labels.[35] The subject of downloading and sharing class songs is always brought to the attention of my students, serving as an entry point into important discussions on the nature of copyright law and protocols—Indigenous and otherwise.

My students may bring a digital recorder or iPhone to class, but I notice that most do not these days. I find this point interesting, as my memory of taking AIS 220 is that most students brought recorders, and some collected the recordings that came from those classes. My sense is that most students tend to focus on the listening examples provided online rather than recording rehearsals because class assessments are based upon the online material. I also find that contemporary powwow prohibitions against audio and video recording lead many students to fear bringing recorders to class. On the one hand, I respect the impetus to lessen the potential invasiveness of digital technology

Figure 2.2. The Sweetwater Singers performing at the Forty-Fifth Anniversary of the College of Ethnic Studies at San Francisco State University, October 26, 2014. *Left to right:* C. S. Gomora, Nicholas Gomez, Dr. Robert Collins, Dr. John-Carlos Perea, Dirk Alphin, Tonya Joe Dollente, Dr. Jacob Perea, Steven Alvarez. Photo by Luigino De Grandis. Courtesy of the College of Ethnic Studies at San Francisco State University.

by limiting its use where appropriate. On the other hand, a YouTube search of "powwow" returns 261,000 hits from all over the country and the world. The difficulties mediating between these issues notwithstanding, I hope to find ways to bring the social activity of recording back into my classroom by emphasizing how to do so in a respectful way that is context sensitive.

When I create listening examples for AIS 320, I do so either with Dirk Alphin, a former Blue Horse Singer and Sweetwater Singer since the inception of that group, or with the core group of Sweetwater Singers, which currently numbers between five and six singers, depending on the singers' availability. In the fall of 2012, I began a sabbatical project to revisit the Blue Horse and Sweetwater archives in order to refresh my SFSU music curriculum with the goal of training a new group of singers and teaching them to sing Dr. Hoehner's repertoire. The medium for those recordings will be digital, but our reference material remains analog. Our most recent recorded examples were made as part of the sabbatical project using a MacBook to record the listening examples direct to hard disk; a Zoom H2 recorder as a microphone; and Audacity, a popular free audio program, as my software interface. My reason for recording direct to hard drive was to make the process of eventually uploading the mp3 files to iLearn more expedient.

Sweetwater Singers rehearsals still take place as needed before events. Interestingly enough, where once we used to try to record every rehearsal and listen regularly to tapes, we now rely more on singers' memories to shape the course of a given rehearsal. We begin with drum "standards" that are familiar to the group in order to warm up and focus. Once we are warmed up, either Dirk or I will begin remembering older songs and rehearse them with younger drum members. At least one digital recorder is always on, and rehearsal recordings are edited afterwards and made available to the group for download by private cloud storage.

Implications

In their description of traditional ecological knowledge, Marie Battiste (Mi'kmaq) and James (Sa'ke'j) Youngblood Henderson (Chickasaw, Cheyenne) state: "What is traditional about traditional ecological knowledge is not its antiquity, but the way it is acquired and used. In other words, the social processes of learning and sharing knowledge . . . lies at the heart of its traditionality."[36] If one extends their understanding of traditional knowledge to the realm of music, then the music archives created by Dr. Hoehner and his students and singers stand as repositories of traditional knowledge defined not by their age but by the circumstances that created the conditions of possibility for their existence. I would further argue that the social experience of different recording technologies might be situated as part of traditional Native music knowledge in both urban and rural contexts. It is therefore vital to consider the implications of my reflections, as they can guide future investigation into both my students' and my own experience of the intersections between musicking and technology.

Primary among these is that a recording of Dr. Hoehner in 1993 does not sound the same when played in 2014. I hear and interpret Dr. Hoehner differently today than I did eighteen years ago. In this way, I find that my own traditioning—my sonic sense of identity as a powwow singer—must be understood as a fluid process, since the social experience of playing those tapes is unique each time I press the play button. My archives are not static entities of unchanging information; they are in fact dynamic, given the fact that the classroom interpretation of the material contained on those cassettes must change over time in order to remain relevant to those who wish to learn. I may return to a given tape because it features a particular song, but I have to teach that song to students who are traditioned by digital technology and other generational factors.

If my traditioning is fluid, then I must also assume at this point that the traditioning of my students is similarly fluid. I require that my students find ways to make what they learn in AIS 320 relevant to their own lives. In some cases this entails representing the songs through different perspectives or even making new songs to specifically address a context or need for which there is no precedent. At one time in my career I saw this change as dangerous to the maintenance of these ways and worked to try and minimize any differences. Now I hear those changes as part of the continued health of these musical practices. Powwows are not practiced the same way today as they were fifty years ago. Part of the beauty of powwows is that they change every weekend in response to the needs of the people who attend them in a manner that could be thought of as "strategic traditionalism."[37] If the event can change, then it follows, in my interpretation, that the songs must also be allowed room to change, grow, and remain healthy. Referring back to Battiste and Henderson, this type of musical knowledge is important not because it is preserved and reenacted, but because it is continually remade.

The foundation of that health lies in the social activity of powwow musicking. When I first recorded powwow listening examples for my Stanford class by overdubbing myself, I gave very little thought to the changes I was making. When I presented those mp3s to my students, I remember a large number of them remarking that the sound seemed strange and that it was odd to hear me singing with myself. I realize now that my students were reacting to the fact that I had taken a social activity they were first exposed to as involving multiple voices through analog traditioning and changed it to something that I made individual through digital traditioning. While every musician's response to technology is unique to their lived experience, I find that for myself, it is possible to combine the convenience of digital technology with the social character I associate with analog technology. I would further argue that innovations in Native American musicking, such as the harmonized powwow singing of Alex E. Smith (Pawnee/Sauk & Fox) and Cheevers Toppah (Kiowa/Diné) or the peyote singing of Louie Gonnie (Diné), are but two examples of how others have come to find technological and musical balance in their own performance practices through the use of overdubbing and other studio technology to communicate their own traditional musical knowledges.[38] I hope, through future explorations into this topic, to better understand the ways in which I and other musicians negotiate these balances between technology and musicking, since those skills will remain essential to singers and listeners as technologies continue to change in the future. It is certainly a balance I will continue to teach, study, perform, and advocate for in my own life.

Notes

This chapter was developed from a paper that was originally intended for presentation at the Symposium on Music, Indigeneity, and Digital Media held April 2010 in the Music Department at Royal Holloway, University of London. I was unable to attend the symposium due to the passing of my maternal grandmother, Gertrude Mohr, earlier that same month. I would like to thank Drs. Thomas Hilder, Henry Stobart, and Shzr Ee Tan for inviting me to stay involved in the creation of the present volume and for their supportive commentary on the development of this work. This work is dedicated with love to the memory of my grandmother and with thanks to Dr. Hoehner, the Hoehner family, the Blue Horse and Sweetwater Singers, my colleagues in American Indian Studies and the College of Ethnic Studies, and the students of AIS 220 and 320 at SFSU. I am also grateful to Dean Kenneth Monteiro and Associate Dean Amy Sueyoshi in the College of Ethnic Studies, Luigino De Grandis (luiphotography.com), and Monica Magtoto (magtotoart.com) for their kind assistance with the images included in this chapter.

1. I follow ethnomusicologist Tara Browner's (Choctaw) example with regard to the names used to refer to the original inhabitants of the United States and Canada in scholarly and public discourses. Browner employs the terms *Indian, American Indian, Native American, Native Canadian, Native North American, First Nations,* and *indigenous,* "because all are used by Native American Indians when writing about themselves." See Tara Browner, *Heartbeat of the People: Music and Dance of the Northern Pow-Wow* (Urbana: University of Illinois Press, 2002), xi, original emphases.

2. Powwows are Native American social events that employ an intertribally shared repertoire of music and dance to both maintain and create intertribal and intercultural communities. While these events do incorporate a sacred component for many participants, I have found in my years of participating in and teaching about powwows that it is impossible to generalize the unique individuality of that sacredness without doing violence to it. In my own classroom, I therefore approach powwow music as primarily social in character and introduce the complexity of those sacred intersections over the course of a given semester. Powwows have long featured as a topic in ethnomusicological studies of American Indian musics. For recent examples, see Browner, *Heartbeat of the People*; Clyde Ellis, *A Dancing People: Powwow Culture on the Southern Plains* (Lawrence: University Press of Kansas, 2003); Clyde Ellis, Luke E. Lassiter, and Gary H. Dunham, eds., *Powwow* (Lincoln: University of Nebraska Press, 2005).

3. McAllester as quoted in John-Carlos Perea, "Preface," in *Intertribal Native American Music in the United States* (New York: Oxford University Press, 2014), xiv.

4. I will provide an individual's tribal affiliation(s) where applicable in parentheses following the first mention of their name.

5. Hilder, introduction to this volume. I chose to remove "repatriate" from the original quote in order to respect the legal implications of that term in relation to the Native American Graves Protection and Repatriation Act.

6. Jeffrey Sissons, "Urban Indigeneity," in *First Peoples: Indigenous Cultures and Their Futures* (London: Reaktion, 2005), 61–84.

7. On the Federal Relocation Program, see Donald Lee Fixico, *The Urban Indian Experience in America* (Albuquerque: University of New Mexico Press, 2000). On the 1969 Occupation of Alcatraz Island see Troy R. Johnson, *The Occupation of Alcatraz Island: Indian Self-Determination and the Rise of Indian Activism* (Urbana: University of Illinois Press, 2008).

8. Hilder, introduction to this volume.

9. I situate my classroom as "intertribal" rather than "pan-Indian," as "intertribal" is more representative of my lived experience attending powwows in the San Francisco Bay Area. Ellis and Lassiter suggest "replacing the term *Pan-Indianism* with *intertribal,* a term widely preferred by powwow participants themselves, and one that we believe more accurately describes both the common and negotiated ground of powwow culture." Clyde Ellis and Luke Eric Lassiter, "Introduction," in *Powwow,* ed. Clyde Ellis, Luke Eric Lassiter, and Gary H. Dunham (Lincoln: University of Nebraska Press, 2005), xiii.

10. Pamela Wilson and Michelle Stewart, "Indigeneity and Indigenous Media on the Global Stage," in *Global Indigenous Media: Cultures, Poetics, and Politics,* ed. Pamela Wilson and Michelle Stewart (Durham: Duke University Press), 3.

11. Jack D. Forbes, "Intellectual Self-Determination and Sovereignty: Implications for Native Studies and for Native Intellectuals," *Wicazo Sa Review,* 13 (1998): 11–23.

12. Faye Ginsburg, "Rethinking the Digital Age," in *Global Indigenous Media: Cultures, Poetics, and Politics,* ed. Pamela Wilson and Michelle Stewart (Durham, NC: Duke University Press, 2008), 302.

13. Deborah Wong, "Pham Duy at Home: Vietnamese American Technoculture in Orange County," in *Speak It Louder: Asian Americans Making Music* (New York: Routledge, 2004), 89.

14. For more information on both record labels, see Canyon Records online store, http://www.canyonrecords.com, and Indian House Records online store, http://www.indianhouse.com, both accessed September 2, 2016.

15. Beverley Diamond, "Media as Social Action: Native American musicians in the recording studio," in *Wired for Sound: Engineering and Technologies in Sonic Cultures,* ed. Paul D. Greene and Thomas Porcello (Middletown, CT: Wesleyan University Press, 2005), 118–37; Anna Hoefnagels, "Powwow Songs: Traveling Songs and Changing Protocol," *The World of Music* 44, no. 1 (2002): 127–36; Christopher Scales, "The Politics and Aesthetics of Recording: A Comparative Canadian Case Study of Powwow and Contemporary Native American Music," *The World of Music* 44, no. 1 (2002): 41–59.

16. David Ake, "Jazz Traditioning," in *Jazz Cultures* (Berkeley: University of California Press, 2002), 146–76.

17. Ibid., 146.

18. Jocelyne Guilbault, "Audible Entanglements: Nation and Diasporas in Trinidad's Calypso Music Scene," *Small Axe* 17 (2005): 40–63.

19. For example, see Susan Rodgers, "Batak Tape Cassette Kinship: Constructing Kinship through the Indonesian National Mass Media," *American Ethnologist* 13,

no. 1 (1986); Paul D. Greene, "Sound Engineering in a Tamil Village: Playing Audio Cassettes as Devotional Performance," *Ethnomusicology* 43, no. 3 (1999): 459–89; Charles Hirschkind, "The Ethics of Listening: Cassette-Sermon Audition in Contemporary Egypt," *American Ethnologist* 28, no. 3 (2001): 623–49; Karin Bijsterveld and José van Dijck, eds., *Sound Souvenirs: Audio Technologies, Memory and Cultural Practices* (Amsterdam: Amsterdam University Press, 2009).

20. Wong, "ImprovisAsians: Free Improvisation as Asian American Resistance," 321–38; Wong, "Moving: From Performance to Performative Ethnography and Back Again," in *Shadows in the Field: New Perspectives for Fieldwork in Ethnomusicology*, ed. Gregory F. Barz and Timothy J. Cooley (New York: Oxford University Press, 2008), 76–89.

21. Wong, "Moving," 78.

22. Norman K. Denzin, *Performative Ethnography: Critical Pedagogy and the Politics of Culture* (Thousand Oaks: SAGE, 2003).

23. Carolyn Ellis and Arthur P. Bochner, "Autoethnography, Personal Narrative, Reflexivity: Researcher as Subject," in *Handbook of Qualitative Research*, ed. Norman K. Denzin and Yvonna S. Lincoln (Thousand Oaks: SAGE, 2000), 739.

24. Mary Louise Pratt, *Imperial Eyes: Travel Writing and Transculturation*, 2nd ed. (New York: Routledge, 2008), 9, original emphasis.

25. Gregory F. Barz and Timothy J. Cooley, eds., *Shadows in the Field: New Perspectives for Fieldwork in Ethnomusicology*, 2nd ed. (New York: Oxford University Press, 2008).

26. Thomas King, *The Truth about Stories: A Native Narrative* (Minneapolis: University of Minnesota Press, 2005), 2.

27. Jimmie Durham, "A Certain Lack of Coherence," in *A Certain Lack of Coherence*, ed. Jean Fisher (London: Kala Press, 1993), 147.

28. Paul Chaat Smith, "After the Gold Rush," in *Everything You Know about Indians is Wrong* (Minneapolis: University of Minnesota Press, 2009), 36.

29. In my experiences performing and studying with Dr. Hoehner, I recall him referring to "making songs" rather than "composing songs." Browner's research on powwow music discusses this terminology in terms of multiple ways of understanding and speaking about musical practices. See Tara Browner, "Making and Singing Pow-Wow Songs: Text, Form and the Significance of Culture-Based Analysis," *Ethnomusicology* 44, no. 2 (2000): 214–33.

30. Frances Densmore, "Musical Composition among the American Indians," *American Speech*, 2 (1927): 393–94; Bruno Nettl, *Blackfoot Musical Thought* (Kent, OH: Kent State University Press, 1989), 96–103.

31. Alan P. Merriam, *Ethnomusicology of the Flathead Indians* (Chicago: Aldine, 1967), 39–40. Other authors highlighting these themes in relation to powwow singing include, Severt Young Bear and R. D. Theisz, "Part III: The Singing Rooster in the Black Hills," in *Standing in the Light: A Lakota Way of Seeing* (Lincoln: University of Nebraska Press, 1994), 67; Christopher A. Scales, *Recording Culture: Powwow Music and the Aboriginal Recording Industry on the Northern Plains* (Durham: Duke University Press, 2012), 130–35.

32. Lassiter, Luke E., *The Power of Kiowa Song: A Collaborative Ethnography* (Tucson: University of Arizona Press, 1998), 148–49.

33. I personally resonate with the discussion of learning pow-wow between Ojibwa singer Gabriel Desrosiers and ethnomusicologist Christopher Scales where Desrosiers reflects on "watching elderly singers . . . these elders would get up and talk about singing, how to treat the song and the drum." Dr. Hoehner fulfilled a similar role for me and for many other students through the vehicle of AIS 220. Desrosiers also notes the responsibility of serving as a "role model" to emerging young singers. Gabriel Desrosiers and Christopher Scales, "Contemporary Northern Plains Powwow Music: The Twin Influences of Recording and Competition," in *Aboriginal Music in Contemporary Canada: Echoes and Exchanges*, ed. Anna Hoefnagels and Beverley Diamond (Montreal: McGill-Queen's University Press, 2012), 94.

34. Paul Winter Consort, *Crestone* (Living Music LMU-41, 2007), CD.

35. For example, Beverley Diamond, *Native American Music in Eastern North America*, Global Music Series (New York: Oxford University Press, 2008); John-Carlos Perea, *Intertribal Native American Music in the United States*, Global Music Series (New York: Oxford University Press, 2014); Scales, *Recording Culture: Powwow Music and the Aboriginal Recording Industry on the Northern Plains*.

36. Marie Battiste and James [Sa'ke'j] Youngblood Henderson, *Protecting Indigenous Knowledge and Heritage: A Global Challenge*, Purich's Aboriginal Issues Series (Saskatoon, SK: Purich, 2000), 46.

37. "Indeed, all of the contributions to this collection can be seen as strategically traditionalist in that they endeavor to protect the distinctive values of community traditions while simultaneously recognizing that culture itself is a living, dynamic organism." Pamela Wilson and Michelle Stewart, "Indigeneity and Indigenous Media on the Global Stage," in *Global Indigenous Media: Cultures, Poetics, and Politics*, ed. Pamela Wilson and Michelle Stewart (Durham: Duke University Press), 31; Wilson and Stewart are referring to Ginsburg's use of "strategic traditionalism" in the conclusion to that volume. See Ginsburg, "Rethinking the Digital Age," 302. Ginsburg notes that her use of the term is borrowed from Tony Bennett and Valda Blundell, "First Peoples," *Cultural Studies* 9 (1995): 1–24.

38. Alex E. Smith and Cheevers Toppah, *Intonation* (Canyon Records CR-6395, 2005), CD; Louie Gonnie, *Rhythms within A Turquoise Dream* (Canyon Records CR-6454, 2009), CD.

Chapter Three

YouTubing the "Other"

Lima's Upper Classes and Andean Imaginaries

Fiorella Montero-Diaz

Some years ago I worked as a music teacher at a wealthy school in Lima. Most of my students lived in gated neighborhoods far from Lima's center and were driven to school by the family chauffeur instead of using public transportation. Their friends mainly lived in the same four exclusive districts, and therefore they did not need to go to other parts of Lima. Teaching a lesson to a fourth grade (nine-year-olds) on contemporary Andean music, I asked the students to name their favorite singer. They all started to laugh, watching each other and looking at me as if I were mad. Nobody said anything, but then one little blonde girl stood up and told me, blushing and looking at the floor, that she liked Dina Paúcar. A bunch of girls whispered "*chola*" and laughed behind her back.[1] I asked how many of them had maids—everyone had one, "of course"— so the immediate assignment was to interview their maids about contemporary Andean singers in Lima. There was an awkward silence. Another girl stood up saying: "Miss, my father will kill me if I talk to my maid." Others saw it as a radically different music assignment (they were accustomed to receiving Western art music lessons), so they did not complain. I was expecting letters from angry parents and even being fired for this. But the girls amazed me with interesting interviews, posters, CDs (or VCDs borrowed from their maids), and some were quite moved by sharing something with their maids again: "Maria was like my mother, she raised me, I don't know why I stopped talking to her."

Similar experiences motivated me to explore the Lima upper-class relationship with Andean music (be this traditional, contemporary, or fusion), their ideas of the Andean person (*el Andino*) and the articulation of people from different ethnic and socioeconomic backgrounds through music. I am aware that, strictly speaking, nearly all music is likely to be a fusion of previous genres. However, in Lima, only a limited range of music is considered as such by the public, or even by musicians. Fusion in this context consists of blendings between traditional Andean music and foreign genres such as rock, reggae, electronics, and jazz. Yet although many Peruvian genres, such as chicha, cumbia, huayno con arpa, música criolla, música latinoamericana, and Afro-Peruvian music are quite easily recognized as fusions, given their structure, they are not branded by people or performers as such. Therefore, I decided to focus only on what young *Limeño* upper classes would refer to as the "fusion circuit" or "Peruvian fusion music," even though it could just as easily be called "*Limeño* fusion music," as the scene is in Lima and the majority of musicians are from Lima, too. This is also the reason why I have chosen not to use terms such as *hybrid, world mix,* or *bricolage,* which are commonly used in music literature when referring to cross-cultural music blending.

This chapter is a discussion of a virtual survey I conducted in 2010 in Lima.[2] The survey was designed to expose how the upper classes perceive Andean indigeneity and indigenous culture, as well as how they themselves fit into their own imaginary of national identity. It presented three models of indigeneity expressed in YouTube music videos seeking to determine which resonates most with the upper-class imaginary and why.[3] In this chapter, I will first explore the seclusion of the upper classes in Lima. Then, I discuss the potential of YouTube to break this seclusion, mainly as a means to access diverse representations of indigeneity. After analyzing the results of the YouTube experiment, I arrive at some conclusions regarding not only upper-class imagery of Andean indigeneity and what exposures challenge the prevailing essentialized idea of Andean indigeneity, but also the upper classes' own imagined social position in relation to the "other" Andean subject.

This contribution builds on the observations of a number of scholars. Pamela Wilson and Michelle Stewart have written about how indigenous groups master and harness mass media technologies, generally associated with the dominant sectors of society, a process in which the technologies themselves transform ideas of indigenous subjectivity.[4] Likewise, Kyra Landzelius highlights the potential of new technologies to reverse power relations between dominant and indigenous communities.[5] Furthermore, Arjun Appadurai has explored how communication technologies can precipitate new subjectivities that go beyond the cultural realm permeating politics.[6] Beyond *how* the dominant elite imagines indigenous Andeans, I here explore how new technologies, such as YouTube, shape and challenge this imaginary. I will focus on YouTube dissemination of nonindigenous and indigenous music representations and self-representations among the upper classes, evaluating their potential to transform notions of citizenship and models of fixed and hyperreal indigeneity. I argue that online ethnographic tools (e.g., anonymous virtual surveys linked to YouTube) may help researchers look at separate factors underpinning dominant imaginaries of indigeneity and uncover upper-class vulnerabilities, fears and dilemmas of identity, which are not frequently communicated and merit further study to deepen our knowledge of a wider social spectrum.

It can be difficult to engage the Lima upper classes in conversations about indigenous, national, and personal identity, but the anonymity of the survey facilitated the discussion of difficult aspects of *Limeño* reality.[7] Within two weeks of launching the survey, I had already received seventy answers, which itself was testimony to the value of using YouTube to elicit opinions, to measure the virtual dissemination or collection of knowledge, and to discuss sensitive issues. The survey was sent out in three rounds and directed to upper-class school and university students with whom I had maintained contact since working as a music teacher in Lima.[8] I asked the respondents to take the survey and then forward it to their friends and colleagues.[9]

The survey's first questions were designed to establish the respondent's socioeconomic and ethnic background by eliciting information about their school, university, and family origin. Respondents who did not match the target group for the research were filtered out (data from students attending state schools and people living in the Peruvian provinces were excluded). In total, I received one hundred answers, seventy-three fitting the criteria for this study, and I followed up with the respondents who chose to include their e-mail addresses.

The Internet proved a valuable tool for my purposes, but also has its limitations. Attracting respondents to virtual surveys is a challenge. Not many people feel compelled to answer a virtual survey, and among respondents there may well be an overrepresentation of people who already feel sympathetic or who already have an interest in these topics. Perhaps people who are less sympathetic to indigenous people are less likely to complete a survey on representation and indigeneity. However, I was satisfied with the number of respondents and by the interest evident from the thorough answers and time dedicated to completing the survey.[10]

So Close, Yet So Distant

According to a market research study conducted in Lima, different socioeconomic classes are concentrated in different neighborhoods where people have very different types of jobs and sources of income.[11] Most of my students grew up in a highly protected environment, studied at an exclusive school (I had to pass three checkpoints to reach it), and only attended concerts at their school or exclusive venues. They moved "freely" in only four Lima districts. Some of them would even go to universities in the same district, which are also the most exclusive universities in Lima, and, as already mentioned, some without even having to commute using public transport. In another more recent survey (late 2010), I discovered that 14% of respondents were attending university abroad and 45% were studying at exclusive universities in two districts: Monterrico and La Molina.

In a previous study about music trends and concert attendance among the Lima upper classes (2008), I observed that teenagers from such backgrounds recognized Andean music as the most representative of Peru, but most of them did not prefer it to rock, salsa, or other traditional Peruvian styles, such as Afro-Peruvian music. Respondents usually attended concerts in exclusive districts, near where they lived. Some acknowledged that the upper classes avoid central Lima venues because "most people who listen to Andean music in Lima are of low socioeconomic status and have a strong Andean ethnic background." These upper-class individuals feel it is "unsafe and uncomfortable to attend folkloric concerts where they will be among people with whom they do not identify or share tastes."[12] This is a clear indicator of the self-imposed physical constraints of the upper classes in Lima, whose lives are policed by fear.

Andean music in Lima is practiced mostly in the city peripheries (formerly known as *conos*, home to 62% of Lima's population). Due to the fact that people in these sectors are mostly Andean migrants of different generations, the further from the *conos*, the more stylized Andean music becomes. Young Peruvians from privileged economic backgrounds who still depend on their parents do not have access to traditional Andean music knowledge, only to folkloric music in schools, restaurants and shows—that is, urban interpretations and adaptations of Andean reality and traditions. This lack of access and transmission of tradition is due less to geographical distance than to lack of social interaction. This, combined with physical distance, reinforces ignorance of Lima's pluricultural reality.

In contrast with many other capital cities in Andean South America, Lima is situated on the coast, and its origins are Spanish and creole. The geographical distance between the Andes and the coastal capital also contributes to the physical and psychological distance from Andeans and Andean culture that the upper classes seem to have imposed upon themselves. However, as evidenced in my example from teaching music in Lima, this distance is relative. Many of these youths have an Andean maid living in their home whom they see every day and who may spend more time with them than their own parents do. This might also be one of the reasons why they think from an early age of Andeans as subalterns.

How do the upper classes construct an idea of "the others" and therefore of themselves? Andean traditions, the notion of an Inca essence, indigeneity, and music are often used to construct national identity, as has been noted by several scholars.[13] Yet this imagined iconic Andean world is often inconsistent with their perceptions of subaltern Andeans in Lima (maids, *guachimanes*,[14] street vendors, etc.). So, how do the upper classes acquire knowledge about what they perceive as an "authentic" Andean reality?

The media, especially television, often heavily stereotype Andeans; through sounds and images portraying them as ignorant, inarticulate, alcoholic, smelly, and poor (e.g., the television program *Paisana Jacinta*; sketches in comedy programs; or movies such as *Madeinusa*, directed by Claudia Llosa). Either way, whether in romantic or negative stereotypes, Andean culture only reaches the Lima upper classes through the lens of an urban interpretation. But, what is the role of the Internet? Is the Internet facilitating interethnic and interclass encounters?

YouTube and the Lima Upper Classes

YouTube is the "most popular destination on the Internet for viewing video"[15] and is visited by millions on a daily basis (90 million in March 2009).[16] It is a virtual "place,"[17] where one can play the identity tourist—"one who engages in a superficial, reversible, recreational play at otherness, a person who is satisfied with an episodic experience as a racial minority."[18] It is also a place where people can be anonymous and cross social boundaries and "interact on a regular basis with others whom they may have never met in person";[19] where people become celebrities overnight, construct identity, interact with other people, and enable nation-building.[20]

Do the privileged in Lima use YouTube? According to the survey, half of the respondents visit YouTube to explore new music or when curious about a group or genre (see fig. 3.1). They recognize and use these virtual tools widely: 94% of the respondents watch music videos and links at least monthly,[21] 70% watch music videos on YouTube daily and 52% state they learn about Peruvian music on YouTube.[22]

But how active are these users in discussing and interacting with other people? Do users really interact? A YouTube account allows the user to upload videos, comment, and rate videos uploaded by other users, and have a personalized virtual space or channel that shows their user profile, history, and video uploads. Accounts allow visitors to actively use YouTube and to build a sense of community.[23] However, even though half of the respondents had an active YouTube account, only 18% of them had ever written a comment on a video.[24]

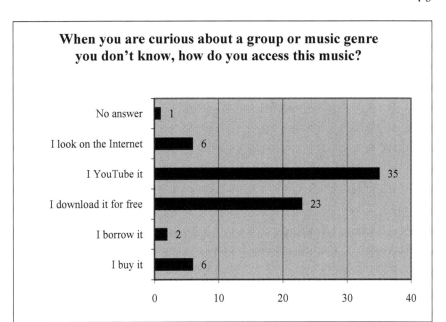

When you are curious about a group or music genre you don't know, how do you access this music?

Figure 3.1. New music discovery and exploration (numbers of individuals responding to each option).

It does not seem that YouTube is facilitating direct class interaction, at least on the part of the upper classes. Nevertheless, the fact that most respondents visit YouTube and play a passive role, watching videos and perhaps also reading the comments, allows them to construct opinions and reinforce (sometimes stereotyped) ideas. Accordingly, I concluded that this popular virtual tool could serve as an effective means to elicit reactions to three music videos that portray the idea of Andean culture (*lo Andino*) in very different ways.

The YouTube Experiment

The fusionists I chose were Miki González, Damaris Mallma, and Magaly Solier—all well-known Peruvian artists with contrasting music expressions and backgrounds. The particular music videos I chose for this survey can be characterized as follows:

1. Miki González's romantic and idealized version of the Andes and Andean music. It is set in the Andes with people who appear to be "authentic *indio*" participating in an "authentic ritual," but the song is in Spanish;

2. Damaris Mallma's video presenting a mixture of faces, languages (the song is in Quechua and Spanish), urban locations, and music genres that suggest a modern and multicultural Peru; and

3. Magaly Solier's collage of pictures (which could be interpreted as a modern indigeneity) that show Magaly in Huanta working the land, in movies, and accepting prizes at European festivals. The song is in Quechua.

Respondents were asked for their impressions to these music videos. My objective was to examine respondents' reactions as a means to assess their opinions, ideas, and images of indigeneity and how these were negotiated and confronted. A more detailed description of each video follows.[25]

The first video was Miki González's "Hoja verde de la coca" (Green coca leaf), directed by Lucho Barrios.[26] The song was released in 1994 in *Hatun Exitokuna* ("Big hits" in Quechua).[27] The song is sung by González and Andean singer Rosita de Cuzco. It has a traditional Andean *huayno* structure. The video features González traveling to Cuzco to visit Don Jesús Qhana, a local *paqo* or *paqu* (Quechua healer) of the Amaru community in Pisaq, for coca leaf divination.[28] The actions are interspersed with images of the coca leaf ritual. The video clip starts with González and Qhana speaking in Quechua with an instrumental background and continues with the lyrics in Spanish. This video was uploaded in December 2006, and when last visited in March 2010, had received 72,965 views and 209 comments from viewers in general, most of these highlighting the love that González professes for Peru, regardless of his Spanish nationality.

The second video link was to Damaris Mallma's "Tusuy kusun" (Let's dance) directed by Percy Céspedez.[29] Mallma was born in Huancayo and is the daughter of Saywa, a well-known singer from Ayacucho. This song was released in 2007 as part of the CD *Mil caminos* and won first place in the category best folkloric song at the Chilean Festival de la Canción de Viña del Mar 2008 (Viña del Mar song festival 2008). It follows the structure of an Ayacucho carnival song and is sung by Mallma accompanied by charango, Andean violin, electro-acoustic guitar, and electronic samples, with Andean and Afro-Peruvian percussion. The video is visually complicated; it features many extras and iconic musicians, including Saywa, from various folkloric music genres, and the well-known Andean guitarist Raul García Zárate, also from Ayacucho.

The video clip presents two parallel stories. The first was filmed inside the recently finished electric train. It features several scenes with diverse Peruvians photographed inside an old colonial house in Lima. It also features a wide assortment of Peruvian musical genres and dances (street dancing, scissors dance, Afro-Peruvian dance). All this is intertwined with symbolism, such as Mallma's baptism or purification by Saywa's hands, and the presentation of

DNIs (national identity cards) to a white official (the only white person in the video). The video clip ends with a shot of an empty stool and then Damaris' face as if she is inviting us to take our place for the next picture. The lyrics are in Spanish and Quechua. This video was uploaded in December 2008 and had received 107,588 views and 451 comments when last visited in March 2010. As in the case of González's video, the comments are very positive and show pride and nostalgia about being Peruvian.

The third video link is to Magaly Solier's "Citaray." Solier is an Andean actress and singer from Huanta-Ayacucho.[30] This song was released in 2009 on the album *Warmi* (Woman) and tells the story of a woman—Citaray—who lost her son at the hands of the terrorist group Shining Path and has decided to live her life as if her son had never been killed.[31] Solier sings both voices in this song that takes the form of a dialogue between Citaray and Maribel, a young woman who tries to help other women in her village, as they talk about their disappeared relatives. Solier has sung this song unaccompanied at various press conferences and interviews, making "Citaray" her signature song. The instruments used for the recording are violin, cello, bass guitar, percussion, charango, guitar, quena and panpipes. As there is no official video clip yet, the images used are a collage of stills from Magaly's life in Huanta-Ayacucho and the movies *Madeinusa* (2006) and *Milk of Sorrow* (2009), both directed by Claudia Llosa. The lyrics of the song are in Quechua. This video was uploaded in March 2009 and had received 75,829 views and 311 comments when last visited in March 2010. The comments vary; most discuss binaries between white and Andean Peruvians, with encouragement from some users to be "more Peruvian"—prouder of being Andean and speaking Quechua. Some even include praise for Solier as an "Andean Goddess, Inca Princess, Andean Messiah."

Quechua use emerges as a key issue in the comments on Solier's video. Many YouTube users asked what the lyrics meant and others offered translations from Quechua. There are questions about where to learn Quechua in Lima and comments on how bad people feel about not understanding the lyrics and not speaking this Peruvian language.

It is worth noting that up until March 2010, Solier's video (uploaded for about one year) had been viewed more times than González's, even though his had been available on YouTube for over three years. Mallma's video (available for over two years) was the most viewed and commented upon. However, when comparing the respondents' reception of these videos, the majority appeared to prefer González's "Hoja verde de la coca." When asked if they liked the music, although many respondents seemed to like all three songs, most respondents preferred Mallma's song "Tusuy kusun." Could it be that González's romanticized version of the Andean was more representative of the Indian "hyperreality,"[32] which the upper classes seem to associate with the indigenous?

The Responses

In Miki González's video, respondents highlight the "real" representation of Andean culture, beliefs, and cosmology together with "beautiful and millenarian" Andean landscapes. The exaltation of the Andes' natural beauty, the apparent knowledge of what a "real Andean" is, and the number of people who equated the Andes, or Cuzco to be more specific, with the image of Peru is remarkable. When discussing the music, they recognized it was a catchy fusion of a "typically sad *huayno* mixed with pop." So, it seems respondents felt able to recognize what is "truly Andean" and how Andean melodies should typically sound.

When respondents argued that González's music video clip represents the "true culture and tradition of Peru," some said it was because it shows diversity and cultural fusion: "It exposes certain aspects of our most indigenous tradition fused or processed through the filter of Westernized tradition and contemporary culture that also belong to us and define us." Some of these respondents also liked the fact that the video portrayed González, a white man, and Don Jesús, an Andean man, singing together "because it represents the diversity; although we are not all represented it still shows that Peru is a country with more than just one face," "the Andean [*lo Andino*] and the *Limeño* together."

In direct contrast, a third of respondents did not think this music video clip represents Peru. Many of these insisted that Peru is more than just the Andes and Andean music: "It represents part of Peru . . . BUT NOT ALL!" "It's annoying to know that in the whole world Peru = Andean customs . . . and that is not the case . . . we also have jungle music plus *criollo* music . . . the *huayno* and waltzes aren't everything." One respondent noted González's wish to appear more "Peruvian": "It presents an idealization of the Andes seeking to elevate the Andean to a national status, which it is not entitled to. It even seems to me that Miki as a white person from the coast is making an effort to deny his origin and appear more 'Peruvian' in the Andes. It leaves out many very Peruvian groups."

In comparison, respondents liked Mallma's video because it is an innovative and artistic way to show the "real [*real*] Peru": diverse, traditional, but urban-modern. Both Mallma's and González's videos were praised as "true" (*verdadero*)—one authentic and natural and the other diverse, traditional, but modern. Respondents tended to equate González's Andes with millenary Peru and Mallma's urban modernity with modern Peru, and not necessarily just with a modern Lima. When discussing Mallma's music, diversity and cultural fusion came into focus. Most respondents liked the fusion of musical genres and styles and the fact that they saw and heard many cultures in one song: "It encompasses many cultures of Peru in one single melody."

According to some respondents, Mallma's music video clip represents Peru because it shows a multicultural and diverse country.[33] For them it reveals the reality of a modern Peru, with migration to the coast and the mixing of

Quechua and Spanish. For others, however, it offered a very mestizo depiction of the country, which "only represents Lima." They considered that Andean indigenous and white people were missing from the video. A few said that the music was not Peruvian. It is important to acknowledge the fact that around one in ten respondents left the questions about representation blank. I am aware that it was a difficult question and that these issues are not always open for discussion among the upper classes.

When discussing Magaly Solier's video, the language used by respondents was more familiar, as if they knew more about her. They dared to say things like: "I don't like her as a person" (*no me cae*); "she's a bit crazy" (*es un poco loca*); or "I love Magaly" (*me encanta Magaly*). Respondents reacted with a more informal and familiar tone, but did not have as strong views about the actual music as they did in response to the other videos. This could be due to Solier's massive exposure in the media through movies and interviews. She was perceived as an articulate, but still humble "authentic" Andean woman. This is reflected in survey answers: "because it [the video] . . . shows our robust, harsh Andes and how it is, our strong and bold Andean woman, who always wants to say that she is in charge and should be respected." Interestingly, a few respondents said that they "love Magaly" (*me encanta Magaly*) and therefore they liked the video. These are strong phrases that invoke a sense of belonging—or perhaps possession; "our Andean woman," and "our Andes" were common expressions.

For many respondents (62%), Solier's music video clip represents Peru. Several reasons were given for this, including its depiction of Peruvian landscapes (18%), the use of Quechua song lyrics (13%), the typically Andean quality of its sounds (13%), and the ways it shows the reality of people in Peru/Andes (13%). For example, one respondent observed that "it shows the truth of life in the highlands, it doesn't lie, it's natural, it's truth." Its representation of Peruvian women was also noted (5%), including the observation that Solier was an "authentic indigenous woman." Again, a third of respondents did not think this music video clip represented Peru, and most of these insisted that Peru was more than just the Andes.

Overall, around 60% of respondents found these music videos representative of Peru. Nevertheless, when asked if they would usually listen to this kind of music, around 82% in each case said no. These answers show the upper classes' disconnection from what seems to be representative of the country's culture and image; and as they do not participate in it, listen to it, nor identify with it, they see themselves excluded from what they perceive as being Peruvian. Perhaps, this is why some respondents assume González was trying to become "more Peruvian" through Andean music.

Respondents were also asked to choose the music video that best represents the indigenous Andean (see fig. 3.2): 54% of respondents said González's video, 32% Solier's, and 10% Mallma's.

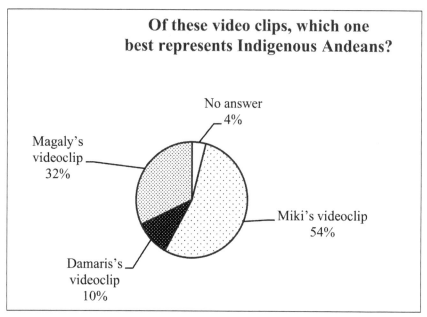

Figure 3.2. Indigenous Andean exploration.

These results go hand in hand with the answers to another question: What is it to be an indigenous Andean? (¿Qué es ser indígena Andino?) This was an open question, and respondents could list more than one idea. Most respondents (63%) considered that to be an indigenous Andean involved being born in and actively living in the Andes. Very few of these respondents said it could also be someone born in the Andes, but living somewhere else. For 25%, being indigenous involved keeping the cosmology, culture, and tradition of the Andean ancestors; 11% stressed the notion of authenticity, using such words as "pure" (*puro*), "non-urban or modern," "still not civilized" (*aún no civilizado*); 7% related it to Andean pride; and 5% said it was to speak Quechua. A few respondents also said that an indigenous Andean person was someone who was discriminated against (3%), poor (3%), or who had no opportunities (1%). They saw these characteristics as intrinsic features of their indigeneity. Some of these answers are reflected in the following quotes:

1. "People who live in the Andes mainly support themselves through agriculture or mining. They maintain customs from precolonial times because of their environment and poverty in which they usually live, due to the limited opportunities they are offered to develop themselves."

2. "I would define them simply as individuals born in a native Andean population who maintain and preserve their own ancient characteristics,

which clearly identify them, and have not been extremely modified by interaction with the Westernization of the rest of the surrounding areas of the country they belong to."

3. "A person with Indian physical traits, who lives in the Andes and who has not chosen to modernize. Probably still working the fields."[34]

To the question "When you think of indigenous Andeans what is the first thing that springs to mind?" the most common answers were: traditional dress—*pollera, chullo,* and poncho, in order of popularity (19%);[35] *Serrano* (11%);[36] soil, mud, field (10%); *huayno* (7%); culture (5%); hard work (5%). Other terms used included sadness (4%), *cholo* (4%), mestizo (4%), poverty (3%), and humbleness (3%).

All this tells us that the image of indigenous Andean people shared by most of these upper-class respondents is quite idealized and romantic. It is therefore not surprising that most chose Miki González's video clip as the one that best represented indigenous Andeans. The majority of these respondents seem to imagine the native Andean as someone living in the Andes; working the fields; without money, education, or any ties to what they describe as the "Western world"; and therefore physically and culturally far away from Lima and themselves.

Interestingly, most of the respondents who did not think that Mallma was a good representative of the Andes said it was because she seemed "already mixed and Westernized" (*agringada*) and that her music was not "real Andean music," although some thought that it was a real representation of "modernity." It appears that Mallma is seen as less authentic than Solier, because of her mestizo status, even though both singers were born in the Andes and have lived in Lima from an early age. In his review of Solier's album *Warmi*, influential Peruvian journalist Sandro Mairata writes: "Solier could have made a typical mediocre actress-wannabe-artist album, filling it with tropical rhythms, hanging an acoustic guitar over her shoulder and using flirty skirts while proclaiming false love with lyrics produced by the professionals of the business. . . . *Warmi* is pure, original, complex."[37]

What seems to appeal to the upper-class respondents and critics is the music and people that they perceive as authentic. This notion of authenticity remains shaped by the romantic and paternalistic imaginary of the Andean Indians developed by early twentieth-century *indigenismo.*[38] The upper-class imaginary is still fixated on the notion of Andeans as people who "publicly embrace their traditions risk[ing] self-positioning in the semantic extremes of exotic primitivism"[39] or as "mythical monsters who possess museum legacies."[40] Orin Starn (1992) calls this essentialist phenomenon *Andinismo,* and Alcida Rita Ramos (1994) describes it as the construction of a "hyperreal Indian." However, for the upper classes, this imagined Andean "museum piece" possesses rich cultural capital and traditions, which are iconic of Peru as a whole and symbolic of Peruvianness, although distant from their daily reality. Thus, the imaginary evidences a contradictory simultaneous over- and underrepresentation of the contemporary indigenous Andean.

No Longer Museum Pieces?

In a process of customizing indigeneity, some indigenous peoples assimilate foreign elements and make them their own, thereby stressing agency.[41] Today, some Andean and South American indigenous organizations seek to challenge indigeneity's association with an idealized and natural past.[42] Indigenous communities have gained increasing agency "not just about their issues, but about the whole country's issues."[43] However, Peru is at a great disadvantage when it comes to indigenous organizations and indigenous political movements, particularly compared to other Andean countries like Bolivia, Ecuador, and Colombia. In Peru, the development of indigenous political agency has been particularly difficult, due to the absence of indigenous organizations and political movements.[44] However, things are starting to change, and these changes challenge the image most upper-class *Limeños* have of the indigenous Andean as a "noncivilized museum piece."

For Shane Greene, President Alejandro Toledo and his embodiment of the returning Inca in 2000 contributed to changing Peru: "He [Toledo] helped to provide a political context in which the overt ethnic language of indigeneity is being revalorized. Certain emergent Andean social movements, particularly those rooted in environmental concerns, have begun to explicitly reindigenize their political image and even to forge initial alliances with indigenous Amazonians. This effectively challenges the norm that has been dominant for the last several decades."[45]

Things are changing not only in politics and election campaigns, but also in public debate. Furthermore, I posit that the music scene has contributed greatly to this process. Fusion music has created a platform where indigenous performers can collaborate with urban upper-class musicians, acquiring more visibility and representing themselves with their own creative voice. This is certainly the case with Magaly Solier, who has challenged the upper-class image of the Andean woman. Especially after the triumph of the film *La teta asustada* (Milk of sorrow), 2009, starring Solier and directed by Claudia Llosa (a white *Limeña* from the high class), at the Berlinale film festival (2009) and its nomination for an Oscar (2010), there was more discussion in national media about racism, segregation, and cultural appropriation in Peru. White-criollo-versus-Andean binaries started to emerge in the national debate on YouTube, in blogs, and on TV programs.[46] Peruvians were divided by the movie, the nomination, and their opinions about Solier and Llosa, whose ethnic back-grounds were impossible to ignore. This spurred multiple online debates on themes such as cultural appropriation, the white/criollo cinema industry in Peru, and Solier as Llosa's "puppet," or as her "Quechua-singing manipulated clown."[47] According to the well-known blogger Carlos Quiróz "Peruanista":

> So just like any self-serving folklorist, Claudia Llosa appropriates Andean cul-tures to make films that impress foreigners and the ignorant. She doesn't care about our Peruvian indigenous people nor about Andean women as human beings, but rather as odd characters and objects of ridicule, to be looked at askance, objects of capitalist exploitation. Claudia Llosa wants to impress Europeans, and for them she has brought along the woman from Ayacucho, Magaly Solier, as her exotic pet.[48]

Some academics argued that Llosa's movies *Madeinusa* and *Milk of Sorrow* promoted a racist and Eurocentric view of the Andean woman.[49] However, I argue that Solier—as an artist, an Andean woman, and a public speaker—has achieved visibility and greater social agency to promote antiracist messages through participation in the Peruvian media, cinema, and music industries. Solier sang and composed most of the songs featured in *Milk of Sorrow*. On her first CD, *Warmi*, she sang mostly in Quechua, and during 2009 and 2010, she usually presented her music at exclusive venues in upper-class districts of Lima. She has collaborated with iconic Peruvian musician Juan Diego Flórez, a renowned young Peruvian operatic tenor who had to take Quechua lessons in order to sing with Solier.[50] Quechua then also became a subject for the main Peruvian newspapers, which found its use quite remarkable, as Quechua is seen as a strong indicator of Andean indigeneity and is therefore often hidden and stigmatized in Lima and the urban Andes.

In 2008 I conducted a similar survey on elite music trends and concert attendance. To the question "Would you learn Quechua?" before the "Solier boom," 41% of respondents did not see any reason to, but in 2010 this per-centage decreased to 22%. In 2008, 30% of respondents felt Quechua was an important language; by 2010, 46% thought so. In 2010 there were more songs in Quechua in the media and on the Internet by Solier and others. Solier, a self-declared Andean *campesina*, was seen as an iconic cultural bearer who represented the indigenous not only in Lima, but at cinema festivals abroad; perhaps this was starting to impregnate the upper classes' imaginary and chal-lenge some perceptions of indigeneity.

According to the (2010) survey, 76% of respondents thought that Magaly Solier was a better representative of Peru than white director Claudia Llosa. Only 7% of respondents were uncomfortable choosing between the two or insisted that both women represent Peru equally well, even though Llosa and Solier have both achieved international success. This illustrates the white/

indigenous dichotomy for the upper classes, as Magaly is seen as more representative of Peru than a white upper-class woman. Given that many of my respondents described themselves as whites (in other words, they look more like Llosa than like Solier), what does this dichotomy mean for them?

Respondents recognized Magaly Solier's music-video clip as the second most authentic representation of indigenous Andeans (32%). To the question "How do you imagine indigenous Andeans in 2030?" 22% of respondents said "the same as now" (*igual*); 21% said "more modern, successful, and innovative"; 19% said "more mixed and articulated, but always incorporating Andean culture"; 18% said "always preserving Andean values and culture"; 12% said "with more voice and agency to do what they want with their legacy"; 10% said "with less 'culture'"; 8% said they imagine them as "more valued and recognized, like Magaly Solier"; and 3% considered that "they would become a threat."

Mixed views were again in evidence regarding acculturation. Some respondents thought that indigenous people should not lose their culture or mix it with that of metropolitan Lima:

1. "I think that the true Andean indigenous people will never lose their essence. They will be the same, peaceful, but fighters, working the land, very sentimental, very guided by nature. They may be influenced, if they leave their original environment, but inside they must not forget their roots."

2. "Just like now, it will be very difficult to change the stereotype we have of the indigenous Andean, because *deep down we don't want to lose our identity and our roots* [my emphasis]."

This last quote is interesting, as it reflects the respondent's admission of an Andean stereotype coupled with insecurity about their own identity. It appears to be an Andean person's responsibility to maintain the roots of the nation and, by extension, to maintain the identity of those who do not share their culture, but who reflect their vision of "Peruvian-ness" as Andean. Furthermore, it hints at their feeling of cultural disadvantage, as they themselves know they are not representative of the culture they seem to associate with Peru.

It is also remarkable that many other respondents, despite their previous choice of González's idealized music-video clip and their romantic vision of the indigenous Andean, recognized that things are changing in Peru and hoped that they continue to change. In response to the question "How do you imagine indigenous Andeans in 2030?" some included Magaly Solier as a good model for the future of the indigenous Andean and some respondents even recognized that essentializing the Andean (*lo Andino*) is a way to force them to remain distant reminders of their iconic past:

1. "A fused indigenous person, but not someone who is alienated. Capable of protecting their roots and opening up to change. Just like Magaly Solier."

2. "I imagine them totally evolved, jazzed (if that is how you say it), so that more places, like the Cocodrilo Verde, take an interest in Andean fusions with other music genres. I imagine them fused, because the vast majority of them are aiming to go global."

3. "I'm not one of those selfish people who want to keep native communities in the stone age if they don't want it, just because 'I' want them to remain like that, so that I can go see them from time to time. If they want to change their way of life, they are fully entitled to do so and we cannot criticize them. The world changes, everything is dynamic. We must not make stereotypes of people or places."

In a country where the main icons of success are white upper-class Peruvians and mostly *Limeños*, the incursion of Magaly Solier as a Peruvian and indigenous icon is remarkable. She is not only an icon for indigenous and mestizo women, but—as previously stated—she is also widely seen as both "authentically" indigenous and as a person with her own voice and agency, who, borrowing Garcia Canclini's words, has the keys to enter and leave modernity at will.[51]

At this point, the question arises again: who would the upper classes be without the essentialized Andean? Part of the upper classes' national identity relies on indigenous Andeans "keeping their traditions," and therefore, they insist on keeping their romanticized vision of the Andean. Could it be that fusion music may be challenging this idea and encouraging upper-class youths to fuse their sounds and identities with those of the Andeans? The word *fusion* and references to music are often used by respondents to illustrate what seems to be a change in attitude toward stereotyping and essentializing the Andean, which also shows the influence of music in this matter. As a respondent wrote:

> More than the indigenous Peruvian, I imagine a stable Peru, with a better quality of life, more modern and more inclusive. Because Peru is not just made up of indigenous or bronze-skinned or people of any particular race, today's Peru is the product of a mixture and, as products of this mixture, we are proud of our origins. Why do you think Bareto now plays music from the Amazon, why is Tongo popular at Asia Boulevard, Grupo 5 was on the cover of Cosas, why is neo-Andean [*novo Andino*] music being heard, etc.? Peru is changing.

As evidenced in this chapter, fusion music, as well as online and mainstream discussion about representation, indigeneity, and citizenship are contributing greatly to the dissemination of modern indigenous voices in Peru. I hope to continue to explore the interethnic and intercultural music dialogues that will be emerging from what appears to be a product of fused and modern Andean identities.

Notes

I would like to thank all the anonymous survey respondents who took the time to fill out my sometimes rather extensive virtual music surveys, allowing me to write this book chapter. Thank you for your detailed, thorough replies; the virtual discussions; and the e-mail exchanges on indigeneity, music and media. I would also like to thank my former high school students for their constant support in the dissemination of surveys and for the friendly online chats. Thanks to Miki González, Damaris Mallma, and Magaly Solier for the time and the conversations. I would like to acknowledge Thomas Hilder, Shzr Ee Tan, and Henry Stobart for the organization of the RHUL symposium. Thanks to Henry Stobart for his continued enthusiastic and expert guidance; and, last but not least, a big thank you to my wife Marita for the late nights, the shared coffees, and the infinite patience.

1. In this context, *chola* was a derogatory term used to refer to a mestizo with strong Andean features and background. In recent years, the word *cholo* has undergone a process of revindication and revalorization, reducing some of its former connotations as an insult to become a positive self-identification among certain *emergente* Andean migrants.

2. Upper classes in the context of this paper are the wealthy and wealthiest *Limeños*. Not necessarily the historical economic power groups or families in Lima, these are people with a high income who have attended wealthy schools and private universities and who have chosen to live in wealthy neighborhoods. In this particular research, I do not make a distinction between white upper classes and new or emergent migrant upper classes.

3. Participants were asked to view YouTube videos by fusionists Miki González, Damaris Mallma, and Magaly Solier.

4. Pamela Wilson and Michelle Stewart, "Indigeneity and Indigenous Media on the Global Stage," in *Global Indigenous Media: Cultures, Poetics, and Politics*, ed. Pamela Wilson and Michelle Stewart (Durham, NC: Duke University Press, 2008).

5. Kyra Landzelius, *Native on the Net: Indigenous and Diasporic Peoples in the Virtual Age*, ed. Kyra Landzelius (London: Routledge, 2006).

6. Arjun Appadurai, *Modernity at Large: Cultural Dimensions of Globalization* (Minneapolis: University of Minnesota Press, 1996).

7. The survey was anonymous and this proved beneficial because of the protection it afforded respondents from sectors of society that are seen as "antagonistic" to most *Limeños*. Also, on the Internet, people "are able to explore aspects of themselves they might otherwise be reluctant to share with others, and can do so in relative anonymity and in the safety of their own homes" (Katelyn Y. A. McKenna and John A. Bargh, 1998, 2000, as quoted by Edward

Sargis and Linda Skitka, "Social Psychological Research and the Internet: The Promise and Peril of a New Methodological Frontier," in *The Social Net: Human Behaviour in Cyberspace*, ed. Yair Amichai-Hamburger (Oxford: Oxford University Press, 2005), 6.

8. Each round consisted of ten surveys: First round: school students (10), second round: university students (10) and, third round: upper-class friends (10). In total, I sent out thirty surveys, which were multiplied due to the snowball effect of people forwarding the survey.

9. I am indebted to all the people who took the time to ponder my questions and share their thoughts.

10. I am aware that social class may not be the only potential dimension to analyse in these YouTube videos, and that other social classes could share the upper classes' views on indigeneity. However, for the purpose of this chapter, I will be focusing solely on the relationship between class and ideas of Andean indigeneity.

11. *Estudio sobre Niveles Socioeconómicos 2007–2008* (Lima: Asociación Peruana de Empresas de Investigación de Mercados [Peruvian Association of Market Research Companies]).

12. These are quotes from the survey.

13. Zoila Mendoza, "Performing Decency: Ethnicity and Race in Andean "Mestizo" Ritual Dance," in *Music and the Racial Imagination*, ed. Philip Bohlman and Ronald Radano (Chicago: University of Chicago Press, 2000), 236; Zoila Mendoza, *Creating Our Own* (Durham, NC: Duke University Press, 2008), 8; Shane Greene, *Customizing Indigeneity: Paths to a Visionary Politics in Peru* (Stanford, CA: Stanford University Press, 2009), 29, 105; Maria Elena Garcia, *Making Indigenous Citizens: Identities, Education, and Multicultural Development in Peru* (Stanford, CA: Stanford University Press, 2005), 18.

14. *Guachimán* is an Anglicism. It comes from the English word *watchman*. In Peru a *guachimán* usually guards the main entrances of businesses, private buildings, gated neighborhoods, and exclusive residences.

15. "YouTube," *New York Times*, November 1, 2011.

16. Pelle Snickars and Patrick Vonderau, eds, *The YouTube Reader* (Stockholm: National Library of Sweden, 2009), 11.

17. It could also be defined as an anthropological "non-place," following Marc Augé's categorization of transitorial places (1995).

18. Lisa Nakamura, *Cybertypes: Race, Ethnicity and Identity on the Internet* (New York: Routledge, 2002), 55.

19. Sargis and Skitka, "Social Psychological Research and the Internet," 6.

20. It is notable that Internet penetration in Peru is higher than average for Latin America; it is the fifth highest in the region. This makes it possible for people from different ethnic and socioeconomic backgrounds to meet online and comment or discuss a video clip from YouTube.

21. Through YouTube and social networks such as Facebook.

22. Most of the people who said they do not spend any time on YouTube were older than thirty-five years of age. Also, people who would not normally visit YouTube daily were more than twenty-six years old. The five respondents who

visit YouTube for more than two hours daily (up to five or six hours a day) were all between seventeen and twenty-five years old.

23. William Uricchio, "The Future of a Medium Once Known as Television," in *The YouTube Reader*, ed. Pelle Snickars and Patrick Vonderau (Sweden: National Library of Sweden, 2009), 34.

24. See also the discussion about the 90-9-1 YouTube interaction rule: "90 percent of online audiences never interact, nine percent interact only occasionally, and one percent do most interacting" (Jose van Dijk, 2009 as quoted by Pelle Snickars and Patrick Vonderau, in their introduction to *The YouTube Reader*), 12.

25. All these videos were accessed on March 30, 2010. The number of views and comments were recorded on that specific date.

26. This was a popular video and song that was censored by MTV in Spanish, as it was believed to encourage cocaine consumption. González has contested this claim several times during his career, setting out the difference between cocaine and the sacred coca leaf.

27. "Hoja verde de la coca" by Miki González, YouTube video, 4:01, posted by "LearnspeakSpanish," July 11, 2009, https://www.youtube.com/watch?v=gT3bt94xmW0. Note: This is a link to the video analyzed in this chapter. However, this is not the same upload as the one that was originally analyzed. That upload has since been deleted. The information about views and viewer comments herein refer to the original upload of the music video available when this research was carried out.

28. See comments and discussion on ibid.

29. "Tusuy Kusun" by Damaris Mallma, YouTube video, 4:21, posted by "Lunazul Producciones," December 4, 2008, http://www.youtube.com/watch?v=AMKr9 0k6HeA&feature=related.

30. "Citaray" by Magaly Solier, YouTube video, 4:18, posted by "SkrrishC, March 30, 2009, https://www.youtube.com/watch?v=1CVOWtoAfbY. Note: This is a link to the video analyzed in this chapter. However, this is not the same upload as was originally analyzed. That upload has since been deleted. The information about views and viewer comments herein refer to the original upload of the music video available when this research was carried out.

31. From 1980 to 2000, Peru was immersed in a period of political violence between the state and the guerrilla group Movimiento Revolucionario Túpac Amaru (MRTA), as well as Sendero Luminoso (Shining Path). The latter group was founded in Ayacucho, the Peruvian province that was most affected by this terrorist organization. Sixty-nine thousand people, many of them rural peasants, died in the internal war over this period. For more information, see "Comisión de la verdad y reconciliación," accessed April 25, 2010, www.cverdad.org.pe.

32. Alcida Ramos, "The Hyperreal Indian," *Critique of Anthropology* 14, no. 2 (1994): 153–71.

33. An example of this is a respondent who wrote: "Peru is a country that is too divided and segregated, which through history has chosen to be blind to the minorities for there to be a representation capturing one Peru; there is

no such thing as one Peru. However the video does seem to me like a good approximation and a conscious effort."

34. The numbers do not refer to specific people; I use them to separate different voices.

35. A *pollera* is a skirt commonly worn by Andean peasant women. In some traditions multiple *polleras* are worn in layers.

36. Strictly speaking, the word *serrano* simply refers to a person from the mountainside (*sierra*). In Lima, however, the word is often used as a disparaging term to denote that someone is backward due to their Andean origin.

37. Sandro Mairata, "Crítica: Warmi de Magali Solier," *Quemarropa* (blog) March 18, 2009.

38. Thomas Turino, *Moving Away from Silence: Music of the Peruvian Altiplano and the Experiment of Urban Migration* (Chicago: University of Chicago Press, 1993), 170; Efrain Rozas, *Fusión: Banda Sonora del Perú* (Lima: Instituto de Etnomusicología. PUCP, 2007).

39. Marisol de la Cadena and Orin Starn, eds., *Indigenous Experience Today* (New York: Berg, 2007), 9.

40. Julián González and Maribel Arteaga, *La representación de lo indigena en los medios de comunicación* (Medellín: Hombre Nuevo Editores, 2005), 85–86.

41. Shane Greene, *Customizing Indigeneity: Paths to a Visionary Politics in Peru* (Stanford, CA: Stanford University Press, 2009).

42. González and Arteaga, *La representación de lo indigena*, 85–86. I am aware that some indigenous communities play on the hyperreal Indian role in order to gain something from the system, something Spivak described as "strategic essentialism" (1987). As an example, see Elayne Zorn, "From Political Prison to Tourist Village," in *Natives Making Nation*, ed. Andrew Canessa (Tucson: University of Arizona Press, 2005), 156–80.

43. González and Arteaga, *La representación de lo indigena*, 143.

44. Luis Millones, "Hay un país sin indigenas entre Ecuador y Bolivia," in *Conversaciones para la convivencia*, ed. Marta Bulnes (Lima: GTZ, 2000), 79. For more information about several factors that might explain why so many Peruvians still choose not to acknowledge their indigenous origins see Garcia, *Making Indigenous Citizens*, 7–10).

45. Shane Greene 2006 as quoted in Shane Greene, *Customizing Indigeneity: Paths to a Visionary Politics in Peru* (Stanford, CA: Stanford University Press, 2009), 140.

46. Since I first wrote this chapter in 2010, these debates have decreased in intensity, but I argue that the incursion of Magaly Solier in movies, music, and public debate on issues of race, representation and agency made these issues less of a taboo and promoted an open discussion in public media.

47. This comment was made in reference to her singing in Quechua when receiving the Golden Bear in the Berlinale 2009. "El Oso de Oro ruge en quechua gracias a La Teta Asustada," YouTube video, 2:36, posted by "Idealterna Peru," February 16, 2009, http://www.youtube.com/watch?v=DKAFxm1AJhE. Discussions followed in Facebook group debates and YouTube video comments.

48. Carlos Quiróz Peruanista, "La teta asustada: Una pelicula racista dirigida por Claudia Llosa y producida por España y Alemania," *Eterna nada de nada* (blog) February 13, 2009, http://eternanadadenada.blogspot.com/2010/05/critica de-cine-la-teta-asustada.html.
49. On "invisible" racism in *Madeinusa*, see Iliana Pagán-Teitelbaum, "El glamour en los Andes: La representación de la mujer indígena migrante en el cine peruano," *Revista Chilena de Antropología Visual* 12 (2008): 1–30.
50. "Juan Diego Florez estudia Quechua para cantar tema a dúo con Magaly Solier," *El Comercio*, October 25, 2009, http://elcomercio.pe/noticia/359831/ juan-diego-florez-estudia-quechua-cantar-tema-duo-magaly-solier.
51. Néstor García Canclini, *Culturas híbridas: Estrategias para entrar y salir de la modernidad* (México: Grijalbo, 1989).

Chapter Four

An Interview with Russell Wallace

Russell Wallace

I am a composer, a producer, and a traditional Lil'wat singer. My education has encompassed numerous disciplines, including performing arts, information technology, creative writing, and ethnomusicology. I compose soundtracks for film, television, and theater productions; I produce my own CDs, which have been nominated for awards in Canada and the United States; and I have been composer in residence for the Aboriginal Dance Program at the Banff Centre for the Arts. Currently, I teach at the Native Education College, Capilano University, and the Vancity Office of Community Engagement at Simon Fraser University. This interview arose out of an invitation by Thomas Hilder, whom I met at the ICTM Colloquium "Indigenous Music and Dance as Cultural Property: Global Perspectives" in Toronto, May 2008. The questions, developed by Thomas, inquire specifically about issues of Indigenous music and digital media. My responses reveal my own personal experiences with musical media throughout my career and my views on pertinent issues of Indigenous musical transmission, production, composition, as well broader political concerns. The interview was conducted via e-mail over the course of numerous months and is thus the result of an extended digital dialogue between colleagues and friends.

Describe briefly your education and current work with music as a singer, composer, producer, and pedagogue.

Most of my knowledge comes from my mother, Flora Wallace, who was a traditional singer from the St'át'imc Nation (which is part of the Salish linguistic group). These teachings have helped me form my own views of music and philosophically inform my compositions. I grew up in Vancouver in the Mount Pleasant area, which back in those days was a diverse working-class neighborhood. I was exposed to a variety of songs from different musical cultures. I also started in radio at a young age (through the high school I was attending), which further broadened my musical exposure.

When I speak of my education, many things have contributed to it that were not necessarily academic. I started at a community radio station called Vancouver CO-OP Radio and that had many music programs that specialized in many music forms (electro-acoustic, experimental, reggae, punk, and many other forms). At that time (1982–83), I was also part of the first wave of Indigenous radio shows in Vancouver, which made me realize that there were very few recordings of Indigenous music.

The lack of Indigenous recordings would inspire me to explore new things. As a teenager, I went through the usual voice-altering experiences, which made me self-conscious and retreat to the safe corners of technology. I took to the recording, editing, and airing of protests and political events that were part of Indigenous life in Vancouver—events like the Constitution Express of the early '80s, where Aboriginal leaders such as George Manuel led people to Ottawa to press the government to include Aboriginal rights in the proposed Canadian Constitution or the discussion of Bill C-31 of the Indian Act (which changed how status Indian women were defined by the Indian Act). The airing of such events with interviews from people involved in these movements helped give voice to that which was missing or distorted in the mainstream media. Those were the days of real-to-reel life.

I tended to fall into opportunities and not recognize them until much later. After radio I went into print journalism, where I learned how to elicit responses from people I interviewed and think about a broader and somewhat objective perspective of what was going on. From there I attended Spirit Song Theatre School and developed my voice, which I had missed for so long, and became comfortable with my inner bass. This is where I started doing music for theater. I had been playing guitar since I was seven years old but it was not a serious pursuit at that time. I loved running the guitar through effects and that sound and exploration opened doors for me, as the music fit well with the theater and dance presentations. I learned how to converse with directors and choreographers, since I understood some of the theater terminologies.

How would you describe your role in the transmission of Salish expressive culture, particularly music?

I have been told to share and pass on the songs. Indigenous people in Canada were not so free to share songs, language, and culture for many years because of laws and policies. My mother was beaten for speaking and singing in her own language. Her resistance to the church and government ensured that the songs and language would survive.

She said, as with anything we try to hide, if we hide the songs we will lose them, and if we want to be proud of our heritage, then we need to share the songs proudly and not feel any shame or fear in singing or sharing them.

Now that she is gone, it is up to me to share the songs in the family along with my brothers and sisters and teach our children and grandchildren those songs.

What do digital media bring to or how do they threaten Indigennous musical performance, composition, and transmission?

Intent is key to how a technology is used by a cultural or linguistic group. If the intent is to document a language, a song, or a dance, then the use of digital media is very good for its intention. If the intent is to construct a new work based on traditional forms then, again, the use of digital media is good. If, however, the intention is to appropriate or to exploit a cultural or linguistic aspect of a group, then the use of digital media is not so good.

How did you learn Salish song, and what role did musical media play in this process?

I learned the songs from my mother, who sang everyday. She would teach us the songs and tell us to accompany her at social and community gatherings.

There was very little access to any recordings of our songs. In fact, there was so little documentation of Lil'wat songs or Salish songs in Canada that I did not hear any recordings until 2004, when I came across an archival recording from 1911, when St'at'imc chiefs went to Ottawa to present the 1911 Declaration of the Lillooet Tribe. Historically, British Columbia (BC) did not have very many treaties negotiated with First Nations communities. British Columbia was a British colony until 1871, when it joined the Canadian Federation. So many lands were being occupied and seized by settlers with no intervention by Canada. The Lillooet People needed a way to address this and so put together the declaration in order to save what little they had left of their territories. To this day, no acknowledgment has been made by Canada to address this issue, and the modern treaty process does not work in the best interest of First Nations communities.

My family group was the first to record and release the songs to the public in CD form in May 2000. The CD was an important step in Salish music because, first, it documented songs my mother learned; second, it put a contemporary spin on the songs with the arrangement of harmonies; and last, it included new songs created by members of the group which followed the traditional Salish music form. I worked as the recording producer on the project (in which I raised funds and negotiated with recording studios) and as a primary arranger along with my mother. Over the years we have taught singing workshops at theater schools, at university composition classes, schoolteacher conferences, and in the community at events and festivals.

What is the role of musical media (e.g., recording technology, studio work, computer software, CDs, MySpace, YouTube) in your work as a singer, composer, and producer?

The biggest breakthrough for me in terms of singing and technology was getting access to multi-track recording. I had intermittent access to multi-track recorders, but it was in studios where time was expensive, so there was really no room to improvise and play with layering. It was around 1991 when I rented an eight-track recorder and played with layering my voice. The results can be heard on Dana Claxton's "Tree of Consumption" performance art piece from 1993.

This opened up ways of singing in which I could sing a melody and then add harmonies. I have always sung harmony since I was really young—it was something that I heard and was able to sing. It was a big transition to sing a melody part.

At the end of the '80s, I had acquired a synth and a computer, and this made me visualize Salish music. The patterns of MIDI notes reminded me of baskets that were woven by Salish peoples for thousands of years. MIDI programs such as SMPTE tracks (on Atari) and later on Vision and Studio Vision (on the Macintosh platform) were based on graphic user interfaces. Musical phrases could be moved around, and the notes were represented from the perspective of a piano keyboard (where the lowest notes would be on top and the higher-pitched notes on the bottom of the track) and the length of each note was shown as a long line rather than as represented in Western notation. As the bars of music grew, patterns were formed and I could see the repetition creating woven designs. I could now see a visual representation of Salish music. This made the form clear to me, and how it could relate to weaving and to the landscapes of Salish people.

Back in the '80s and '90s the vinyl record, cassette tape, and compact disc were the ways of sharing music. It was an expensive and arduous process to record, mix, master, and then duplicate or press music for release. In the last few years I have been able to share my music on YouTube or other social media sites. I still release songs on CD or on Internet music sites, but for the most part I create videos from random images and add my music.

This opens up new questions in terms of what is being presented. Are people interested in the music or images? Are both necessary for the observer/listener to understand a song? My visual interpretation of a song may lead people to understand that work of music in only one way. Just as a writer might read his or her work and color how the poem could be interpreted, do visualizations of music create only one available interpretation? Or, how a director might interpret a book could change the meaning from the original intent of the author.

The videos I create are informed by the lyrics, for the most part, or the mood. Mostly it is finding random images (on the Internet or created by myself) that might fit the song. The video poem for "The Snows" is pretty much a literal interpretation of the words.

I do the videos to make some songs publicly available, since other routes of releasing material can be expensive and time consuming.

What musical media did you use in the process of composing, recording, and distributing your CD's "Through the Cracks" and "Tzo'kam," and how did the media impact the musical aesthetics and political messages of these projects?

Through the Cracks and *Tzo'Kam* were recorded at home (for the most part) and mixed at the Factory Studios. I was the producer for both projects, but the focus for each one was different; the solo CD showcased my efforts in writing pop/folk songs based on Salish forms of music, whereas the group CD showcased traditional songs with contemporary arrangements.

Tzo'kam is political just for existing in Canada. What I mean by that is *Tzo'kam* shares songs and language that were not free to share in Canadian society (through laws and institutional practices). The fact that we have these songs today stands as a testament to the strength and determination of our elders to keep these songs and traditions alive.

My solo efforts in writing songs has a political message in that I focused the lyrical material on alienation, social injustices, and contemporary Aboriginal experiences in Vancouver.

The fact that these CDs were broadcast on radio (CBC, CFRO—Vancouver CO-OP Radio on various programs, CJSF, and other university stations across Canada) demonstrates that things are slowly changing—that is, Aboriginal music is reaching a broader audience.

In terms of technology, things are changing all the time. The studio in which these CDs were mixed or recorded has since closed its doors. The same studio in which many well-known rock and pop bands have recorded is gone. The big boards and gear that were seen as the pinnacle of recording technology in the '70s and '80s are too big to maintain in this digital era, at least in Vancouver, where the price of real estate has pushed all big spaces to convert to condominiums. There is a loss of theater spaces (some historical theaters have been torn down) and many large recording studios are closing their doors because the cost is way too high to maintain. The opportunity of creating a home studio is more viable with the falling prices of recording equipment.

So why do we still make CDs? Most of our support and market come from our communities that have limited access to the Internet. So in a place where you might have limited electricity and perhaps no Internet access, you would most likely have CD players. Most of our market would prefer to have a CD rather than have a downloaded version.

Describe your composition work for film.

My work in composing for film, theater, and dance is all about collaboration— collaboration with the director or choreographer. My approach is to provide a work that helps the narrative or that evokes what the director or choreographer wants. Although I am rooted in my Salish music forms, I investigate other music forms and expressions.

For the film *Cedar and Bamboo* (a film about people of aboriginal and Chinese descent in BC), I played the guzheng and sang a Salish-influenced song over the top. I studied Chinese music at UBC and learned to play the guzheng years before and saw this soundtrack as an opportunity to combine the two musical cultures. Knowing the scales of Chinese music and knowing the form of Salish music, I had no problem blending the two together. The music could exist without the film, but the overall context of both the film and the music leave a lasting impression. These types of collaborative efforts can fail on so many levels, but the training I had in both traditions and the narrative of the film brought together a cohesive music expression that I feel good about.

Sometimes I feel that my best work comes from the challenges set out by a collaborator, and other times I feel that my sensibilities or initial impulses are my best work. It is always interesting to negotiate a sense of collaboration and sharing.

How do you employ musical media in your work as a singing and composition teacher?

I don't really use any musical media in my teaching. I encourage self-awareness of voice through exercises and repetition of song. I learned by doing, and so even though we all learn differently, I want the participants to get in touch with their voice through hearing and singing with others in real time rather than by singing to a recording. I will give people recordings if they need it, but a cappella singing changes and the nuances of pronunciation are never clearly heard on recordings. For me I learn best by seeing the shape of the mouth as well as hearing the sounds.

Singing is a physical activity. Singing with people is a social activity. Singing is also about listening and responding. For me, it took years of listening to my mother and the people in our communities singing and then singing the songs on my own, but it was in the layering of my own voice on recordings that I clearly understood the nature of Salish singing. The difference between coastal singing and interior singing is vast. On the coast, the men sing low in pitch, and in the mountains, the men tend to sing higher up in pitch. The landscapes play an important role in this distinction. You sing what you see around you in the physical environment. When we say the songs are from the land, we mean it. From these recording experiments I learned to blend my voice in with both types of singing. As I live in Vancouver, which is on the coast, my voice leans to a coastal way of singing that complimented my mother's and sister's voices in our family group. Who I sing with affects the way I sing.

To teach this type of singing would be difficult with just a CD. It is something that must be heard and felt by the singer. Most of the people who come to learn to sing have little or no experience, so I guide them through at their pace and sing songs that are suited to their voices, whether they are traditional songs or songs created from traditional forms.

How has your use of and attitude toward musical media changed over the last decade(s), and how has this change impacted your work?

Music used to be accessible through recordings released on vinyl, CDs, or cassette tapes. The Internet, of course, has changed many things. We live in a world full of data and information and different means of transmitting ideas and knowledge. Whereas before we used to go to the record store or library to find the music that impacted us, we now utilize search engines and must find the right tag words that will bring us to online stores or other online resources.

I upload music onto the Internet through video sites and tag the videos with words like "Salish" or my own name. If someone is looking for me they can find me and other similar types of music. I am finding new artists all the time and have passed on what I find to others through social media. The danger, of course, is being distracted by all the music and videos.

In the early 1990s I started in information technology at Capilano College. This was when the World Wide Web was in its early stages. One of my fondest memories of that time was getting to know Buffy Sainte-Marie through e-mail correspondence. We had both been at a round-table discussion on Native New Media, and we all exchanged e-mail addresses. We both used the Roland D50 keyboard a lot and so had discussions on that.

I realized the possibilities of the Internet after learning that Buffy had recorded her album by e-mailing MIDI files back and forth with her producer. The Internet is a tool, and it can be an effective means to create, collaborate and disseminate.

In your work, what impact has digital media had in changing representations of and strengthening Indigennous culture?

It is hard to say what impact my work has had, since I am usually not present when it is played on TV or on the radio. People have come up to me and said that the music I composed for a certain film moved them and that is really nice to hear. In terms of other Indigenous artists it is nice to make a connection through the work and have collaborations spring up through different projects. Working with Inuit artists such as Eva Adams, Donna Bernhardt, and Sylvia Cloutier, who come from different parts of the North in Canada, in creating new works based on those traditions have made me look at my own traditions in a more focused way. Traditions such as those which incorporate voice in relationship to drum, breath, sounds of the land, and narrative made me connect to both Inuit and Salish musics at the same time.

In North America there is still an entrenched mindset that anything Indigenous is inferior. In music we still find that traditional music is thought of as folk music and academic institutions have little or no representation of local musics. The lack of formal Western music training affects traditional singers and composers in grant opportunities, in teaching, and in working on productions that would represent our own culture (awards shows, national/provincial celebrations, and in cultural institutions like theater, dance, and opera productions). So, my feeling is that there is a cultural mindset that will take generations to change; however, with greater access to these traditions through social media, people are connecting. My video poem for "The Snows" was part of a university literature class in Alberta, and my work in AIDS awareness was part of an exhibit in New York simply because the people involved had seen the work on the Internet.

How do debates concerning access and ownership of Indigennous cultural heritage impact your use of digital media in your work as a singer, composer, producer, and pedagogue?

In 2000, our family group finished recording our first CD. I called up to our band office and asked about correct spellings of some of our songs and was told at that point we were not allowed to release the CD without permission from the chief and council. I spoke with my mother about this, and her response was that she did not need to get permission when she had learned these songs from her aunts or in-laws; she did not need to get permission to be beaten at school for singing these songs and keeping them alive; and she did not need to get permission to keep singing them from an elected council consisting of people who were not even born when she learned them. "Why would I learn something that I am not allowed to share?"—a sentiment that informs my own work.

I understand the importance of protecting our songs, but what is the price of doing so when so few know the songs? We copyrighted the recording and the arrangement of the songs and listed them as traditional compositions. By doing this we protect the song through the arrangements. As traditional music is public domain, the copyright of the arrangement helps protect the songs in small ways. We have never been asked by the reserve to perform since then, but the community still supports the group through CD purchases and coming to shows outside of the community. Chief and councils are unstable and there are always shifts in power, but the people still support the music in its different forms.

We recorded songs the way my mother recalls them or have taken them and put new arrangements to them to reflect our singing style, and we share them with the community. We have created new songs based on the old forms using the language and have also arranged the songs to have Western instrumentation and have recorded them. Technology should be a tool of culture. That is, we must use technology to advance our culture (songs, language, dance, and art). When culture becomes a tool of technology (that is, when music is mined for source material to utilize in TV or film and put in a completely different context without anyone knowing it), that is when the gray areas begin to appear and our understanding of the culture can become distorted. Technology needs an informed, consensual, and contextual agreement with cultural practitioners. I, as a traditional singer, need to know that the music I share will not be used to sell beer or put into any other context that might bring harm to the songs.

The importation of technology for the sake of technology can have devastating effects on the culture and language. If you think of food technology and how that has been widely imported by many different cultural groups, we can see the physical effects through obesity, diabetes, and cancer where there was none before.

If we look at it from a cultural or arts perspective we can lose a worldview (present in language or songs) that comes directly from the land. One example would be asking someone's age: in English you would ask, "How old are you?" as in "How many years are you?" In St'at'imc you would say, "How many snows are you?" as in "How many winters have you survived?" This question brings up the fact that winters are hard, and if we are not prepared we may perish during the winter months. The question asks for a fact, but is also a poetic way to get information.

Another example of the importance of language and its revelation of worldview would be the words in St'at'imc that mean "to sing" and "to eat." Both sound very similar: ílhen (roughly sounding like "eet'lin") means "to eat" and ít'em (sounding like "eet' lum") means "to sing." One means to nourish your body by having something go in your mouth and the other means nourishing your body by having something come out of your mouth. We cannot go through life without eating, so why would we go through life without singing?

As an individual I do not own the songs, but I am part of a larger community that collectively owns the songs. Some would say that the songs are part of what has gone on before and we honor those before us by keeping the songs alive and sharing them. To give the power of ownership to a select few inhibits the transmission to the future.

What is your participation in pan-Indigenous forums (either within Canada or internationally) in the realm of music, and how have digital media impacted this participation?

Pan-Indigenous forums have many streams to work from. In my collaborations, certainly there have been many opportunities to be a part of pan-Indigenous expressions. In my work with choreographers I have had to work within another cultural expression. The choreographer or director would supply music from their cultural group and ask me to compose something around that music. Sometimes there are a number of different music ideas that have to fit within one composition. This process is more about collaboration and fusion.

There is another process of finding the "lowest common denominator" type of expression (not the best way to express this work but the only one that I can conjure up that can be understood). This collaboration within a larger group finds a way that everyone involved is represented in the music. The reduction of the music to vocables and generalized traditional forms is what is present in a lot of media soundtracks. We as cultural presenters must find a way to present music that is inclusive but also relates to the soundtrack or function of the song. In some ways this pan-Indigeneity is the only thing people understand as Indigenous music from North America. This creates a reductionist interpretation and does not go very deeply into specific cultural expressions.

It seems that to be acknowledged as being Indigenous to North America, all music that represents "Native American" culture must have a powwow-based style of singing, and all music that represents Inuit culture must have throat singing. When there is a deviation from that set of interpretations of Indigenous music, then the music is considered to be too localized for international consumption or is considered "world music." I have encountered this interpretation of Indigenous music at awards shows, music juries, and music festivals across North America.

In terms of digital media, composers must deal with this reductionist view when they apply for jobs writing music for soundtracks or awards shows. In some way this feeds into stereotypes of Indigenous music. In acting for TV and film there is a stereotype of Native Peoples that defines the spectrum of Indigenous people within a small frame. That is, you must have long hair and have dark skin to even be considered to be cast as a Native person in the industry. Things are changing, for sure, but that same sort of stereotyping can be applied to other art forms as well. Have I done this type of composition? Yes, of course, because that is what the producers wanted for a project. I have stopped marketing myself in this arena, because I prefer to work with producers and directors I know and with whom I have developed respectful professional relationships.

Of course there is the flip side to this discussion which I have encountered a number of times. The flip side is defining Indigenous music as having no Western-influenced instrumentation. Again the definition of the music becomes narrow in scope and creates limits in production. As someone who makes a living from composition, I must make sure the funders are happy with the work; but as an artist I must ensure that I am learning something or moving my music into an area that I am comfortable with. That balance is always negotiated, and I am happy with most of my work presented in the public.

Chapter Five

Mixing It Up

A Comparative Approach to Sámi Audio Production

Beverley Diamond

In 1989, in a significant article on "Globalization as Philosophical Issue," cultural theorist Fredric Jameson elaborated some of the tensions between aspects of what he has identified throughout much of his career as "late capitalism." Noting that the extent to which world markets now require "a global division of labour on an extraordinary scale,"[1] he observes that, on the one hand, cultural difference can be asserted and celebrated to a larger extent than ever before, but, on the other, standardization on an unparalleled scale threatens "forced integration into a world system."[2] He clearly inclines to the latter (pessimistic) side of the equation, observing that "American mass culture, associated as it is with money and commodities, enjoys a prestige that is perilous for most forms of domestic cultural production."[3] While, like many ethnomusicologists, I am motivated to emphasize the distinctiveness and agency of local cultures, this article recognizes that it is less useful to take sides on the issue of standardization than to attempt to understand the intertwining factors that impinge on local cultural production. The attention I pay here to comparative recording aesthetics addresses such factors in relation to issues examined in the anthology's introduction. I explore, to some extent, the way contemporary Sámi musicians have used the opportunities that modernity has presented in order to resist marginalization by drawing upon local aesthetics, indices of place as well as styles of social interaction, and archival memory. I agree with

Wilson and Stewart's statement that "the major executives of the hegemonic media do not always define the terms of 'excellence' for Indigenous media makers. Indigenous artists and activists are using new technologies to craft culturally distinct forms of communication and artistic production that speak to local aesthetics and local needs while anticipating larger audiences."[4] By emphasizing comparative responses to distinct Indigenous processes, however, I hope to nuance the discussion, challenging a simplistic idea of "resistance" by insisting on the complex array of social contingencies, media memory, styles of relationality and cultural values that contribute to the divergent "readings" of Indigenous audio production in the digital era.

More than twenty-five years after Jameson's prognosis, then, it is instructive to reexamine the tension between local distinction and transnational standardization in the context of Indigenous music production, for several reasons.[5] Counter to Jameson's pessimism, Indigenous music industries have burgeoned in the intervening decades, at times converging with struggles for land, resources, and cultural rights. Furthermore, Indigenous production has been generically diverse—"a maelstrom of experimentation," as Lehtola described Sámi music in particular.[6] Have Indigenous musicians and music producers been able to create and retain a distinctive "voice" in the commodified forms that were central to this cultural flourishing? This chapter will address this question through a comparison of audio production aesthetics, using recent Sámi recordings from Scandinavia as a case study.[7]

The small comparative study described here was inspired by another statement in the Jameson article. "Globalization," he wrote, "is a communicational concept, which alternately masks and transmits cultural or economic meanings."[8] His thinking related again to the broad dialectic between cultural distinctiveness and standardization. Assertions of "identity" that seem to present cultural distinctiveness are more and more masks that obscure diversity and effectively present the opposite: standardized "brands" or stereotypic representations that contradict cultural distinctiveness and heterogeneity, or present a rigid and limited trace. I will argue that recording studio practices are cultural arenas where this alternate masking and transmission are complex and powerful for a second reason.[9] The processes of production are literally hidden from the listeners—and often from the musicians, as well—because they take place "behind the glass" of the studio or in back offices where mixing and mastering are done. How is difference asserted or denied in such spaces? Furthermore, because the recording industry takes local music to transnational audiences, how does a recording with distinctive cultural markers fare in the transnational marketplace? I first assumed that difference is asserted in the early stages of production and played down in the marketing and commodity distribution phases. But there is evidence that the opposite is also true. Independent and culturally specific recordings are given new layers of meaning within the larger music industry, and their distinctive sounds can generate financial return for local artists or communities.[10] Because recording studio processes are often hidden from public view, the tension between the cultural and economic meanings alluded to by Jameson is germane. This paper reports on an experiment that begins to bring those practices into view by comparing cross-cultural production aesthetics.

Since the late 1980s, I have been working (off and on) with contemporary Native American and Sámi recording artists in an attempt to better understand how digital technologies function in their creative practice and social networks. My motivation is strongly influenced by the fact that technological processes are hidden, and by my desire to demystify technologies of the ear (which are every bit as important as other "technologies of the self").[11] At times, this work has involved studio ethnography, interviews with sound engineers, recording artists, and others involved with Indigenous CD production; investigations of intellectual property; and feedback listening. It has been readily apparent that Indigenous producers often have unique approaches to studio production— approaches in which cultural values are embedded, rearticulated, and resignified in the recording/mixing processes.[12] I wrote about Sámi musicians' and producers' approaches in a 2007 article, focusing on the ways Indigenous concepts are articulated in the recording studio, especially in the hands of two very skilled musician/producers, Frode Fjellheim and Wimme Saari. I often wondered how non-Indigenous producers and sound engineers who know industry conventions might respond to the Sámi studio work. In this paper, I report on a small step in the direction of finding out by comparing two recording producers' responses about production processes in a wide range of Sámi recordings. The two producers are Anglo-Canadian Spencer Crewe and Norwegian Sámi Frode Fjellheim. I also draw on earlier interviews with Sámi performers and producers.

I worked through a number of Sámi audio tracks with Spencer Crewe, a talented engineer who works in the Research Centre for Music, Media and Place at Memorial University of Newfoundland, asking what he hears and how he would "read" various production decisions. Crewe enjoys "deconstructive listening," in which he identifies audible production and postproduction techniques, and he is patient and generous in response to my sometimes ill-informed questions. In his own words, he likes "talking nerd." Crewe has recorded, mixed, mastered, or produced recordings by a number of bands that have considerable regional and national success and one that has a large measure of international renown.[13] Furthermore, he has worked in diverse genres including rock, traditional Celtic, blues, country, world music and, to a lesser extent, classical. Like any listener, he brings both personal taste and learned experience to this exercise. He clearly doesn't "represent" North American studio producers, but he is aware of certain norms and conventions. Sámi producers are, of course, also aware of mainstream norms and conventions, but they are arguably disinclined to regard them as normative. The rest of this article will elaborate how conventions may at times be adopted but at other times ignored or resignified.

Trondheim-based Fjellheim is a remarkably adept collaborator, since he is thoughtful and generous about explaining both traditional *joik* production and the ways he uses traditional *joiks* in modern live and recording projects. As a "crossover" musician with traditional, jazz, and classical training, he has worked with musicians in many genres, and created intercultural works, among them an opera, *Skuvle Nejla*, and an Arctic Mass. As a postsecondary instructor and curriculum designer, he also understands academia.[14]

Like most producers whom I have met, both Crewe and Fjellheim regard recording and audio production as a distinct art form not an imitative one.[15] Fjellheim expressed this as follows: "I always consider the recording format as an artistic expression on its own, rather than a recreation of a 'reality.'"[16] His use of the word "reality" in quotes is noteworthy, since it recognizes that recording and mixing never simply replicate acoustic sound, but always mediate the sound source. Fjellheim's comment further implies some skepticism about interpretations that read social nuances into studio production. He asserts that the imaginative spheres evoked in the artistic processes of recording are neither determined nor limited by conventional codes.[17]

Sámi Cultural Identities in the Recording Studio

Phase one of this work began about twenty years after the boom in the Sámi recording industry had kicked off. As Hilder (2015) describes at more length, Sámi music of many kinds (live performances, exhibitions, recordings, festivals) have become powerful means of negotiating the politics of Indigeneity in Arctic Europe in recent decades. Furthermore, most of the recording production was in the hands of Sámi themselves, first through the companies DAT and Iđut and later joined by Rieban and Vuelie (Fjellheim's company). By 2010 approximately 380 CDs had been produced, with eight to ten emerging each year.[18] As in many parts of the world, Indigenous audio and video production flourished in the digital era. In Sápmi (the region of northern Scandinavia where Sámi reside), music production was tied to local developments, central among them challenges to Indigenous land rights relating, in part, to hydroelectric development. It was enabled by the expansion of arts subsidies within oil-rich Norway, albeit with conditions that the traditional genre known as *joik* be featured in all productions.[19]

Audio recording was not without its challenges. The live tradition of subtly altering a *joik* to reflect a specific situation or of responding to a person's *joik* by *joiking* back was now changed to a fixed, one-way communication. As political leader Ole Henrik Magga told me, "In one generation, we have taught them how not to participate."[20] Producer Wimme Saari commented that "personal *joiks* are personal things. Somehow I don't want to put them into the public domain."[21] Indeed many artists prefer to record *joiks* about places, animals, or abstract and imaginary concepts rather than people, thus shifting the repertoire relative to that used in daily life or live performance contexts. For some, the biggest challenge was the recording studio itself. Sámi singers described it as a "dead" space, "unreal," "hard work," or "pale and dull."

These phrases are apt, since the studio lacks people who vocalize responses—yet sociality is central to the tradition of *joik.* Of course, the notion of "liveness" is also implied, and this is a concept to which I return below. Jameson argued in 1998 that "no enclaves—aesthetic or other—are left in which the commodity form does not reign supreme,"[22] and many Sámi musicians and producers of the twentieth century were initially ambivalent and wary about the commodification of *joiks.*

In spite of the challenges, however, studio production helped to create and negotiate Sámi identity, partially by means of communication strategies that had been part of traditional lifeways. The distinctive identity-making processes that musicians and studio producers discussed with me clustered around (1) the particular quality of the *joik* voice and its capacity for mimicry, (2) a particular conceptualization of aural "liveness" in relation both to the way temporality and spatiality are deployed,[23] and (3) a love of polyvalent meanings.

Artists consistently differentiated the sound of the traditional *joik* technique from the sound of "singing." Several artists whom I interviewed—among them Inga Juuso, Berit Risten Sara, and Annuka Hirvasvuopio—demonstrated the difference, pointing to the body for *joik* and the head for song. Johan Sara emphasized the diaphragm, adding that "the color is so fantastic" when *joiking* is done well. Song, on the other hand, has "a lot of breathing in the voice."[24] Annukka Hirvasvuoppio explained that "you *joik* with your whole body,"[25] and Ante Mikkel Gaup taught that you have to find the break in your voice and push the voice out at that point in your register.[26] Radio producer Ola Nakkalajärvi explained that "traditional *joiking* doesn't aim at pleasing somebody, so the voice formation doesn't have to be beautiful."[27] Its role is to characterize or mimic people, animals, or landscape features. Sámi musicians consistently emphasized the individuality, timbre changes, and the throatiness/rawness of the voice, features that contrast rather with pop music production norms.[28] The individuality of vocal quality is, then, in itself an assertion of distinctiveness, "restoring political potential to art in a different sense than we have been accustomed to thinking about [it]."[29]

Indigenous producers are respectful of the individuality of vocal styles, but find a variety of ways to highlight the distinctive vocal "colors." Johan Sara Jr.

described the vocal technique itself as reverberant.[30] "We make a big hall of a voice," he explained. In the studio, Sara emphasizes "reverb and the right mics . . . but not compression." No standardized production or postproduction values have emerged, however, but rather a range of diverse production techniques.

For the deconstructive listening sessions with Spencer Crewe, I selected forty-three tracks that reflect such variety, but only fifteen of these are referenced in this chapter (see Appendix).[31] We started by listening to four excerpts of traditional *joik* recording—chosen for the extreme variety of recording and mixing approaches that they represented. I asked Crewe to compare them. In the first (#1) he noted places where he perceived a bump in the low-frequency range to enhance the rich bass colors of Mathis A. Oskal's voice. He describes the production of Inga Juuso (especially #2) as having the clarity of a modern pop recording ("clarity" in his terms involved a close mic, and a bump to the mid-range and high-end frequencies), but the reverb and echo are extreme, a feature he maps as "dreamy," "fantasy-like," perhaps relating to the representation of midsummer's eve, the subject of the *joik* presented; the third example (#3) is overdubbed twice, with the voices spread from left to right to sound like a trio of voices instead of one. The fourth (#4)—Wimme Saari's representation of the mountain *háldi* or spirits—sounds like it was recorded outdoors; it is dry and distant (as Crewe noted, both environmental noise and the pre-amp sound are quite audible). This particular example raised questions for me about the presumed "ideal" space in which to hear a *joik*. Zagorski-Thomas has argued that rock production, for instance, was functionally "staged" in the recording studio to evoke memories for listeners of large-venue arenas where live concerts took place, even though most rock recordings were listened to in domestic spaces.[32] Saari may have been using an opposite kind of "staging" by suggesting a distant mountaintop as the "ideal" space for *joik*. The main point, however, is that production of the traditional *joik* recordings is extremely varied. There is no standardization.

Some differences reflected technological change. Aware that some *joik* recordings of the '90s really sound edgy and that many joik performers emphasize the contrast between the vocal production of song and *joik*, I played Berit Risten Sara and Ravna Anti Guttorm's "Ivváar-Máret" (#5) to Crewe. He noted that the harshest production values coincided with early digital technology that is now regarded as less warm than either analog recordings or more recent digital recordings. The discursive distinction between *joik* and song, then, might have been partially facilitated by the coincidence of a particular stage of the technology with an important political moment when Sámi assertions of their rights were reaching a broader public.[33] The aesthetic distinction became further established by a play produced for the Lillehammer Olympics, in which the different timbres of song and *joik* served as sonic metaphors for colonial oppression and cultural sovereignty.[34]

Genre and Gender

The organization of music industries around "genre cultures," as Keith Negus has labeled the phenomenon, which "inform the organization of music companies, the creative practices of musicians and the perceptions of audiences" is well proven by now but not often tested cross-culturally.[35] While a label such as "world music" attempted to define and homogenize a new genre culture in the 1980s, the diverse nature of the music encompassed in such a catch-all category often defied categorization or, as is the case with much Indigenous music, was generally placed outside of the category altogether. Furthermore, as Tom Porcello notes about the ethnographic studies in the anthology that he coedited,[36] media theory has often ignored the "everyday *uses* of technology by social actors in crafting sonic artifacts and environments. Here the value of ethnography as the principal methodology of anthropology and ethnomusicology bears fruit by providing a window into how people deploy technology to engineer (whether by making, listening to, or circulating) their musical and sonic lives."[37] Indigenous producers and Spencer Crewe tended to place different emphases on genre, on the one hand, and social functionality, on the other. Where their interpretations of production strategies were more often coincident was in the imaginative spatialities of some of the most innovative Sámi work.

The range and variety of recording and mixing techniques used by experienced Sámi producers such as Johan Sara Jr., Wimme Saari, and Frode Fjellheim led Crewe to describe some of the production values as "anti-pop" in one session and "informed by classical music" in another. He thought Mathis Oskal (#1) sounded "traditional," the recent recordings of Angelit (#6) "commercial pop," and Per Tor Turi (#9) "very electronica." In spite of the sheer variety, then, there was a constant pull in Crewe's experience toward genre definitions. The strength of genre expectations often influences the circulation of Indigenous recordings. Peter Dunbar-Hall and Chris Gibson quote the veteran Murri recording artist Kev Carmody about the fact that mainstream radio "has an obsession with 'radio friendly' music. They won't even touch anything that's not 'safe' to play. They don't like anything or anybody that's singing from outside the system and communicating messages that criticize that system."[38] While the "system" is described in terms of the political content of the lyrics, it is likely that part of "radio-friendly" is the genre expectations of radio's clientele since most "format" radio is so defined.

In Sápmi, on the other hand, Indigenous radio stations broadcasting in the Sámi language were open to playing a wide variety of styles.[39] Most musicians with whom I have spoken regarded radio airplay as less restrictive than CD production due largely to the funding mechanisms. CD production has relied extensively on government grants, initially through national programs, but after the founding of the Sámi Parliament in 1989,[40] through a Sámi Culture Fund to which artists, writers, and musicians as well as organizations could apply.[41] Since 2001, funds continue to be distributed through the Sámi Parliament, but the administrative structures have changed. I was told that there were expectations that elements of "traditional" sound—*joik*—would be part of Indigenous production, an expectation that Australian musicians also encountered.

On the other hand, Sámi musicians and producers often ignore or challenge the relevance of genre boundaries, or the need to sound traditional, using at times a strategy that Tim Taylor has labeled "strategic inauthenticity."[42] Even the lengths of songs or the track boundaries that separate them might be regarded as part of this strategy. Wimme Saari, for instance, often continues one electronic element from one track to the next so that there is no silence between tracks. In this way, he adjusts the time between vocalizations, since "some pieces can be such that another cannot begin straight after, but there has to be calm water before the next one begins. And some pieces require that the next one must begin at once."[43] For the most part, though, Saari encourages listeners to respond independently: "I don't want to direct or guide or lead the feelings they get." On the other hand, producer Magnus Vuolab explained that he often lays down bed tracks to create a groove and then records and overdubs the vocal lines (that usually involve *joiking*) quite separately, a process similar to that of Crewe and many other North American popular music producers.[44]

In addition to genre references, gender constructions were frequently mentioned in conversations with both the Sámi producers and in earlier interviews with performers. The earliest recording technologies were often said to reproduce male voices better than female voices.[45] Techniques for moderating any harshness in female vocals are still part of some sound engineering training. The *joik* sound, on the other hand, is consistently said not to be gendered. The "colors" of every range are savored. Sámi women, then, who perform popular music (*joik*-derived or not) have encountered problems in mainstream recording studios when they used a variety of timbres. Some were told to sing more lightly and were further "feminized" in the mixing process. Sofia Jannok, who describes herself as "bicultural" (Sámi and Swedish), and who was one of the new solo stars on the Sámi scene in 2007, commented on the instructions of her producer to sing only with a light tone quality that she calls her "small" voice:

> On stage I like the dynamic of a very, very small voice to a very, very big voice; so it was hard for me to only use the small voice. It was a little bit frustrating sometimes, but in the studio it is hard to get the feeling of the big kind of voice. . . . You get a very close, almost whispering feeling in the studio which you can't really bring on stage.[46]

From a non-Indigenous engineer's perspective, "Ija Salas" from Jannok's debut album (#7) was standard pop production. Crewe described that mode of production as follows:

> Very close to the microphone, intimate with the microphone (there's a sweet spot). But you kind of have to sing like that. Give a sense of closeness. They have the air going, using a Neumann 87 or [some other microphone that has a] sweet high-end response, smooth sounding, tube technology as opposed to solid-state stuff. It starts with mic choice and they accentuate that with EQ and over-easy compression. But it takes a particular voice to do that. You can hear the compression on the high notes where she makes a bit more effort. She is playing with the microphone, turning away from time to time.

Sofia responded to this vocal containment by adding a hidden (unlisted) track at the end of her debut CD. The "naturalness" of this track is reinforced, since, at the beginning, she is rehearsing and warming up off-mic, then seeming to walk toward the microphone where she *joiks* unaccompanied, on mic, with a voice that is closer to her "big voice." Crewe described it as a "happy accident" that the mic was still turned on to capture this informal moment.

Other female artists have had similar experiences. Ulla Pirttijarvi told of the experience of recording one track for her first CD that "perhaps wasn't so peaceful as the other pieces" and it was left out of the track list.[47] The first attempts to record for her first album were furthermore not to her liking. "It was too much like pop music," she says. "It didn't have a soul." Annuka Hirvasvuopio confided that she didn't like the way the *joiks* sound on her own first album, *Vilddás*.[48] All of these artists have assumed more control over the sound of their voices in subsequent recording projects.

Sounding Temporality

Both live *joik* performance and recordings can become a sonic trace of lineage at times, when a singer could hear a family relationship through voices four or five generations removed, regardless of gender differences. As mentioned earlier, Wimme Saari feels the memory and the existence of past generations when he performs: "So sometimes when I *joik*, I have this feeling that I am not alone, or only with my band, but that there are bigger forces with me, the past generations. And all these, they move in my surroundings and I am one factor in that flow."[49]

Old recordings can also evoke similar memories and feelings. Ulla Pirttijarvi recognized a sonic connection in an archival recording of a man she subsequently learned was her relative, a *noaidi* (shaman) of note. She incorporated the recording into a song about him, "Čalkko Niillas" (They said he was a shaman) (#8). In conversation, we agreed that the timbre of her lowest notes was similar to her relative's, and thought Fjellheim had digitally enhanced this similarity. As Fjellheim reflected, he said: "I don't remember if I intended Ulla's voice to sound like the archival sample. Most likely my choices were based on aesthetic preferences. But of course those preferences might have come from somewhere."[50] He did intentionally bridge their voices by performing the call-and-response part himself: the part from around 2:18 up to the synth solo is "put together using the archive recording (a small part—now pitch transposed) and my voice, not Ulla's."

Crewe heard contrasts, not similarities, between the voices, especially in the middle section:

> They still kept a great contrast between the older and newer sound. Still [it is] more matched than if they could just treat it as a pop song. They wanted to keep that contrast. [The drum sound] could be just a sample or a drum [recording] with a whole pile of reverb and they kept the beater sound lopped off—cut the high-end frequencies out. I've done that a lot with bodhran, especially to get that heartbeat feel. . . . It's still a fairly warm and intimate sound as opposed to the overdone typical pop sound. [In the middle call-and-response section, they] tried to create the intimacy of the recording. That's what we call "ear candy"—moved her [voice] back, rolled back the high frequencies to give a very narrow bandwidth. In North America we call it the AM radio mix, the car stereo. It's just a way to break it up a bit and give the listener something different, just to give it a bit of contrast. [It's] another way to differentiate which is the call and which the answer.

Crewe notes the drum sound in the quotation above and Fjellheim responded to this, saying: "The drum track is Snorre [Bjerck, purcussionist and frequent collaborator with Fjellheim] playing in a big staircase. We wanted it *big*." The warmth that Crewe perceived, then, was the natural acoustic of the space in which the recording was made.

It is not surprising that Crewe's concept of sonic temporality would be oriented differently from that of the Sámi musicians, nor that his comments are often related to technological change. This is one of seven or eight places where he cast old sounds as the "AM radio" sound and saw it as a means of creating contrast by harkening back to an older sound aesthetic.[51] This perception is quite different from that of the Sámi performers, who see the "old sound" of the archive sample as a means of bringing the liveness of the past into the present.

A significant part of traditional *joik* performance in a community context is the fact that one *joik* may be "answered" by another. Of course, stage performance has lessened the tendency for this to happen, as I have discussed elsewhere.[52] As Chris Scales has noted with respect to Native American powwow recordings, the notion of "liveness," references not only the inclusion of "live" recordings but also the indexing of place and spaces of social interaction.[53] Just as the powwow musicians with whom Scales worked wanted to overdub the sound of bells worn by dancers in order to invoke the powwow grounds (and the necessity of dance as a component of powwow), so too, the Sami producers found ways to reference the centrality of "answering" by contrasting archival and modern recordings or by manipulating a contemporary recording to evoke an older sound aesthetic to contrast with a modern one. But the "liveness" of the moment is a continuing value that challenges studio production for many, and inspires others.[54]

In the very different genre world of electronica, Crewe hears Per Tor Turi's track "Vuoibmi (Power)" (#9), produced by Vuolab, as almost the reverse. The structure of the arrangement (see left column of table 5.1) is necessary to make sense of Crewe's comments (right column of table 5.1). Each of the sections consists of four phrases, the third of which (like some choruses in a thirty-two-bar pop- or jazz-song structure) has the greatest concentration of new elements.

Crewe hears Per's voice as old, vintage-sounding, "like a field recording." The association with Moby is partly a reference to ambient music but also to Moby's use of old media, as in the earlier example.

Table 5.1. Spencer Crewe's comments on Per Tor Turi's track "Vuoibmi" (Power)

1. Introduction. Very rapid electronic groove (over 400 bpm), augmented by electronic cymbal elements, single hits of other percussion, and, in the fourth phrase, more legato string-like synthesized melodic elements that are not quite coinciding with the beat but are being constantly changed timbrally.	Very electronica. VERY electronica. The [introduction] music creates space between "in your face" and a "dream-like" atmosphere.
2. Vocal section begins and the string-like elements stop. There is big reverberation on the voice and echo effects when he utters the single syllable "Huh." The electronic groove stops and the nonrhythmic string-like elements return.	[Once the voice enters], that's a very different feel. More of the field-recording kind of sound. You know what it reminds me of? It reminds me of Moby. He used to take vinyl recordings, keep them old-sounding and layer these beautiful musicscapes over it. He's keeping the clear mid range under control— a bit smaller, not in your face (like Sofia). Heavier compression to keep it a bit linear instead of dynamic.
3. Denser textured vocal section with electronic elements, so that the voice seems to be partially buried in the mix. The single syllables have changed to "Heh" and are more rapid and intense.	

(continued)

Table 5.1.—*(concluded)*

4. Sparser-textured vocal section where the voice is heard at its most intense over a stripped-down electronic groove. Very extreme echoes are created throughout the first two phrases. In the third phrase, the voice stops, but an AM radio voice enters. Then the string-like synthesized elements, return, with occasional voice gestures in the distance, though becoming more intense. Two electronic sputters end the arrangement.	[The echo is] digital delay [so as] not to have it too far inside the modern-pop era. [He uses a] low-frequency filter that moves through the [pitch] spectrum. [There's] a lot of effects to give it deep down a "dark cave" kind of effect. The vocal is used more as a texture as opposed to a focus. It's as if he's disappearing. That's pretty crafty stuff right there. He's definitely a Moby fan.

Sounding Spatiality

Producers Fjellheim, and Spencer Crewe seem to find the most common ground when they speak about acoustic space and the kind of spatial sociality that it implies. As Peter Doyle has stated in his book *Echo and Reverb: Fabricating Space in Popular Music Recording 1900–1960*, "there was no one-to-one relationship between the effect and what was signified by its deployment."[55] Echo and reverb effects might connote the supernatural, or desolate, wide-open landscapes, "murderously large waves," but also deterritorialization, haunting or eerie qualities, sacredness, exoticism, or psychic inner spaces.[56] Doyle demonstrates, nonetheless, that certain genres were constructed with different spatial terrains in mind: the intimacy of crooners and pop music, the slapback guitar echo of rock, as well as the signature qualities of certain record labels (Chess Records, for instance). Simon Zagorski-Thomas has written about the imagined spaces that were sometimes consciously evoked in some genres. Describing the highly reverberant "functional staging" of 1970s rock recordings as "the stadium in your bedroom,"[57] he contrasts the actual domestic spaces where most listeners played records and imaginal spaces of large arenas that had an aura of authenticity. Quantitative work by Serge Lacasse, on the other hand, has revealed that North American listeners are rather consistent in associating echo and reverb with space on the one hand and spirituality on the other.[58] The acoustics of large cathedrals are perhaps partially responsible for the latter connotation. In the realm of Indigenous music, one could see Native American music within his paradigm. Recordings have frequently been produced with lots of reverb, particularly those marketed as New Age. I've argued that only a few Native American genres—Inuit throat games, for instance—were immune to this stereotype (arguably a stereotype of spirituality). Sámi CD production, on the other hand, is more diverse. Producer Wimme Saari describes echo and reverb as "some kind of merry-making," without a trace of the serious "spiritual" or supernatural connotations often ascribed to these techniques in the North American or Australian studies.

Spencer Crewe agreed that the spatial imagination of both Frode Fjellheim and Wimme Saari was exceptional, more idiosyncratic and creative than any he had ever encountered. We both laughed at Saari's spatial humor in "Morning Coffee" (#10), a track where we hear him moving around what we presume to be his kitchen, hear his pre-coffee gravelly voice ("a boost at about 8K," says Crewe), and then hear the voice become clearer, presumably after the first cup.

On the other hand, Saari's spatial designs are often more remote or imaginative spaces, as in "Milky Way" (#11), coinciding to some extent with Doyle's "psychic/inner" effects. Saari has explained that "when a child is born, the essence of that child comes from the Milky Way, and when the person dies, this essence goes back to the Milky Way and goes on being there. So it doesn't come from nowhere, and it doesn't disappear to nowhere."[59] Crewe was not aware of this explanation when he "read" the production of the song as follows:

> Sounds like falling down a well, one of those huge [ones]. Everything has this falling off quality to it. [It's] getting further and further away. Radio noise. That's RF, radio frequency interference. Is this song about going out into space or something? Radio frequencies travel that far. . . . That's what it's got to be, the vastness, what it would be to be out in the Milky Way somewhere. [The sounds] might have acoustic origins but they've been warped enough. That's just dragging down the pitch wheel. Definitely gives you the feeling of being alone and in the middle of absolutely nothingness.

Reverberation is not the only way to suggest spatiality with sound. Referencing place is another strategy. There are many contemporary tracks named for cities where these cosmopolitan Sámi artists have toured or worked.[60] In the studio, however, spatiality is frequently referenced through the use of sampled sounds. Both Wimme Saari and Frode Fjellheim use live samples extensively in the recorded mix. Fjellheim values liveness over high-fidelity sound. He has, for instance, recorded voices over his cell phone preferring the spontaneity to the result he gets in a formal recording context. He records all rehearsals and even the responses of participants in *joik* workshops that he conducts, claiming (with a mischievous gleam in his eye) that he might use them in a subsequent recording project. On tour, he records many samples. Saari has also used field recordings, among them sounds of birds from Africa, Sámi performers at the Nordic Roots Festival in Minneapolis on the CD *Barru* (Wave; 2003), waves of the Indian Ocean, and samples of a power tool in a room under construction next door to his in a Brussels hotel where he stayed on tour. These recordings enable "the creation of sound worlds into a musical form," says Saari (2001). "They are not the masters. They are good tools." He emphasizes, though, that "it isn't imitation or mimicry. You can hear in it [the resulting musical composition] that you yourself have been there, that you have felt the atmosphere." The Sámi concept of "liveness" then, was not simply a reference to a "raw" recording but a recall of emplaced experience and relationality.

Polyvalence

A third aspect of the recording and mixing processes that I tested in this cross-cultural experiment with a Canadian sound producer is the Sámi delight in polyvalent meanings. Comparative literature scholar and North Sámi Harald Gaski has written eloquently about this subject, describing *joiks* as a "secretive text" that have overt but also hidden meanings that are comprehensible only to Sámi speakers and local residents. "Being aware of this extra potential of the text, and also being able to explain it, is of course the advantage, superiority and pleasure of the 'insider.'"[61] Gaski notes that some of these insider meanings are products of the colonial encounter whereby criticisms or references, that were disguised so that clergy or others could not understand them, could be exchanged. Until quite recently, many Sámi recording artists preferred not to include text translations or even transcriptions, since they did not want to pin down meaning or even assist non-Sámi listeners with the verbal dimensions. But sound itself can, of course, be polyvalent. Examples are easy to find. I think of Niko Valkeapää's debut CD, where a sample of a herd of reindeer is used in the intro to "Rain" (#14) and then, filtered slightly differently, in the track "Wings" (#15). A significant aspect of polyvalence in Wimme Saari's recordings in particular (but others as well) is the ability to blur the lines between species (animal, human, spirit,) or between human and machine. Thomas Hilder gives the example of Wimme Saari's *joik* to the old fox, in which Saari's voice sounds at one point like a snowmobile (panned left to right to imply movement or travel) and at another like the fox's voice.[62] In other tracks, Saari conveys sounds of mosquitos buzzing, children playing, and puppies whimpering. He also plays with the human/machine boundary a great deal. When bass clarinetist Tapane Rinne was part of his band, recordings often highlighted the resemblance between the clarinet and Saari's voice. In a track called "Lips" (#12) the bass clarinet seems to modulate the voice sound. When the clarinet drops out, the voice is "naked" (Crewe's descriptor) and vulnerable. In these cases mixing extends the central importance of polyvalent meanings. Wimme Saari was particularly intent on this, stating that he wanted the listener to "fly as they want to."

Hidden meanings might simply be personal narratives that frame the sound production but are known only to the composer/improviser. In one *joik*, Saari references his awareness of two worlds when he worked in Helsinki as a sound engineer at the Finnish Broadcasting Company (Yleisradio, often abbreviated to YLE). "Iḋitidja" (5:00 a.m.) describes his morning routine and his bike ride to work in the early hours. It includes a reference to the train tracks that lead to his northern home, and finally to a difficult steep hill at the end of the route. It's a personal narrative that audiences cannot share unless he chooses to explain it.

While Crewe could not possibly have known the hidden meaning of such a private narrative, he was very attuned to contrasts that he described as "urban" and "organic." Perhaps the distinction that Saari felt between Helsinki, where he resided, and Karesuando, where he felt at home, was evident even without explanation. Crewe used a similar description of another track, "Rock of the Thunder God" (#13): "That [part] is processed. That [other part] is nice and organic. The processed stuff is living . . . left of center, and the organic stuff is right of center. He's keeping a very clear separation. Vocals very clean. Electronica drumbeat is very much in-your-face. Responsive. This guy's really good. Whoa. . . . Those little shots of electronica; dark at that. If that's not painting a picture—"

Conclusion

This study represents a small step toward an intercultural dialogue about the meanings of technological processes. How other Sámi producers respond to some of Crewe's hearings would be an interesting further step, perhaps best accomplished by getting not one but a number of Indigenous and non-Indigenous producers, mixers, and arrangers together. In this case study, however, a number of differences were arguably "unmasked" through a comparison of production techniques and interpretations. Crewe's distance from the culture sometimes allowed him to see the influences of changing technologies. He often thinks historically about technologies. He emphasized and often referred to generic patterns where Sámi producers attempted to defy or resignify them. In some cases, archival recordings are transformed in the process, reinforcing and reinterpreting cultural memory.

Such strategies often disrupt expectations about "genre." Genres have been identified as epistomologies of purification that govern expectations about how groups of people or places should sound.[63] Genres, similarly, have often been described as structures of listening or, to refer again to Jameson, as "the modes and forms of thought in which we inescapably have to think things through" but, he continues, "which have a logic of their own to which we ourselves fall victim if we are unaware of their existence and their in-forming influence on us."[64] The fluidity of traditional *joik* improvisation, for instance, is both maintained and transformed by electronic manipulation, layering of other sounds, and postproduction. Crewe referenced genre more often than any of the Sámi musicians. Comparative perspectives exposed both the existence of and resistance to such structures of listening. They also revealed distinct Sámi concepts of relationality (socially, and across the categories of human/other species or human/machine), spatiality (in Sápmi, internationally, and imaginatively)—themes that are theorized in the introduction and emerge in other chapters of this anthology.

Crewe's casting of some techniques as "old" when Sámi producers saw them as reciprocity, alive in the present, was another interesting difference among the comments. In this regard, the views of Sámi musicians reflect a unique cosmological imaginary—one of the themes that has emerged in this anthology. What Crewe described as an industrial/organic divide contrasted with descriptions of the ways mixing could blur the boundaries between species, humans and machines. The amazing spatial imagination that Westerners cast so often as magical or sacred, was more often described by Crewe as fantasy. Is this a trace of exoticization? Perhaps. But, given that this is a young man whose office is filled with characters from Transformer movies and a Homer Simpson clock, I'm inclined to say that fantasy may be pretty close to real life for him.

The sonic associations we make and the conceptual frames we read onto sound, are indeed power laden. They constitute one of the potentially dangerous aspects of the separation of recorded sound from its sources, as Murray Schafer first taught us and as Steven Feld, among others, has so usefully elaborated. The ways in which studio producers shape listening experience, then, and the way they speak about their studio decisions constitute rich discursive fields that may be initially hidden from view but can nonetheless be revealed through reflective and reflexive conversations. While, as the anthology editors discuss in the introduction, the digital world is a global public sphere, its structuring and reception are still clearly shaped by both group and individual cultural engagements, among them Indigenous histories, spatialities, and relationships as well as cosmopolitan artistic careers and intercultural experiences. If we study these processes through an intercultural dialogue, some of the globalization processes—and localized alternatives—that Jameson speaks of may be unmasked.

Appendix: Audio Tracks Referenced

1. Mathis A. Oscal, "Ruvaš nieiddat ja buolaš bártnit"
2. Inga Juuso, "Jonsána"
3. Anders P. Bongo, "Nášša"
4. Wimme Saari, "Háldeduottar/The Mountain Háldi"

5. Berit Kirsten Sara and Ravna Anti Guttorm, "Ivvár-Máret"
6. Angelit, "Gárkit"
7. Sofia Jannok, "Ija Salas" (plus hidden yoik)
8. Ulla Pirttijärvi, "Čálkko-Niillas"
9. Per Tor Turi, "Vuoibmi"
10. Wimme Saari, "Iđđesdolla/Morning Coffee"
11. Wimme Saari, "Lodderáidaras/Milky Way"
12. Wimme Saari, "Baksamat/Lips"
13. Wimme Saari, "Dierpmesbákti/Rock of the Thunder God"
14. Niko Valkeapää, "Rain"
15. Niko Valkeapää, "Wings"

Notes

1. Fredric Jameson, "Notes on Globalization as a Philosophical Issue," in *The Cultures of Globalization*, ed. Fredric Jameson and Masao Miyoshi (Durham, NC: Duke University Press, 1998), 55.
2. Ibid., 57.
3. Ibid., 59.
4. Pamela Wilson and Michelle Stewart, eds. *Global Indigenous Media: Cultures, Poetics, and Politics* (Durham, NC: Duke University Press, 2008), 2.
5. Standardization has been identified as an effect of recording music that was traditionally orally transmitted. Usually the emphasis is on broader access to what had previously been highly localized repertoires, rather than on conformity to hegemonic norms. See John Baily, "Modi Operandi in the Making of 'World Music' Recordings," in *Recorded Music: Performance, Culture and Technology*, ed. Amanda Bayley (Cambridge: Cambridge University Press, 2010), 107–24; Richard Jones-Bamman, "'Greetings from Lapland': The Legacy of Nils-Aslak Valkeapää (1943–2001)," in *Ethnomusicological Encounters with Music and Musicians: Essays in Honour of Robert Garfias*, ed. Timothy Rice (Farnham, UK: Ashgate, 2011), 97–110.
6. Veli-Pekka Lehtola, "Folklore and Its Present Manifestations," in *Siiddastallan: From Lapp Communities to Modern Sámi Life*, ed. Jukka Pennanen and Klemetti Näkkäläjärvi (Inari, FI: Inari Sámi Museum, 2000), 182.
7. Both the techniques of recording and their aesthetic implications have been studied rather widely in recent years in contexts that range from the multinational big four music groups—Universal, Sony, EMI, Warner—to the very local community level. See, for example, Alf Björnberg, "Learning to Listen to Perfect Sound: Hi-Fi Culture and Changes in Modes of Listening, 1950–80," in *The Ashgate Research Companion to Popular Musicology*, ed. Derek B. Scott (Farnham, UK: Ashgate, 2009), 105–30; Paul D. Greene and Thomas Porcello, *Wired for Sound: Engineering and Technologies in Sonic Cultures* (Middletown, CT: Wesleyan University Press, 2005); Louise Meintjes, *Sound of Africa: Making*

Music Zulu in a South African Studio (Durham, NC: Duke University Press, 2003). Comparative projects in which local producers from different cultural backgrounds comment on specific recordings are, thus far, rare.

8. Jameson, "Notes on Globalization as a Philosophical Issue," 55.

9. A growing number of ethnomusicologists have demonstrated that recording studios are important sites for ethnography, places where power is negotiated and sonic identities are constructed. See Meintjes, *Sound of Africa: Making Music Zulu in a South African Studio*; Christopher A. Scales, *Recording Culture: Powwow Music and the Aboriginal Recording Industry on the Northern Plains* (Durham, NC: Duke University Press, 2012); Greene and Porcello, *Wired for Sound: Engineering and Technologies in Sonic Cultures.*

10. Keith Negus points out that top-selling artists are marketed as placeless and hence "global," but that ethnically distinctive recordings are harder to classify, and constitute a second-tier market niche. Keith Negus, *Music Genres and Corporate Cultures* (New York: Routledge, 1999), 153–73.

11. See Luther H. Martin, Huck Gutman, and Patrick H. Hutton, eds. *Technologies of the Self: A Seminar with Michel Foucault* (Amherst: University of Massachusetts Press, 1988).

12. Several publications dealing with Australian or Native American recording production support this statement. See Philip Hayward, ed. *Sound Alliances: Indigenous Peoples, Cultural Politics, and Popular Music in the Pacific* (London: Cassell, 1998); Peter Dunbar-Hall and Chris Gibson, *Deadly Sounds, Deadly Places* (Sydney: UNSW Press, 2004); Beverley Diamond, "Native American Contemporary Music: The Women," *The World of Music* 41, no. 2 (2002): 9–35; Christopher A. Scales, "The Politics and Aesthetics of Recording: A Comparative Canadian Case Study of Powwow and Contemporary Native American Music," *The World of Music* 44, no. 1 (2002): 41–60.

13. Winner of numerous East Coast Music Awards and Juno Awards (the Canadian equivalent of the Grammies), the trad-rock band Great Big Sea has nine CDs and a DVD to date, some of which have been released in the United States and Europe, as well as in Canada. They have collaborated with Russell Crowe, contributing to the soundtrack and acting in the movie *Robin Hood.*

14. Of the Sámi producers mentioned in this chapter, only Frode Fjellheim has thus far had a chance to read a draft and to respond briefly.

15. By way of comparison, on the ways that concepts of "hi-fidelity" played out in Swedish society between 1950 and 1980, see Björnberg, "Learning to Listen to Perfect Sound."105–30.

16. Frode Fjellheim, e-mail April 23, 2012.

17. When this paper was presented in 2010, studio-savvy audience members offered further reflections on the audio examples played.

18. Thomas R. Hilder, *Sámi Musical Performance and the Politics of Indigeneity in Northern Europe* (Lanham, MD: Rowman & Littlefield, 2015), 55.

19. I discuss these issues in more length in Beverley Diamond, "'Allowing the Listener to Fly as They Want to': Sámi Perspectives on Indigenous CD Production in Northern Europe," *The World of Music* 49, no. 1 (2007): 23–49.

20. Ole Henrik Magga, in conversation (not recorded) with author, 2001.

21. Wimme Saari, in interview with author and Pirkko Moisala, 2001.

22. Jameson, "Notes on Globalization as a Philosophical Issue," 70.

23. In "'Allowing the Listener to Fly,'" I discussed traditional ownership protocols and the challenges that digital production presents to them.

24. Johan Sara, interview with author, 2001.

25. Annukka Hirvasvuoppio, interview with author and Pirkko Moisala, 2001.

26. Ante Mikkel Gaup, Joik workshop at Riddu Riđđu Festival, 2004.

27. Ola Nakkalajärvi, interview with author and Pirkko Moisala, 2001.

28. Of course, there are exceptions to this statement about pop production norms—think of the strained male voice in much rock music and the gravelly texture of blues singers' voices.

29. Stuart Hall, quoted in Jameson, "Notes on Globalization as a Philosophical Issue," 70.

30. Johan Sara Jr., interview with author, 2001.

31. Most of the tracks are available on iTunes.

32. Simon Zagorski-Thomas, "The Stadium in Your Bedroom: Functional Staging, Authenticity and the Audience-Led Aesthetic in Record Production," *Popular Music* 29, no. 2 (2010): 251–66.

33. The Alta River crisis of 1979 and 80 was one instance when Sámi took their protest to the streets of Oslo. The formation of the Norwegian Sámi parliament in 1989 was another event that got international attention.

34. Originally produced in 1985, the Beaivváš Theatre Company remounted *Vaikko čuođi stálu* (Even if a hundred ogres). *Joik* and song were contrasted in the presentation, the former style having more intensity and texture, the latter being more legato and timbrally light. Several references to the distinctiveness of *joik* and song are presented and also problematized as a politics of difference in Hilder, "Sámi Musical Performance," 35–69.

35. Negus, *Music Genres and Corporate Cultures*, 3.

36. Greene and Porcello, *Wired for Sound*.

37. Thomas Porcello, "Afterword," in *Wired for Sound*, 270.

38. Dunbar-Hall and Gibson, *Deadly Sounds, Deadly Places*, 63.

39. Issues of "radio-friendly-ness" are also important to Tore Skoglund of NRK Sámi Radio. See Hilder, "Sámi Musical Performance," 54.

40. *Sámediggi* in Sámi or *Sameting* in Norwegian or Swedish.

41. The website of the Resource Centre for the Rights of Indigenous Peoples (www.galdu.org) offers a publication, *The Sami People—A Handbook* (2006), that includes some details about the financial resources provided by this fund. In 1989, the annual allocation was approximately 8 million Norwegian kroner (approximately US$1.4 million). An article by Harald Gaski indicates that almost 35 million in Norwegian kroner was distributed in 2000 to Sámi in Norway, Sweden, and Finland; see Harald Gaski, translated John Weinstock, "Sámi Culture in the Nordic Countries—Administration, Support, Evaluation," accessed September 2, 2016, http://www.utexas.edu/courses/sami/dieda/hist/nordic.htm.

42. Taylor's term plays on related concepts such as "strategic essentialism" (Spivak) or "strategic anti-essentialism" (Lipsitz). See Timothy D. Taylor,

Global Pop: World Music, World Markets (New York: Routledge, 1997), 125–46; Gayatri Chakravorty Spivak, *In Other Worlds: Essays in Cultural Politics* (New York: Methuen, 1987); George Lipsitz, *Dangerous Crossroads: Popular Music, Postmodernism and the Poetics of Place* (New York: Verso, 1994).

43. Wimme Saari, interview with author and Pirkko Moisala, 2001.

44. Magnus Vuolab, interview with author and Pirkko Moisala, 2001.

45. For a good analysis in relation to girl groups of the '50s and '60s, and for salient quotations by Theodor Adorno, see chapter 2 of Jacqueline Warwick, *Girl Groups, Girl Culture: Popular Music and Identity in the 1960s* (New York: Routledge, 2013), 33–50.

46. Sofia Jannok, interview with author, 2007.

47. Ulla Pirttijarvi, interview with author and Pirkko Moisala, 2001, and subsequent conversations.

48. Annuka Hirvasvuopio, interview with author and Pirkko Moisala, 2001.

49. Wimme Saari, interview with author and Pirkko Moisala, 2001.

50. E-mail from Frode Fjellheim, April 2013.

51. Popular music historian Greg Milner also discusses "low-fi" production, influenced in part by the widespread use of transistor radios in the 1950s. He mentions that producers such as Phil Spector in the United States and Joe Meek in the United Kingdom "aggressively rejected traditional ideas of high fidelity," knowing that the postwar generation embraced sound that emulated the "tinny" quality of the transistor radios on which they listened to it. Greg Milner, *Perfecting Sound Forever: An Aural History of Recorded Music* (New York: Faber & Faber, 2009), 154.

52. Diamond, "'Allowing the Listener to Fly.'" 23–49.

53. Liveness has been studied in a number of different contexts. Philip Auslander (1999) references the energy of live performance and also the way that energy has been captured on video and "remediatized" subsequently. Liveness has also been discussed extensively by Louise Meintjes (2004) in her studio of South African recording studio work. She describes a preference for high sociality, even at the expense of low fidelity, and reports on some unexpected mapping such as the attribution of "liveness" to a very mechanical drum machine beat. Her findings resonate with mine and those of Scales.

54. Extended discussions of the constructedness of "liveness" in specific studio contexts are can be found in Philip Auslander, *Liveness: Performance in a Mediatized Culture* (New York: Routledge, 1999); Meintjes, *Sound of Africa: Making Music Zulu in a South African Studio*; Thomas Porcello, "Music Mediated as Live in Austin: Sound Technology and Recording Practice," in *Wired for Sound*.

55. Peter Doyle, *Echo and Reverb: Fabricating Space in Popular Music Recording, 1900–1960* (Middletown, CT: Wesleyan University Press, 2005), 5.

56. Even a browse through the index of Doyle's book reveals the range of associations in the popular music repertoires that he describes.

57. Zagorski-Thomas, "The Stadium in Your Bedroom," 251.

58. Serge Lacasse, "'Listen to My Voice': The Evocative Power of Vocal Staging in Recorded Rock Music and Other Forms of Vocal Expression" (PhD diss., University of Liverpool, 2000), 32.

59. There are similar beliefs in many First Nations traditions.
60. Saari has created "Havana," "Paris," Calcutta," and others.
61. Harald Gaski, "The Secretive Text: Yoik Lyrics as Literature and Tradition," in *Sámi Folkloristics*, ed. Juha Pentikäinen et al. (Turku, FI: Nordic Network of Folklore, 2000), 196.
62. Hilder, "Sámi Musical Performance," 140.
63. Ana Maria Ochoa Gautier, "Sonic Transculturation, Epistemologies of Purification and the Aural Public Sphere in Latin America," *Social Identities* 12, no. 6 (2006): 805–25.
64. Jameson, "Notes on Globalization as a Philosophical Issue," 75.

Chapter Six

Creative Pragmatism

Competency and Aesthetics in Bolivian Indigenous Music Video (VCD) Production

Henry Stobart

Although several of the case stswudies in this book feature indigenous people based in countries with strong economies, it is important to stress that a disproportionate number of the world's indigenous people live in poverty.[1] A particularly notable aspect of the so-called digital revolution is the way it has provided low-income consumers and creators with access to cheap audio-visual technologies. Massive reductions in prices alongside exponential growth in unlicensed copying (so-called media piracy) have given rise to an abundance of new media consumers and producers among the world's poorer populations, especially in parts of the global south. In such regions, the Internet is often available only in larger towns and cities, primarily accessed in public Internet cafés.[2] In these rapidly transforming technological environments, the number of home computers has risen exponentially, but a large proportion of them remain offline. Meanwhile, in smaller towns and rural areas, television reception is often poor; thus, where electricity is available, audiovisual entertainment often takes the form of videos.

Arguably, the most ubiquitous form of digital hardware in low-income homes of the global south[3]—especially during the first decade of the twenty-first century—was the VCD (Video Compact Disc) player.[4] Such machines were usually found alongside a stack of (mostly "pirated") VCD discs of films and music videos. The VCD format, which is almost unknown in the global north and a kind of low-tech version of the DVD, enables video to be copied onto CD discs and played, on low-cost players, through a television.[5] Originally launched in China, this technology rapidly spread to many areas of the global south, escalating both the creation of massive new markets for audiovisual entertainment among low-income groups and rampant "media piracy."[6] It also motivated indigenous musicians—often with negligible technical training or financial resources—to grasp the entrepreneurial opportunities offered by this cheap audiovisual technology to create music videos for these new low-income local and regional markets. Here we might make a distinction between outwardly orientated indigenous media created for a global stage or international indigenous community[7]—as featured in certain chapters of this book—and media created with more local or regional audiences in mind—the primary focus here.

In this chapter I examine the VCD music video production processes of Gregorio Mamani Villacorta (1960–2011), an *originario* (indigenous) musician and cultural activist who grew up and lived well into adulthood in the rural community of Tomaykuri in northern Potosí, highland Bolivia. Along with my long-term familiarity with the rural music of this region,[8] I draw on eleven months of ethnographic research based in the city of Sucre (September 2007–July 2008), where Mamani lived with his family and created a home studio. This provided me with the opportunity to participate, as a technologically unskilled assistant, in the production of three *originario* VCD music videos. Mamani's productions proved hugely popular among the low-income indigenous rural and urban migrant consumers for whom they were intended. However, for outside viewers accustomed to the high technical standards of mainstream television and film, they might appear "amateurish." Indeed, I heard Mamani's—and other similar *originario* music videos—disparaged by Bolivian middle-class media professionals for their low standards of production and technical inadequacies. But how should we understand such comments? How much should production values and notions of technical competency be viewed as normative, enabling them to be judged objectively? Alternatively, to what degree do such judgments reflect convention and the viewer-listener's aesthetic values, which are necessarily subjective and culturally contingent? What is the relationship between production techniques and aesthetics, and to what extent are these interdependent or separable?

In this chapter I attempt to navigate some of the complex terrain between notions of technical competency and aesthetics. Firstly I explore these issues in the context of the rich scholarship on indigenous film and video production, which I then relate to the relatively understudied but locally and regionally influential genre of *originario* (indigenous) music video. This focus on production competencies and aesthetics is then briefly placed into wider debates about "low-tech" aesthetics and amateur/professional distinctions in media production. The second half of the chapter is ethnographic in approach and dedicated to the *originario* music video production work of Gregorio Mamani. It examines his working practices and aesthetic priorities in the light of negative evaluations from Bolivian media professionals, arguing ultimately that such practices and priorities might usefully be understood in terms of what I call "creative pragmatism." This expression, which stresses local realities and praxis, benefits from avoiding the dangers of, on the one hand, essentializing or romanticizing indigenous media aesthetics and, on the other, devaluing so-called professional media practices.

Bolivian Indigeneities

Bolivia is regularly presented as among the poorest, most economically informal, and most indigenous countries of South America. It made international news in late 2005 with the election of its first indigenous president, Evo Morales, who was reelected in both 2009 and 2014. Together with the creation of a new constitution, ratified by a national referendum in 2009, the official name for the country was changed to The Plurinational State of Bolivia, largely in recognition of its diversity of indigenous peoples. Discourses of indigeneity have been fundamental to Bolivian politics over the past decade, yet while lowland groups are happy to refer to themselves as *indigena* ("indigenous"), highland groups have tended to distance themselves from this term, preferring the label *originario* ("originary"). While from the global perspective of this volume, *originario* is essentially interchangeable with "indigenous," out of respect for this preference and given my focus on highland Bolivia—I use the term *originario* in this chapter.

While physiognomy suggests a notably indigenous aspect to the majority highland population, formal identification of indigeneity is steeped in historical complexity, and measures such as blood quantum are irrelevant to the Andean context. In the colonial Andes, indigenous ("Indian") and nonindigenous people were separated into distinct populations and parishes, with *originario* status and usufruct land rights dependent upon the payment of tax and labor—what Platt has called the "pact of reciprocity."[9] The burden of tribute, among other factors, led many indigenous people to move away from the land into *mestizo* status and occupations, thereby avoiding taxation. Such migration and changes in fiscal status was usually accompanied by cultural—even if not racial—mixing (*mestizaje*) and the incorporation of aspects of the hegemonic European-derived or *criollo* culture. Thus, while *originario* status was associated with indigenous claims to land, *mestizaje* often became connected with perceptions of superior cultural status linked to exogenous knowledge and power. Indeed, *mestizo* is often understood to mean "nonindigenous." The tribute system was abolished long ago and rural-to-urban migration has escalated for many other reasons. Arguably, however, vestiges of the historical rights connected with *originario* status resurfaced with the rise of indigenous politics in the 1990s[10] and the social movements opposing global capitalism in the early 2000s that swept Evo Morales to power.[11]

The fluid nature of indigenous identity in Bolivia has been especially notable in the two most recent national censuses. While for the 2001 census, 62% of the population (over 15 years of age) self-identified as "indigenous,"[12] in the 2012 census, only 48% self-identified as such. In 2001, most of those registered were urban dwellers—20% not speaking an indigenous language— and no option was included for identifying oneself as *mestizo*.[13] Similar urban predominance in registration probably applied in 2012, when again—controversially—no *mestizo* option was included. Andrew Canessa suggests that the high number of people self-identifying as indigenous in 2001 was not about an intimate attachment to the land or genealogical descent from preconquest populations, but rather about claims to difference, rights, and possibly "moral authority in the face of encroaching globalisation."[14] In 2012, after six years with an indigenous president, a pro-indigenous government, and a relatively buoyant economy (aided by the nationalization of the country's rich natural gas reserves)—alongside cynicism about indigenous privileges—it would seem that fewer people felt the need to assert indigeneity. This suggests a tension between a kind of fluctuating urban indigeneity, often linked to rights and perceptions of exclusion, and a more rural indigeneity that may include the maintenance of close connections with the land, indigenous languages, and distinctive cultural traditions.

This distinction is played out in some of the *originario* music videos I helped Gregorio Mamani produce. Two of these featured music, dance, and festive dress associated with rural feasts from his region of origin, where video of the artists was interspersed with footage from actual feasts—Carnival (February/ March) and the Feast of the Holy Cross (May). These kinds of productions of rural music are referred to by vendors as *cultura* (culture) and aim to represent indigenous rural traditions and practices. However, a more fluctuating indigeneity was evident in the case of *huayño:* popular Spanish or Quechua language dance songs, accompanied by the charango and Spanish guitar, associated with the *cholo* (or *mestizo*) town dwellers of the Northern Potosí region of Bolivia.[15] It was by performing *huayño* that Gregorio first made a name for himself as an artist; but unlike most other leading exponents of the genre, he had grown up in a rural peasant community. This led certain artists to refer to him pejoratively as *indio* (Indian), distancing themselves from an indigenous heritage they perceived as being connected with shame. However, with the 2006 presidency of Evo Morales, many of these same *huayño* artists began to embrace *originario* identity and to group themselves into organizations such as the Cultural

Association of Indigenous and Originario Artists of Bolivia (ASCARIOBOL)—partly in opposition to more cosmopolitan middle-class musicians who tour internationally. Thus, in certain respects, the discourse of indigeneity acquired political capital—while still potentially marginalizing rural indigenous people[16]—and certain genres, such as *huayño*, came to be presented and perceived as more indigenous.

Indigenous Media Making: Aesthetics and Audiences

Although the indigenous music video (VCD) has attracted relatively little critical attention to date, a useful counterpoint to its study is provided by the rich vein of scholarship on indigenous film and video making dating back to the 1970s. This latter work has stressed the political agency and empowerment offered to indigenous people by producing their own media as a form of "cultural activism"[17] and as a means of "decolonizing the mind" and countering discrimination and misrepresentation.[18] It has also, for the most part, focused on projects facilitated or funded by outsiders, such as anthropologists and NGOs, who provide equipment, training, and technical support. Often evident in such anthropologically motivated work has been the expectation that distinctive aesthetics or styles of media production will result when indigenous people have access to the means to create their own films or videos. Allied to this is sometimes a concern to avoid imposing standardized Euro-American media practices and techniques. Accordingly, some levels of technical training may be intentionally limited. For example, in the case of the Amazonian Kayapo (who have been involved in video making since 1985), Terence Turner observes that he and his collaborators "sought to limit training both in camera work and editing to the essential minimum to allow the maximum room for Kayapo camerapersons to develop their own culturally and individually specific styles."[19] For some commentators, such as James Weiner,[20] the acquisition of even basic filming and editing skills inevitably entails entry into the language, culture, and values of "Western" audiovisual media. Media anthropologists, by contrast, tend to stress how indigenous people adapt media technologies to their own sociocultural environments and political exigencies.[21] For example, Pace and Shepard have identified some of the aesthetic choices made by Kayapo videographers and editors.[22] Lines of dancers are filmed using long-pan medium-distance shots that feature all participants, whereas panoramic shots (in which body ornaments would become indistinct) or close-ups (that "amputate" body parts or show body ornaments out of context) are largely avoided. Complete sequences (which outsiders might find long and repetitive) are preferred over synopsis, and narration, commentary, and subtitles are rarely employed. And, in the case of a soccer game video, as much footage is dedicated to the audience as to the game itself, in a filming style—Pace and Shepherd suggest—that pulls the viewer into the scene as a participant, rather than remaining an outsider observing an exotic spectacle.

These characteristics are perhaps hardly surprising for a community-based video, whose primary audience is the community itself and where it is likely to be important that each participant—and his or her body ornaments—is included and easily recognizable. Similarly, commentary and subtitles may be deemed unnecessary when, as in home movies elsewhere, the subject matter and participants are already familiar to most viewers. Indeed, we might even characterize this kind of video as "participatory style media" to distinguish it from "presentational style media"—adapting Thomas Turino's useful distinction between participatory and presentational styles of music performance.[23] This helps us appreciate how—in the kind of Kayapo video described above—greater priority is afforded to social inclusion and group participation than to technical competency and cultural mediation for outside audiences. When Turner observes that the Kayapo are just as happy to watch an unedited "home movie" as one of the beautifully edited works being created by certain Kayapo video makers,[24] it should be remembered that we all enjoy watching inexpertly produced home movies or other forms of low-tech media when we, our family, or friends are featured as participants; in short, when we experience a sense of close connection or empathy with the subject matter. However, we quickly lose interest if such media are not directly related or relevant to us, or if the content is not captivating for other reasons (such as extraordinary feats or phenomena). In sum, many aspects of Kayapo video aesthetics discussed above might be attributed to a participatory media style, rather than indigeneity per se.[25] However, much indigenous video is more outwardly oriented and presentational in approach, screened not only within the home communities but also at international film festivals. Indeed, according to Juan Salazar, indigenous media "occupies an intermediate and hybrid space between global mass media and local interpersonal uses of communication technologies."[26]

Certain indigenous video makers, including members of Bolivia's CEFREC-CAIB,[27] incorporate a range of stock codes from Hollywood and dominant industry techniques and formats. Yet, rather than seeing this adoption of dominant film language as running counter to Bolivia's decolonization project (as presumably Weiner would have it),[28] Freya Schiwy interprets this as "Indianizing film" (the title of her book).[29] Here, she invokes the revolutionary Aymara politician Felipe Quispe, who called upon indigenous Andeans to reject the discourse of *mestizaje*—i.e., the project of the 1952 national revolution, to unify Bolivians as mixed-race citizens—and instead to "indianise the white man."[30] This, she observes, reflects "a long Andean tradition of integrating what is foreign into traditional cultural and economic forms"[31]—what Brooke Larson has called "adaptive vitality."[32] This leads us to wonder whether, beyond subject matter, it might be possible to recognize aesthetically distinctive aspects of Andean indigenous film and video. Are there culturally characteristic ways of seeing or hearing? This is hazardous territory, where it would be easy to fall into generalization and essentialisms, as highlighted by Steven Leuthold for the case of Native American documentary film.[33] While identifying the aesthetic importance of the themes of nature and religion/spirituality in such film, he is careful to stress the dangers of generalizing an indigenous aesthetic sensibility:

> There is no one set of formal characteristics that comprises an Indian way of seeing. The problem with searching for such a key to unlock the secrets of a group's outlook is that it tends to lead to a minimization of the variation within the group. . . . There is not enough formal consistency in visual style or narrative structures to clearly define a single indigenous documentary genre based on formal considerations alone.[34]

Might it thus be more productive to focus, with an ethnographic eye, on the ways that —in given contexts of such media making—the diverse actors creatively and pragmatically explore the affordances of the technology?

Indigenous Video Projects and *Originario* Music Videos

Many notable contrasts are evident when comparing the indigenous video projects discussed above and *originario* music videos. These include, for example, aesthetics, cultural value, economics, circulation, politics, representation, and technical competencies. First, most indigenous video projects are community-based and facilitated by outsiders, whereas music video tends to be commercially motivated and produced by entrepreneurial individuals. Similarly, whereas community-based video projects usually actively downplay individual authorship, "star" filmmakers, and financial motivation,[35] a primary function of the music video genre (inherited from its Anglo-American ancestry) is precisely to showcase and promote the "star."[36] Indeed, Gregorio Mamani explicitly presented his motivation for creating the music videos on which we worked together as a means to increase his "fame." Having recently resigned from a position in the Culture Department of the Prefecture, he was concerned with returning to the public eye as an "artist," rebuilding his audience, and attracting bookings for live performances. In short, the associations of music video with individualism and commercial motivations fit uneasily with stereotypical constructions of indigenous people.

Second, a striking disparity is evident in the relative cultural value attached to these genres and their respective modes and levels of circulation. On the one hand, productions from indigenous video projects are mainly distributed outside commercial venues[37] and often treated as socially or aesthetically valuable, as well as politically significant—in terms of indigenous rights. They tend to be screened either for local communities or in international settings, such as film festivals, where the context—often involving an introduction by the filmmaker(s)—implicitly constructs such productions as works of "art." Audiences for these international screenings tend to be small; the viewers, characterized by political commitment and discriminating tastes. This already limited circulation is sometimes further reduced by certain filmmakers' concern to restrict distribution in order to prevent media "piracy."[38] On the other hand, Bolivian *originario* music videos, which are often widely circulated, fall into the category of "entertainment" and suffer double disdain. The popular genres they feature, such as *huayño*, are commonly dismissed by the Bolivian middle classes as "trash" (*basura*), while music video—as a medium—is often denied artistic value, an inheritance from its Anglo-American roots.[39] In striking contrast with the limited circulation of much indigenous film, *originario* music videos sometimes achieve immense popularity and massive circulation, which is often greatly amplified and extended by media piracy.[40] For example, the hit video *Vichito Mamani* (featuring Gregorio's son David when he was around eight years old) gained a vast audience due to piracy, not only throughout Bolivia but also in Peru and Argentina. Despite Gregorio's outspoken opposition to "piracy," this enabled the family to make an international tour through which the necessary capital was raised to set up a home studio—albeit a very modest one with cheap secondhand equipment. What I wish to stress here is the potency of *originario* music videos as popular, widely circulating, and influential representations and constructions of indigeneity. Indeed, the agency and visibility such videos afford to indigenous people might be seen as implicitly political. This raises key questions concerning the video makers production processes, priorities and values.

Finally, it is important to consider technical and aesthetic differences between indigenous video and *originario* music videos. As already noted, indigenous video projects are often facilitated by outsiders, who typically provide equipment and varying levels of technical support or training. However unintentional, it is almost inevitable that the mode of facilitation will shape indigenous video making values and priorities in particular ways. For example, I have suggested that styles of camerawork, editing, and representation in Kayapo videos may, in part, reflect the conflict avoidance strategies employed by Turner and his team. Even if the resulting styles or aesthetics are not immediately accessible to outside or international audiences, the technical quality of such videos—in my experience at least—is generally high, suggesting expert support or training. However, the technical quality of *originario* music video and the competency of producers appear considerably less consistent, especially when production has taken place in a low-budget home studio, such as that of Gregorio Mamani. But do limitations in technical resources and knowledge inevitably mean poor-quality productions, or should we approach such videos—as has Tony Langlois for locally produced Moroccan music videos—in terms of a "'low-tech aesthetic"?[41]

Amateurs, Professionals and Imperfect Media

The advent of digital technology means that low-cost domestic audio and video recording and editing equipment is now available that can approach— and sometimes surpass—the media quality of professional equipment of the 1980s. This has led to the emergence of countless digital home studios around the world,[42] which are utilized with varying levels of technical competency. The professional quality of work accomplished in some home-based studios makes a "professional" versus "home/amateur" binary problematic.[43] However, might certain generalized contrasts in working practices be identified between established professional studios and inexpensive digital home studios? In his discussion of (primarily audio) home studios in the Solomon Islands, Denis Crowdy muses on this question.[44] Also, relevantly for this chapter, he relates issues of "access" to technology to "quality standards, and by association, aesthetics." He asks:

> Is it not the case that professionals produce consistent quality through skills and knowledge garnered through experience and criticism from peers? Then again, institutions and associations also relatively easily bind professionals, and the overall aura of professionalism is one of conservatism. One might argue that as production and recording are increasingly creative processes, radical and experimental expressions are more likely to be found in the broader base offered by widening access to the means of production.[45]

This raises interesting questions regarding what access to digital technology might mean with regard to creative practice. In a study of discourses relating to amateur film and video making, Buckingham, Pini, and Willett note how popular books, manuals and magazines often highlight the sense of empowerment and innovation offered by these technologies.[46] The amateur video maker is presented as "a free agent, able to record, edit and exhibit what they like . . . able to use technology in more creative and potentially challenging ways that might ultimately revolutionise "big" media."[47] However, another discursive strand critiques such talk of empowerment as "empty rhetoric," arguing that "amateur video has failed, or more precisely not been allowed, to live up to its radical potential."[48] It remains conservative and stuck in the "home mode,"[49] featuring family moments, some of which, for example, find their way into mainstream media as "video bloopers." Buckingham, Pini, and Willett conclude by arguing against any simple binary opposition between amateur and professional film/video making, noting that "technology is not in and of itself a force of empowerment" (due to its simplicity and accessibility). They also suggest that we should not understand the "home mode" as inevitably naive and conservative—either aesthetically or ideologically.[50] In similar vein, Patricia Lange observes:

> Scholars often assert that "amateur" videos lack aesthetics, creativity, or knowledge of dominant entertainment standards. By lacking "an aesthetic" they often mean, the right kind of aesthetic as determined by certain cultural groups or individuals. Judgements about quality are often problematic not only because they are based on Hollywood standards, but because they are based on idiosyncratic interpretations or *stereotypes* of both professional and amateur idioms.[51]

Evident from such discussion is that the intimacy of the "home mode" can sometimes be powerfully affecting, despite—or even because of—its low-tech aspect. For example, the film *Tren de Sobras* (José Luis Guerín, 1997) incorporates reconstructed domestic movie footage as an expressive and nostalgic device, where the imperfect technical quality is integral to its effect.[52] This film also responds to an aesthetic for found footage, paralleled in music where low-fi effects or resources from older technologies are sometimes employed in new recordings.[53] Nonetheless, the efficacy of such effects relies on familiarity with more recent and higher-quality media (not always available to low income Bolivians). Access to cheaper audiovisual technology has also given rise to a host of low-budget movies, partially bridging the professional-amateur divide. These often set themselves apart from—or challenge—the excesses and obsession with technical perfection of high-budget cinema and build on a more spontaneous "fly on the wall" or "reality television" aesthetic. For example, *The Blair Witch Project* (Sánchez and Myrick, 1999), which cost US$22,000 to make, takes the form of a mock documentary, while *Monsters* (Edwards, 2010), costing around US$20,000, was made driving around Mexico and adopts a journalistic style, using local people as actors.[54] The low-tech quality and documentary style of these immensely successful and innovative films may be seen to enhance their sense of spontaneity and, perhaps, verisimilitude. Yet, in these cases imperfection appears to have been more a function of entrepreneurship and shoestring budgets, than a political statement. By contrast—and decades earlier—Cuban filmmaker/theorist Julio García Espinosa's manifesto "For an Imperfect Cinema" is explicitly political and revolutionary in its rejection of the aesthetics and technical perfection of mainstream cinema.[55]

These various examples suggest that applying professional/amateur distinctions or dismissing *originario* music videos for their low-tech production quality is often analytically unhelpful, as well as risking generalization and stereotypes. However, to ascribe a "low-tech aesthetic" to such videos is also perilous, as well as politically naive. As I have argued, low-tech media can be highly effective, aesthetically potent, and politically charged in certain contexts, but to impute a "low-tech aesthetic" to *originario* producers and audiences, would imply they had a high-tech option. As I stressed in the introduction, for many people, access to digital technology is in itself a breakthrough. A more fruitful way forward, I suggest, is to combine close-up ethnographic study of production, circulation, and reception with a focus on "technological affordances." This latter approach, developed by Ian Hutchby, building on James Gibson's 1979 theory of ecological perception, turns our attention to how people orientate themselves to the possibilities for action offered by particular technologies.[56] It also helps overcome social and technological determinism by highlighting both (a) opportunities for and (b) constraints on interpretation and action when people interact through, around, or with particular technologies. I bring these ideas together in the concept of *creative pragmatism*, which—while arguably necessary for all media makers—is fundamental when economic resources, technology, and training are limited. With these points in mind, we now turn to the *originario* music video production work of Gregorio Mamani.

The Home Studio of Gregorio Mamani

Gregorio's home studio consisted of two small rooms. One contained his two secondhand computers and a simple mixing desk and functioned as the control room; the other was a tiny audio recording studio, with egg boxes on the walls for sound absorption and a single microphone. Other parts of the family's domestic space were invaded during certain parts of the production process. For example, the tiny concrete yard (*patio*) was used for filming in the dry season, and the main living room—which also served a Gregorio and Cinthia's bedroom—became a film studio, with high-power lights, during the rains.[57] A bedroom would also be used for screen-printing recorded VCD discs with Gregorio's CEMBOL logo—a strategy to combat piracy—and the printed discs laid out on a bed to dry.

Gregorio prided himself on his capacity to complete every aspect of the music video production and distribution process himself—except for the color printing of the paper cover sheets (*lamina*) for the display boxes, which was done by a commercial printer. To appreciate the work involved, and the minimal resulting profits, it is worth briefly outlining the numerous aspects of this process. First, based on his own lyrics and compositions or arrangements, Gregorio worked on the performance, recording, and editing of the music in his home studio. He used multi-tracking to record most of the parts himself, bringing in his wife or other singers for tracks featuring female voices, and the occasional additional instrumentalist for special effect. Next, after finalizing the music in an album of 10–12 tracks of 3–5 minutes each (usually also released as an audiocassette), he would commence filming the video. For the most part, this would feature miming and dancing to the audio recording played on a portable CD player, for which dancers and other assistants would need to be found. Using one of his two cheap secondhand video camcorders, he would film on location or at home, often using chroma-key ("green screen"), which enabled him to superimpose video images over existing footage or still photographs.[58] As Gregorio was frequently featured as the "star," he regularly called upon assistants to work the video camera (typically his son David or me), often providing close instructions for the shots required. Then, for the editing (using Pinnacle software), Gregorio would select clips from our filming sessions and combine these with footage and photos from many other sources, including television clips and animation films, to create a sense of visual variety. He would edit these and synchronize them with the music tracks, often adding special effects, stock transitions, and screen text.

In the fourth phase of the project, the finalized VCD would be copied onto CD discs, initially using two computers, but later employing a burner tower that could copy ten discs in three minutes. Also, in order to brand the VCD discs as original productions, each disc would then be screen-printed with the CEMBOL logo, a messy and labor-intensive process involving several family members (see fig. 6.1). Meanwhile, arrangements would be made for the *lamina* for the display boxes to be printed, using artwork Gregorio created using PowerPoint software. Finally, Gregorio and his wife would embark on a three- or four-day distribution expedition to visit poorer market districts of major cities and towns where the new VCD would be sold to local vendors. They would travel in different directions, often taking overnight buses and covering huge distances. This distribution campaign would take place over a single weekend, in order to quickly saturate key regional markets for the VCD before it could be copied and circulated by media "pirates."[59] Along with the immense amounts of time and energy invested into each VCD production, considerable financial outlay was necessary. It is doubtful, in the case of the *Zura zura* VCD, for example, whether this economic investment was fully recouped from sales (let alone any compensation for the time and energy). As Gregorio explained to me on several occasions, paid live engagements—even though these were few and far between—were a far superior source of income than the work of VCD production. He regularly blamed this situation on the effects of media piracy, reminiscing about a former time when he was well remunerated and looked after by the Cochabamba-based label *Borda*, for which he had recorded numerous audiocassettes.

Figure 6.1. Gregorio Mamani screen printing discs with the help of his wife and son. Photo by Henry Stobart.

Production Values and Collective Happenings

Even though Gregorio's work was very popular and he clearly had a good feel for what his low-income rural and urban migrant audience wanted, I heard a number of critiques of *originario* music videos from media professionals. One such perspective came from Laureano Rojas, who, in addition to owning a Cochabamba-based television station and printer, was the founder and director of Lauro y Cia, formerly one of Bolivia's three major record labels.[60] However, the combined challenges of digital developments and media piracy led *Lauro* to cease record production in around 2003.[61] Hardly surprisingly, given that this role has been fundamental to his career, Rojas highlighted the detrimental consequences on quality when video production was undertaken without an experienced producer:

> At the moment technology increases every day . . . so they make their own studio in their house and so on. . . . But we need someone who has the

experience to say whether this is the feeling of the people or, wherever possible, to say what else might be missing. Because if this is not done, things turn out very mechanical, without feeling, without being a music that is felt to be true to life, true to the soul—therefore it doesn't live.[62]

It is notable that rather than alluding to technical aspects, Rojas focuses on the producer's role in communicating the organic and emotional qualities of the music—making it come alive. As a highly experienced producer, he clearly had a strong sense about what would appeal to a mass, largely middle-class audience. Indeed, his vast catalog of *Lauro* recordings since the 1960s—an immensely successful entrepreneurial venture—was fundamental to the construction of a national folklore. In this process of adapting and adding value to oft-disdained indigenous regional expressions, Rojas needed to ensure that the resulting sounds (and, when video appeared, images) appealed to the tastes of his audience and reflected professional production values. In his view, such production values were absent from many *originario* music videos, as he explained to me:

> The images that they are putting out . . . are in effect natural. In the natural position of each artist or each group which appears. . . . This is not something well-prepared, well written, for which scripts have been made, for which the necessary story lines about what is to appear when have been made. . . . It is not a complete work. It is a kind of collective happening, as most filming simply takes place in the moment, it is done simply to demonstrate what the customs are at particular times.[63]

Rojas's criticism of the "natural" aspect of the performers in *originario* music videos suggests a requirement for some kind of artifice or act; this presents an interesting juxtaposition with his previous insistence on the need for a producer to ensure that the production is "true to life, true to the soul." Here he seems to be highlighting the need for presentational skills, where musicians actively perform to the camera, rather than ignoring its presence.

Similarly, Gregorio had strong opinions about the need for musicians to develop the ability to perform to camera, and was critical of those artists who appeared stilted, visibly uncomfortable, or who just ignored the camera. In the light of Rojas's comments, it should be stressed that music video, as a genre, is not usually structured according to a clearly definable story line or narrative. Instead, the sense of narrative or flow is provided by the music and visual discontinuities, such as sudden changes in clothing, and disjunctive edits are seen to enrich the visual diversity rather than threaten the believability of the narrative, as would be the case with a feature film.[64] Nonetheless, the presence of some form of script, to help the planning of particular shots during the production process, would seem beneficial in certain contexts (as I will discuss in more detail below).

It is to Rojas's characterization of location filming for *originario* music videos as "a kind of collective happening" to which I now wish to turn. I participated in a considerable number of filming expeditions in the roles of chauffeur, part-time cameraman, general helper, and occasional "exotic" dancer. Gregorio especially appreciated the provision of transport, using the 4x4 vehicle I acquired for the year, as it provided flexibility and saved him paying for taxis. Our excursions involved traveling to visually interesting locations, usually in the countryside (or a park), and filming video sequences of dancing and mimed singing to the audio recordings of the songs for the video, played back on a portable CD player. A frequent challenge for Gregorio prior to such expeditions was finding enthusiastic and "attractive" girls who could dance well, owned an array of suitably colorful *pollera* skirts and tops, and who were prepared to spend a day filming on location for a low fee.

I will focus here on a day of location filming undertaken on Tuesday, January 15, 2008, at the height of the rainy season—an expedition that, like almost every other, was surrounded by a series of complications. While some of these could be attributed to a lack of planning and informal attitudes, many also reflected factors beyond our control and the challenges of working with a minimal budget and cheap equipment. It should also be stressed that the decision to undertake this trip at all reflected a desire to maintain production standards. We had filmed the video for these songs several months earlier at Chataquila (30 km from Sucre), but Gregorio's dissatisfaction with the girls' infrequent smiles, lack of expression, and poor dancing led him to discard most of this footage.

For our trip on January 15, he worked with a different group of girls, and at his house on the evening prior to filming they rehearsed the dance steps and discussed what they would wear. Gregorio had planned to film very nearby at Siete Cascadas (Seven Waterfalls), but as it had rained heavily overnight, making the dirt road muddy and impassable, he decided to relocate to the suspension bridge over the Pilcomayo River, a beautiful but much more distant site on the main tarmac road between Sucre and Potosi. I arrived at Gregorio's house before 8:00 a.m., and following various last minute errands, including collecting the three female dancers, we got on route at around 10:30 a.m. However, at the roadblock near the village of Yotala (14 km from Sucre), I was required to return to the city to purchase a new tax disc. Gregorio decided to get started with filming and have an early lunch there while I was gone. When I returned, just over an hour later, the group had eaten lunch and consumed several jugs of *chicha* (maize beer). Gregorio explained to me that they had abandoned filming, as the girls' dancing was too self-conscious and stilted. Now fuelled with *chicha*, and supplied with two further bottles of *chicha* and one of *Singani*

Figure 6.2. Getting ready to film at the bridge over the Pilkomayo river. Photo by Henry Stobart.

(grape spirit) for the journey, the party was now very merry. We continued the journey to the Pilcomayo suspension bridge, singing along to the songs for the video, as they boomed out from the vehicle's CD player.

Arriving at the bridge at 1:15 p.m., we set up cameras (see fig. 6.2). Gregorio arranged that his sixteen-year-old son David would film the dancers from nearby on the bridge while, with a different camera, I made a long shot, zooming out from the dancers to reveal their location on this spectacular bridge over the Pilcomayo river. However, after filming a few short sequences, we had to stop, due to torrential rain. This was so heavy that it dislodged several boulders and washed open deep gullies into the narrow and precipitous dirt access road to the bridge, making the cliff-edge drive back to the main road very hazardous (the rest of the party chose to walk while I drove alone). As we set off along the main road back to Sucre, dejected silence overcame us. But fifteen minutes later, the sun came out and Gregorio suggested we stop to film beside the road. Following these various ups and downs, the three female dancers were now very relaxed and merry as they performed. In particular, Clementina Jancko—an artist in her own right who had also made her own music video—was full of imaginative suggestions for shots, in turn fuelling Gregorio's enthusiasm and creativity. These spontaneous ideas included exploiting various features of the landscape, placing dancers in the background of various shots, and dragging me in (for the first time) for comic effect, as an exotic and incongruous dancer. We stopped several more times to film on the journey, exploiting the beauty of the early evening light, and arriving back in Sucre at nightfall with a considerable amount of footage, much of which found its way onto the final music video. Everybody was in high spirits and we rounded off the day by going out to celebrate with a few more drinks. However, I should stress that this was the only occasion—among my many location filming expeditions with Gregorio—that featured alcohol.[65] The day was most certainly a "collective happening" where filming took place "in the moment," but does this mean that the quality or value were somehow diminished, or that the results were not "true to life"?

One of the songs for which much of the video was shot during this filming expedition was "Elenita" (Helen).[66] This was a classic audio recording from the late 1980s that Gregorio decided to rerelease as a music video on his compilation *Exitos de ayer y hoy*, the second and least explicitly indigenous VCD on which we worked together. The video opens with shots taken on a track beside the Sucre-Potosí road, zooming away from the dancers to highlight the landscape—but cut away just before the road comes into view. It then features the improvised coordination of the three girls dancing in matching burgundy skirts and tops, before a star transition—presenting Gregorio as the "charango idol" (in screen text)—leads into the first verse, located in the patio of Gregorio's house, where he and Sandra are superimposed—using green screen—in front of a group of revelers (which includes Gregorio). Screen text in Quechua presents Sandra as "my lover Elenita" and with the end of the verse a picture frame transition transports us back to the track beside the Sucre–Potosí road for the instrumental. A further picture transition leads to Clementina dancing alone on the road, before a love-heart transition takes us to dancers in a maize field (from another filming expedition). For the second verse (in Spanish) we return to the track beside the Sucre–Potosí road, where—with partial miming of the words from Gregorio—the camera focuses on the dancers heads while—to general amusement—Clementina cavorts with "Chinito" (Juan Medina), pushing him to the ground. A transition, showing a magnet pulling a picture frame, leads into the instrumental and more partially coordinated dancing and a further transition featuring a North American-style mail box. The third verse is introduced by a heart-shaped transition. Gregorio and Sandra are shown in a nostalgia-invoking black-and-white sequence, with the screen text "my lover Elenita" appearing once again. For the final instrumental, Gregorio and Sandra are shown getting up from a park bench (filmed in Sucre) and walking off hand in hand, before getting into a taxi together. The video imagery presents a romance between Gregorio and Sandra (as Elenita), albeit highly incongruously, given their thirty-year discrepancy in age. The words of the song are divided between two verses: the first, in the indigenous language Quechua, draws on well-known couplets from a rural dry-season songs, and the second, in Spanish, comically twists the romance though allusions to marrying the girl's sister.

(Quechua)
Jank'a saranichu, yuraq saranichu, (Elenita)
Allinchá nuqaqa ni kasaranichu, (Elenita)
Kasarayman chayqa, khuyayaymanchari, (Elenita)
Agustu wayrapis apawanmanchari, (Elenita)
(Spanish)
Para que mi voy a casarme con otra (Elenita)
Antes puedo casar con tu hermanita (Elenita)
Díganle tu padre, díganle tu madre (Elenita)
Antes puedo casarme con tu hermanita (Elenita)

(Quechua)
Toasted maize? White maize? (Elenita)
I'm fine, not getting married,
If I were to marry, perhaps I'd be sad,
I might be carried off in the August wind
(Spanish)
Why would I marry anyone else?
Before that I could marry your sister
Tell your father, tell your mother
Before that I could marry your sister

Spontaneous Filming and Spontaneous Editing

A further critique of *originario* music video production quality, and specifically related to Gregorio's work, was voiced to me in an interview with Darío Arclénega, an experienced television producer and radio presenter. His comments undoubtedly relate to Gregorio's pre-2007 productions, completed before he had acquired the equipment and skills to undertake his own video editing.

> But there's a little problem, people are not trained or prepared, they don't know much. All they do is film spontaneously and edit spontaneously. There are no, let's say, "technical resources" for editing. People are not trained how to make a good quality edition. So, for example, they don't use a tripod, they don't employ adequate lighting; they don't make use of the different angles, right? [They don't] make the shots they need to have.
>
> Well, what they do is grab [the camera], go off to the countryside, film the singing and that's it. Hey presto, just like that, they put it on DVD. So there's

not any workmanship in the editing of their productions, which is a bit more "professional"—if it's worth saying in quotation marks.[67]

Arclénega's comments raise important and pertinent questions about training, production values, and conventions, and are interesting in light of the expedition to film at the Pilcomayo suspension bridge. We certainly "grabbed" the cameras and went off to the countryside to film the singing, as he describes. As many of the plans fell through, there was also a great deal of spontaneity about the way the filming was finally done. However, Gregorio was particularly concerned to avoid shaky video footage and usually instructed anyone filming for him to use the tripod. (As I found it difficult to track movements effectively using a tripod and much preferred handheld filming, Gregorio made an exception for me.)[68] Gregorio often had strong ideas about the selection of camera angles, particularly when it came to over-the-shoulder shots with a large crowd in the background (to highlight his star status), zooming-out shots, shots from below, and moving shots between close-ups of the singer ("master") and the dancers. In the light of Arclénega's comment about failing to get "the shots they need to have," I was sometimes surprised by the systematic nature of Gregorio's working practices. Prior to setting out for location filming, he often noted down the shots he needed on a piece of paper. For example, the selection below (translated and culled from a much longer list) was prepared for one of our filming expeditions for the third music video on which we worked together, entitled *30,000 Chanchos* (30,000 pigs), which featured the music associated with *tinku* fighting. This video was more explicitly indigenous in character than *Elena*.

> Image = fights with stones
> Image = Head [covered in] pure blood
> Image = man on the ground spews pure blood
> Image = Gregorio kicks Chino in the behind, and Chino falls in the river
> Image = dress like llamas
> Image = when fighting between brothers, Chabela takes scissors and cuts off
>   clothing

The first three images from this list appear in track 4, the song "A la mar" (To the sea),[69] which with comic brutality warns vendors and buyers about the fatal consequences of pirating Gregorio's music videos. The message is very clear: as a "noble savage," he will reap justice with his own hands.[70] The video highlights Gregorio's *originario* identity and background as a formidable Macha warrior participating in the ritual fighting (*tinku*) of the harvest-time Feast of the Holy Cross (May) in the town of Macha.[71] It intersperses footage of actual *tinku* fighting, filmed by Gregorio during the feast in Macha, with specially staged sequences from location filming. In the final sequence of the video, most of which I filmed, we see:

1. (3:30) Gregorio throwing a large stone directly at the camera. This evokes the stone fighting which quite often results in fatalities during the Macha *tinku;*
2. (3:34) the vanquished opponent laying on the ground — his face splattered with blood;
3. (3:43) a close-up of a globule of blood on the ground, as if spewed by the defeated opponent. (For this scene, bulls' blood was collected from a slaughterhouse and transported in a plastic bag.)

Gregorio applied the same systematic approach to his video editing. In his notebook, he jotted down a list of the various transitions that he had researched and wished to use for a particular production. On another page, he recorded various "video effects" with which he wished to experiment, noting down the name and the way he planned to use the particular effect. For example, to create "a dream sequence" he jotted down: "RTFX Vol 1—Radiance of a dream = brighten an image and for brilliance."

Knowledge and Learning: Technological Competency and Consistency

As a videographer, Gregorio was entirely self-taught. Nonetheless, having worked as a recording artist since the late 1980s, he held strong ideas about audio production values, evidently picked up from the producer with whom he had worked very closely. I was also impressed with his competence in multi-track audio recording techniques and editing. For his pre-2007 videos he sometimes undertook some of the filming himself, but always employed a "professional" to edit the video for him. Nonetheless, it is clear that he carefully oversaw the editing process, directing the creative decisions of the video editor to a considerable degree, but also—though viewing the footage—realizing how to improve his own camera technique. The first music video on which we worked together, *Zura zura*, featuring rural Carnival music,[72] was also the first for which Gregorio independently undertook the video editing. He encountered many technical problems during the editing process, often calling upon his fifteen-year-old son, David, for advice. Although, David had not received any formal training, either, like many other young people, he approached computers fearlessly and intuitively, and was able to help solve many problems. As Gregorio's knowledge, competence, and confidence grew, he became less reliant on David and more adventurous in exploring the opportunities afforded by the technology. By the third and final video on which we worked together, Gregorio was much more in command of the editing process; he was able to work much faster and was rarely detained by technical snags. Indeed, the difference in technical quality between this and his first video is striking.

Gregorio's gradual mastery and fascination with particular aspects of the technology can be charted through the three main music video productions in which I participated. A key technical innovation for the first video was the introduction of chroma key ("green screen")—an effect that involves superimposing video images over other video or still shots. I had not previously seen this effect used in Bolivian *originario* music videos. This innovation enabled him to reduce the number of location filming expeditions and to complete much of the filming at home in front of a large blue sheet-like screen.[73] However, chroma key video editing often created problems with color bleeds (for example when the performer wore a white hat) that took considerable effort to overcome. For the second video, Gregorio became fascinated by the stock transitions provided by the Pinnacle video editing software. Many readers might find such transitions kitsch and incongruous, where North American imagery—such as a mailbox or "Happy Christmas" greeting card—flashes across the screen, but Gregorio's audience clearly found them novel and quirky. However, the stock transitions, which had featured so prominently in the second video, were entirely absent from his third. Here Gregorio introduced a range of special effects to highlight action—for example, speeding up sequences for comic effect or introducing curious voice distortion effects over the song.

Gregorio also produced videos for other artists on commission, but it is notable how lacking in imagination and humor these videos sometimes appear compared to his own productions. How much, we might wonder, was this because he was less invested in the projects of other artists and how much because the medium provided fewer challenges and novelties for him, leading him to become more conventional? This takes us back to Crowdy's query as to whether we should expect technical consistency joined with conservatism from professional studios, and more radical and experimental approaches, with less technical consistency, from home studios.[74] For his own productions, Gregorio invested huge amounts of time, creative energy, and technical precision into certain scenes, but in others made minimal effort to catch the imagination or correct technical faults, such as poor lip-synching. His videos seem to lurch unpredictably between lackluster conservatism and radical experimentation, bursting with (sometimes outrageous) humor. The inconsistent technical quality of his work highlights Gregorio's idiosyncratic approach and the difficulty of generalizing about his productions. It also makes it difficult to rebuff accusations about a "lack of professionalism"—if professionalism is defined in terms of consistency in quality.[75] Despite the inconsistencies, compared to many other Bolivian *originario* music videos, Gregorio's VCDs are remarkable for their energy, humor, and sense of life. Indeed, we often discussed the dull, repetitive, and conventional quality of many *originario* music videos.

It is notable that the vast majority of such work is filmed and produced by urban middle-class *mestizo* professionals. Such producers—whose social group would be unlikely to purchase or consume these videos—usually approach *originario* people and their culture with a complex mixture of romanticism, paternalism, protectiveness, respect, and disdain. Their video editing tends to stress indigenous authenticity, with any hints of modernity carefully erased. The indigenous subjects are implicitly contained within the permitted spaces and marginalized social positions constructed for them—what Silvia Rivera, and later Charles Hale, have called the *indio permitido* or "authorized indian."[76] As a music entrepreneur from a rural *originario* background, Gregorio was in many respects exceptional and a pioneer.[77] His videos often confronted the image of the *indio permitido*, serving instead as a platform for self-promotion, to publically play out personal quarrels, and to present himself as a revolutionary leader fighting against injustice. His productions of *originario* music often juxtapose urban and rural images or incorporate aspects of modernity (for example, when—to great comic effect—he appears with long hair and sunglasses parodying a Euro-American rock star). For the *mestizo* producers to whom I spoke, such juxtapositions—or, for example, an indigenous person wearing jeans—were seen as entirely unacceptable. This highlights Gregorio's insider *originario* perspective with its shared cultural references, which stress entertainment and contemporary indigenous experience, where tradition and modernity jostle on a daily basis. Even if outsiders, such as Bolivian middle-class urban *mestizos*, find it hard to look beyond the technical deficiencies of Gregorio's productions, the videos were undoubtedly popular among the local *originario* audience for whom they were intended. For example, according to Gregorio, the third and final music video on which we worked together (*30,000 Chanchos* [30,000 pigs]) had sold around 6,000 copies by the time I returned to the United Kingdom, around six weeks after its release. This number is highly impressive when we consider that, according to larger-scale producers, *originario* music videos rarely sell over 1,000 copies.

Conclusions: Creative Pragmatism

My intention in this chapter has not been to defend Gregorio Mamani's *originario* music videos from the charge voiced by Bolivian media professionals: that they lack "professional" production quality. Gregorio was only too aware of the technical limitations of his productions; had HD and other technical resources or training been available to him, he would surely have been the first to exploit them. Rather, my aim has been to contextualize his work and examine how it relates (a) to the constraints within which he worked and (b) to his *originario* identity and background. Clearly, any artist, musician, or producer faces constraints or challenges which may, on the one hand, limit the quality or potential of the work and, on the other, focus and motivate creativity and innovation, sometimes in the form of solutions or alternatives. I want to characterize this latter process as *creative pragmatism*. Let us briefly examine some of the key challenges Gregorio faced as an *originario* musician-producer and their implications for quality.

His first and most obvious challenge was economic; his low income necessitated relying on cheap and unreliable secondhand equipment and essentially working without a production budget. Even paying for a taxi to travel to the countryside for a location shoot, or providing a modest meal and remuneration for participating dancers was a major consideration. Also, the need to reduce the price of his VCD productions to compete with "pirate" prices meant that profits were usually extremely meager,[78] making it impossible to invest in better-quality equipment or other aspects of production.

Second, Gregorio's lack of technical training in video editing represented a major challenge, leading him initially to rely on the support of his fifteen-year-old son. Nonetheless, through my eleven months of research I witnessed his gradual, but very significant, increase in technical knowledge and competency, a largely independent process of trial and error, alongside a strikingly methodical approach and passion for experimentation.

A third challenge was finding competent collaborators to help with audio recording and filming, and to sing and appear in the video. Gregorio's limited economic means to provide adequate wages or forms of reciprocity often led him to complete the vast majority of production tasks alone—such as multi-tracking all the instrumental parts himself.[79]

A final challenge was temporal: managing multiple projects simultaneously, and ensuring they were completed in time for specific seasonal release dates. For example, his Carnival music video needed to appear around one month before the feast of Carnival and could enjoy only a very short sales window. Thus, although Gregorio could often afford to dedicate more time to his productions than larger-scale commercial studios do, he was nonetheless subject to significant temporal constraints in order to market his productions and recoup some investment. This, in turn, meant that that he sometimes cut corners and production quality suffered.

As this case study highlights, it is necessary to stress that technologies are adapted to specific social, cultural, economic and political contexts of production and reception. Within these contexts, and their diverse constraints and challenges, different types of responses and solutions are likely to surface—what I have called *creative pragmatism*—and in turn to give rise to particular aesthetic priorities or even vocabularies. Thus, rather than searching for some kind of "indigenous" way of seeing or hearing, and thereby falling into generalizations and essentialisms, I suggest that we explore the frictions, interactions, priorities, and creative pragmatics that surround these kinds of engagements with technology and its particular affordances. Such approaches may not reveal the "pure" indigenous aesthetic "essences" that certain outsiders might desire. However, they are likely to tell us things about indigenous experience today and to give insights into how influential constructions of indigenous people are being produced and consumed by indigenous people themselves.

Notes

This chapter is dedicated to the memory of Gregorio Mamani, and my thanks go to his family, and the many other friends in Bolivia who so generously contributed to this research. Special gratitude is due to Cassandra Torrico, who first suggested focusing my research on Gregorio. The ongoing support of the Museum of Ethnography and Folklore (MUSEF), La Paz—especially Varinia Oros and former director Ramiro Molina—are warmly appreciated. Thanks to Thomas Hilder and the anonymous reviewers for helpful and thought-provoking comments on earlier drafts. Finally, I gratefully acknowledge the support for this research received from the British Academy (http://www.britac.ac.uk) and the UK Arts and Humanities Research Council (http://www.ahrc.ac.uk).

1. Gillette Hall and Harry Patrinos, *Indigenous Peoples, Poverty, and Development* (Cambridge: Cambridge University Press, 2012).

2. Although "Internet café" or "cybercafé" is the common term, these kinds of Internet access points do not usually serve food and drink. They consist of banks of computers that customers rent at an hourly rate.

3. I use the highly unsatisfactory terms "global north" and "global south" with considerable reluctance. See Jean-Philippe Thérien, "Beyond the North-South Divide: The Two Tales of World Poverty," *Third World Quarterly* 20, no. 4 (1999): 723–42. Nonetheless, compared to similarly problematic terms, such as "developed/emerging economies," the geographical aspect of these terms has been relevant to the circulation of VCD technology.

4. This has been increasingly replaced by machines that can also play DVD, mp4, mp3 and other formats.

5. Elsewhere I discuss the shift from "analog" audiocassette to "digital" VCD among low-income rural and urban indigenous people in Bolivia, bypassing the digital audio CD, which was largely the preserve of the middle classes. Henry Stobart, "Rampant Reproduction and Digital Democracy: Shifting Landscapes of Music Production and 'Piracy' in Bolivia," *Ethnomusicology Forum* 19, no. 1 (2010): 27–56.

6. Shujen Wang, *Framing Piracy: Globalization and Film Distribution in Greater China* (Lanham, MD: Rowman & Littlefield, 2003), 50; Stobart, "Rampant Reproduction and Digital Democracy," 28; Joe Karaganis, *Media Piracy in Emerging Economies* (New York: Social Science Research Council, 2011), 331.

7. Pamela Wilson and Michelle Stewart, "Indigeneity and Indigenous Media on the Global Stage," in *Global Indigenous Media: Cultures, Poetics and Politics,* ed. Pamela Wilson and Michelle Stewart (Durham, NC: Duke Univeristy Press, 2008), 8.

8. Henry Stobart, *Music and the Poetics of Production in the Bolivian Andes* (Aldershot, UK: Ashgate, 2006).

9. Tristan Platt, *Estado boliviano y ayllu andino: Tierra y tributo en el norte de Potosí* (Lima, Peru: Instituto de Estudios Peruanos, 1982), 20; Brooke Larson, *Trials of Nation Making: Liberalism, Race, and Ethnicity in the Andes, 1810–1910* (Cambridge: Cambridge University Press, 2004), 40–41.

10. Jeff Himpele, *Circuits of Culture: Media, Politics and Indigenous Idenity in the Andes* (Minneapolis: University of Minnesota Press, 2008), 8.

11. John Crabtree and Laurence Whitehead, eds., *Unresolved Tensions: Bolivia Past and Present* (Pittsburgh, PA: University of Pittsburgh Press, 2008).

12. INE (Instituto Nacional de Estadísticas de Bolívia), "Bolivia: Características sociodemográfícas de la población" (La Paz: INE, 2003), 157.

13. Carlos Toranzo Roca, "Let the Mestizos Stand Up and Be Counted," in *Unresolved Tensions: Bolivia Past and Present,* ed. J. Crabtree and L. Whitehead (Pittsburgh, PA: University of Pittsburgh Press, 2008), 35–50.

14. Andrew Canessa, "Who Is Indigenous? Self-Identification, Indigeneity, and Claims to Justice in Contemporary Bolivia," *Urban Anthropology and Studies of Cultural Systems and World Economic Development* 36, no. 3 (2007): 195–237.

15. Most professional *huayño* artists make their homes in the poorer migrant neighborhoods of cities such as Cochabamba, Sucre, and Potosí.

16. Andrew Canessa, "Todos somos indígenas: Towards a New Language of National Political Identity," *Bulletin of Latin American Research* 25, no. 2 (2006): 260.

17. Faye Ginsburg, Lila Abu-Lughod, and Brian Larkin, "Introduction," in *Media Worlds: Anthropology on New Terrain,* ed. Faye Ginsburg, Lila Abu-Lughod, and Brian Larkin (Berkeley: University of California Press, 2002), 8.

18. Freya Schiwy, "Decolonizing the Frame: Indigenous Video in the Andes," *Framework* 44, no. 1 (2003): 117.

19. Terence Turner, "Representation, Politics, and Cultural Imagination in Indigenous Video: General Points and Kayapó Examples," in *Media Worlds: Anthropology on New Terrain,* ed. Faye Ginsburg, Lila Abu-Lughod, and Brian Larkin (Berkeley: University of California Press, 2002), 79.

20. James Weiner, "Televisualist Anthropology: Representation, Aesthetics, Politics," *Current Anthropology* 38, no. 2 (1997): 205.

21. Freya Schiwy, *Indianizing Film: Decolonization, the Andes, and the Question of Technology* (New Brunswick, NJ: Rutgers University Press, 2009), 12–13. This is suggestive of Ali Jihad Racy's distinction between "idiosyncratic" and "adaptational" forms of transmission for the case of musical instrument technologies. Ali Jihad Racy, "A Dialectical Perspective on Musical Instruments: The East-Mediterranean Mijwiz," *Ethnomusicology* 38, no. 1 (1994): 37. Weiner's position resembles Racy's "ideosyncratic explanation," where the instrument is adopted as a cultural "package," arguably exemplified by Japan's adoption of

the piano and violin, alongside their respective techniques, pedagogy, repertoire and aesthetics. For counter-examples of cross-fertilization, see Judith Ann
Herd, "Western-Influenced 'Classical' Music in Japan," in *The Ashgate Research
Companion to Japanese Music*, ed. A. Tokita and D. W. Hughes (Aldershot, UK:
Ashgate, 2008), 363–82. By contrast, "adaptational explanations" stress how
musical instruments transform "in response to different ecological and aesthetic realities" (Racy, "A Dialectical Perspective on Musical Instruments,"
37), debatably evidenced by the way that in the Andes, the European guitar,
harp, recorder, and saxophone have given rise to a multiplicity of distinctive
regional musical expressions, meanings, and aesthetics. See Stobart, *Music
and the Poetics of Production in the Bolivian Andes*; Raúl R. Romero, *Debating
the Past: Music, Memory, and Identity in the Andes* (Oxford: Oxford University
Press, 2001). Importantly, Racy emphasizes that these processes are "basically
inseparable and intertwined" (Racy, "A Dialectical Perspective on Musical
Instruments," 37) and reflect extremes on a continuum. However, they do
help us place audiovideo technologies into broader historical trajectories.

22. Richard Pace and Glenn Shepard, "Miss Kayapó: Filming through Mebengokre
Cameras," *Anthropology News*, April 2012, accessed January 4, 2013, http://www.
anthropology-news.org/index.php/2012/04/02/through-kayapo-cameras/;
Pace and Shepard's article also cites examples from Turner, "Representation,
Politics, and Cultural Imagination in Indigenous Video," 75–89.

23. Thomas Turino, *Music as Social Life: The Politics of Participation* (Chicago:
University of Chicago Press, 2008), 23.

24. Terence Turner, "Defiant Images: The Kayapo Appropriation of Video,"
Anthropology Today 8, no. 6 (1992): 8.

25. It is not hard to imagine how, in the context of such videos, excessive focus
on particular individuals—to the exclusion of others—can provoke social tensions. Similarly, while the role of filmmaker is afforded high prestige within
Kayapo communities—with ambitious young men sometimes using it as a path
to chieftainship—it may also provoke intense jealousies and conflict (Turner,
"Defiant Images," 7). This was clearly a complex issue for Turner and his collaborators to negotiate; in turn, this raises questions about how conflict avoidance strategies adopted by facilitators might impact on the styles of media
produced. Although the Kayapo are very media-savvy in their engagements
with the Brazilian state and international press (Turner, "Representation,
Politics, and Cultural Imagination in Indigenous Video," 84), the videos discussed above are notable for their largely internal consumption. They circulate among Kayapo communities as an expression of pride and inter-village
rivalry, and require filmmakers to be acutely sensitive to local demands and
criticisms.

26. Juan Francisco Salazar, "Imperfect Media: The Poetics of Indigenous Media in
Chile," PhD disertation, University of Western Sydney, 2004, p. 75.

27. Centro de Formación y Realización Cinematográfica–Coordinadora Audiovisual Indígena Originaria de Bolivia.

28. Weiner, "Televisualist Anthropology: Representation, Aesthetics, Politics," 209.

29. Schiwy, *Indianizing Film*.

30. Ibid., 12–13.

31. Ibid., 13.

32. Brooke Larson, "Andean Communities, Political Cultures, and Markets: The Changing Contours of a Field," in *Ethnicity, Markets, and Migration in the Andes: At the Crossroads of History and Anthropology*, ed. Brooke Larson, Olivia Harris, and Enrique Tandeter (Durham, NC: Duke University Press, 1995), 12.

33. Steven Leuthold, *Indigenous Aesthetics: Native Art, Media, and Identity* (Austin: University of Texas Press, 1998), 183.

34. Steven Leuthold, "An Indigenous Aesthetic? Two Noted Videographers: George Burdeau and Victor Masayesva," *Wicazo Sa Review* 10, no. 1 (1994): 49.

35. Gabriela Zamorano Villarreal, "Crafting Contemporary Indigeneity through Audiovisual Media in Bolivia" in *Recasting Commodity and Spectacle in the Indigenous Americas*, Helen Gilbert and Charlotte Gleghorn, eds. (Institute of Latin American Studies, School of Advanced Study, University of London, 2014), 77–95.

36. Carol Vernallis, *Experiencing Music Video: Aesthetics and Cultural Context* (New York: Columbia University Press, 2004), 47.

37. Schiwy, *Indianizing Film*, 27.

38. Zamorano Villarreal, "Crafting Contemporary Indigeneity," 86.

39. Jody Berland, "Sound, Image and Social Space: Music Video and Media Reconstruction," in *Sound and Vision: The Music Video Reader*, ed. Simon Frith, Andrew Goodwin, and Lawrence Grossberg (Abingdon, UK: Routledge, 1993), 30. Diane Railton and Paul Watson, *Music Video and the Politics of Representation* (Edinburgh: University of Edinburgh Press, 2011), 1.

40. Stobart, "Rampant Reproduction and Digital Democracy"; Henry Stobart, "'Justice with My Own Hands': The Serious Play of Piracy in Bolivian Indigenous Music Videos," in *Postcolonial Piracy: Media Distribution and Cultural Production in the Global South*, ed. L. Eckstein and A. Schwarz (London: Bloomsbury, 2014).

41. Tony Langlois, "Pirates of the Mediterranean: Moroccan Music Video and Technology," *Music, Sound, and the Moving Image* 3, no. 1 (2009): 82.

42. Paul Theberge, *Any Sound You Can Imagine: Making Music/Consuming Technology* (Hanover, NH: University Press of New England, 1997), 231–35.

43. Notions of amateur and professional are also highly blurred for the case of music making more generally. See, for example, Stephanie Pitts, *Valuing Musical Participation* (Aldershot, UK: Ashgate, 2005), 26.

44. Denis Crowdy, "Studios at Home in the Solomon Islands," *The World of Music* 49, no. 1 (2007): 144.

45. Ibid.

46. David Buckingham, Maria Pini, and Rebekah Willett, "'Take Back the Tube!': The Discursive Construction of Amateur Film and Video Making," *Journal of Media Practice* 8, no. 2 (2007).

47. Ibid., 186.

48. Ibid., 186–88.

49. Richard Chalfen, *Snapshot Versions of Life* (Bowling Green, OH: Bowling Green State University Popular Press, 1987), 143.

50. Buckingham, Pini, and Willett, "'Take Back the Tube!'" 198–99.

51. Patricia Lange, "Video-Mediated Nostalgia and the Aesthetics of Technical Competencies," *Visual Communication* 10, no. 1 (2011): 40.

52. Éfren Cuevas Álvarez, "En las fronteras del cine aficionado: *Tren de sombras* y el proyecto de la bruja de Blair," *Comunicación y Sociedad* 14, no. 2 (2001): 11–35. Lange also observes how "tropes of amateur video making such as shaking cameras appear in professional productions, reworked as symbolic tokens of authenticity" ("Video-Mediated Nostalgia," 40).

53. Timothy D. Taylor, *Strange Sounds: Music, Technology and Culture* (New York: Routledge, 2001), 96; Crowdy, "Studios at Home in the Solomon Islands," 151.

54. Will Buckingham, "25 Low Budget Films," *Raindance: Write-Produce-Direct Film* (2009), http://www.raindance.co.uk/site/index.php?aid=3790.

55. Julio Garcia Espinosa, "For an Imperfect Cinema," *Jump Cut* 20(1979/2005 [1969]).

56. Ian Hutchby, "Technologies, Texts, and Affordances," *Sociology* 35, no. 2 (2001): 447–50.

57. Henry Stobart, "Constructing Community in the Digital Home Studio: Carnival, Creativity and Indigenous Music Video Production in the Bolivian Andes," *Popular Music* 30, no. 2 (2011): 217.

58. In reality, Gregorio used a blue cloth screen as a backdrop for chroma-key filming, rather than the "green screen" of popular discourse.

59. Stobart, "Rampant Reproduction and Digital Democracy," 218.

60. Laureano Rojas Alcocer and unnamed authors, *35 Años de folklore marcando la soberanía patria: Historia de 29 Festivales Lauro records* (Cochabamba, BO: Talleres Gráfico Lauro, 1994).

61. Stobart, "Rampant Reproduction and Digital Democracy." Although not under the Lauro label, the studios were still sometimes hired out to make recordings.

62. Lauriano Rojas, interview with the author, January 24, 2008.

63. Ibid.

64. Vernallis, *Experiencing Music Video*, 30–31.

65. Usually, as Gregorio had suffered severe health and alcohol problems, which he self-critiqued in several music videos, he carefully avoided drinking. Mestizo producers of *originario* music video, such as GC Records of Cochabamba, informed me that they often provided their performers with alcohol to relax them before recording or filming. I mention alcohol consumption with some hesitancy here, as it is important to challenge stereotypes of indigenous drinking; see Byron Dueck, *Musical Intimacies and Indigenous Imaginaries: Aboriginal Music and Dance in Public Performance* (New York: Oxford University Press, 2013), 9–10. It would, however, be a mistake to pretend that alcohol is not a critical ingredient of indigenous Andean festive contexts when most music making takes place. See Henry Stobart, "Sensational Sacrifices: Feasting the Senses in the Bolivian Andes," in *Music, Sensation and Sensuality*, ed. L. Austern (New York: Routledge, 2002), 107. It should also be stressed that alcohol often poses a special problem for professional musicians—and not just indigenous ones—who perform in festive contexts.

66. "Elenita—Exitos de Ayer y Hoy (2008) Gregorio Mamani," YouTube video, 3:14, posted by "Takirichun," October 25, 2012, http://www.youtube.com/watch?v=GCYOU0QwEVY.

67. Dario Arclénega, interview with author, March 3, 2008.

68. My ability to hold the camera still for handheld filming was especially appreciated by Gregorio, who sometimes joking referred to me as "Enrique pedestal" ("Tripod Henry"). It should also be stressed that handheld filming is common as an effect in high-budget music videos elsewhere, as in Madonna's "Cherish" (Vernallis, *Experiencing Music Video*, 212).

69. "A la Mar—Gregorio Mamani," YouTube video, 4:11, posted by "Takirichun," November 29, 2011, https://www.youtube.com/watch?v=TpcgAhUt1_U.

70. For further discussion of this song in the context of Gregorio's antipiracy strategies, see Stobart, "'Justice with My Own Hands,'" 228–31.

71. Stobart, *Music and the Poetics of Production*, 133–65.

72. Stobart, "Constructing Community."

73. Although commonly referred to as "green screen," this effect also works when filmed against a blue screen.

74. Crowdy, "Studios at Home in the Solomon Islands," 177.

75. Ibid., 144.

76. Charles Hale, "Rethinking Indigenous Politics in the Era of the Indio Permitido," *NACLA Report on the Americas* 38, no. 2 (2004): 16–21.

77. Gregorio was the only *originario* artist from a rural background I encountered during my research who owned a home studio and produced his own music videos.

78. Stobart, "'Justice with My Own Hands,'" 240–41.

79. Stobart, "Constructing Community," 218–20.

Chapter Seven

Keepsakes and Surrogates

Hijacking Music Technology at Wadeye (Northwest Australia)

Linda Barwick

This chapter focuses on some uses of digital recording technology in the township of Wadeye in Australia's Northern Territory, where I worked on a project focusing on *djanba*, a genre of public ceremonial song created and performed by Murriny Patha people.[1] In this chapter, I will draw a distinction between "traditional" song forms like *djanba*—ceremonial genres using Indigenous musical forms and instruments whose origins predate contact with Europeans and that continue to be performed due to their fundamental religious and social role—and "nontraditional" musical forms—recently composed secular songs that use introduced musical instruments (guitar, electric piano) and accompanying musical features such as diatonic scales, two-part harmony, and strophic form.

The chapter will discuss emerging nontraditional musical forms composed by members of one of the local Indigenous groups in Wadeye. These new compositions, disseminated via various digital platforms, embody strategic assertions of cultural and territorial autonomy and identity, thereby continuing and developing one of the fundamental functions of traditional song performance. In Australia, as elsewhere in the world, Indigenous identity is not monolithic: "the voluntary perpetuation of cultural distinctiveness," and the "assertion of territorial (and cultural) autonomy" recognized as common elements of Indigeneity worldwide are cultivated not only in relation to the nation state, but also in relation to regional and local intergroup relations.[2] The deployment of digital media discussed here concerns local distribution, the construction of local collectivities and intergroup politics; a form of "strategic traditionalism," or perhaps, better, a "strategic blend of traditionalism and innovation" intended as an intervention in local rather than global discourses of identity.[3] As discussed by Hilder in the introduction to this volume, nuanced attention to creative practice in case studies such as this is needed for the development of broader insights into contemporary global articulations of Indigeneity, difference, and identity.

Originally established as Port Keats Roman Catholic mission in 1935, the present-day township of Wadeye lies about 250 kilometers southwest of Darwin. It is home to approximately 2500 people, mainly Aboriginal people descended from about twenty clans from the surrounding areas, whose members were originally attracted to the settlement by the availability of food, work, and schooling.[4] The township lies within the traditional estate of the Kardu Dimirnin clan, who continue to assert their special interest in the town and its surrounding areas. Their traditional language, Murriny Patha (also known as Murrinh-patha)[5] is now spoken as a lingua franca by young people of all clans.[6] With about 3000 speakers, Murriny Patha is one of the healthiest Indigenous languages in Australia, no doubt due to the relative isolation of the community: the single access road is cut by wet-season rains for about six months of each year.[7]

Despite the common spoken language, clan identity continues to be highly relevant at Wadeye, being taught and enacted in many dimensions of life in Wadeye, including the school, church, and community governance. The fundamentals of clan-based social organization in this area were described in the 1960s by W. E. H. Stanner and J. Falkenberg.[8] Clan organization predates the founding of the mission, was recognized in mission times (1935–74) and continues today.[9] People, totems, clans, languages, songs, and stories all spring from a common origin in the life force of the relevant country.[10] Each patrilineal exogamous clan has its own set of *ngakumarl* (totems) and *nguguminggi* (Dreaming sites), with associated stories and ceremonial obligations. This connection with the ancestral clan country and its associated language, totems, sites and stories is maintained irrespective of actual residence within the country of another clan (the Kardu Dimirnin clan).

For example, members of the Kungarlbarl clan identify with their ancestral language Marri Ngarr, their *ngakumarl* (totems)—including *ku karnarndurturt* (crocodile) and *nandji bamngutut* ("bottle tree," the boab tree, *Adansonia gregorii*)—and their *nguguminggi* (Dreaming sites) within the clan country—including the places Kungarlbarl, Arrntji, Numurli, Banagayi, Yeperrmi, Yeneri and others.[11] Members of the clan bear one of the four main patrilineal surnames, and each person in a clan bears a personal name of a clan site or totem.[12]

Since the 1970s, when the community became independent of the Roman Catholic mission, there have been many changes, including a population boom and the progressive modernization of the community's infrastructure.[13] As I discuss in more detail later, Indigenous ceremonial musical traditions have always had a key role in creating and channeling relationships between people of the area and outsiders. Although at various times the Church attempted to suppress ceremonial practices, during the 1970s and 1980s the development of syncretic forms was encouraged, including the creation of songs in Indigenous musical style for liturgical performance as well as hymns and other religious-themed songs in Murriny Patha language.[14]

Contact with modern guitar songs had begun in the 1950s, when many men from Wadeye (then Port Keats) worked on cattle stations to the east and south of Wadeye. Furlan reports that at first, sing-alongs accompanied by guitar were the main form of general contact with popular music, but as elsewhere in Australia, as soon as music technologies for accessing, recording, and broad-casting music became available, they were enthusiastically adopted. In the early 1970s, commercial cassette recordings of American popular music artists like Neil Diamond were beginning to become available, and Australian artists like the country singer Slim Dusty presented live concerts in the community. Local guitar bands like the Last Sunset Band and the Iddiyi Bush Band soon formed, initially performing covers in English of commercial songs, and later creating their own songs in Murriny Patha.[15] AM radio broadcasting began in the late 1970s, and then television in 1987 with the commissioning of the Aussat sat-ellite service, although there were many problems with communication net-works for accessing and relaying content. As in many other communities in Australia's Top End, funding to support production and broadcasting of locally recorded material alongside national content was made available through the government-funded Broadcasting for Remote Aboriginal Communities Scheme (BRACS).[16]

Over the years, BRACS has been just one of a number of sources of record-ings documenting the rich traditional cultural life of Wadeye and its various clans; other collections have been made by local educational and cultural bodies, church and government staff, cultural researchers and visitors. In col-laboration with three local institutions—the Wadeye Aboriginal Languages Centre (WALC), the Kanamkek Yile Ngala Museum, and the Wadeye Library and Knowledge Centre (WLKC)—our University of Sydney research team (Allan Marett, Michael Walsh, Joe Blythe, Nick Reid, and Lysbeth Ford with PhD student Alberto Furlan) completed a project to digitize and document all the song recordings held by WALC, and to make them available through a music database in the WLKC.[17] In addition to these recordings of traditional song (many created during previous research projects of our team members), the collection also includes numerous recordings of oral history and language materials; nontraditional song genres such as songs from various rock bands documented by University of Sydney postgraduate student Alberto Furlan in 2002–3; and recordings donated by locals of various church songs and hymns in Murriny Patha, some translated from English-language originals, others created during the 1970s and 1980s in the course of song writing workshops sponsored by the Summer Institute of Linguistics.[18]

Since the establishment of the WKLC database in 2003, almost all new additions have been "funeral songs," an emerging syncretic genre that draws on precedents from both traditional and nontraditional styles, including hymns and Western-influenced popular music. Indeed, according to staff at the Library and Knowledge Centre, the main use for the music database since 2003 has been to provide music for playing at funerals in the Catholic church, a function that was previously provided by live performance of one of the traditional song genres *djanba, wangga* and *lirrga* (these will be discussed in some detail later in the chapter). When a person dies, it is important that their spirit returns to their home site within clan country, so performance of clan-based songs is particularly important at this time. Recordings from the music database, selected to match the clan of the deceased, are burned to CD and played over the PA system of the church during the funeral. On occasion, new songs are also composed and recorded for later use at funerals, and added in turn to the music database.

Through detailed attention to one case study of songs created for a funeral in 2009, this chapter will address the modalities of production of these funeral song recordings, and how the adoption of new technologies for recording, editing, and tagging sound files supports various aspects of traditional social organization while creating new channels for social interaction and displacing old ones. I am particularly interested in the extent to which localized diversity of clan affiliation is played out in the composition, performance, content, and circulation of the songs.

To frame my understanding of the significance of these emerging musical practices, and bearing in mind that readers may have little previous acquaintance with social and musical institutions in this remote area of Australia, later in this chapter I will spend some time explaining the social history of music in the Wadeye area, and in particular the ways in which ceremonial performance has functioned to support different layers of individual and group identification within a complex social fabric. But let us first turn to the case study.

Some Funeral Songs Recorded in 2009

The case study concerns four funeral songs I recorded in 2009, at the request of the family of a young woman from the Kungarlbarl clan who had died some weeks earlier. On the day before the funeral was to be held, I was working on recordings of old *djanba* songs in the Kanamkek Yile Ngala Museum with the deceased woman's brother-in-law and elder sister, and they asked me to come down to their house later that day to record a Kungarlbarl song to be played at the funeral.

The first song was in fact recorded even before I reached my friends' house. Seeing me head out the door with my microphone and recorder, another family from the same Kungarlbarl clan as the deceased woman stopped me on the verandah of the Museum and begged me to record first the song they had composed in memory of the deceased. They pulled out a sheet of paper with the words written down on it, arranged an extension cord to plug into the electric keyboard they had brought with them, and sat down on the verandah with me to record the song. Two women, Kungarlbarl clan members, sang, while one of their husbands played the keyboard.

Example 7.1. Musical transcription of two verses of the Kungarlbarl song composed by MK, as performed by MK and CM, accompanied on electric piano by LD, at Wadeye, June 29, 2009. Recording and transcription by Linda Barwick.

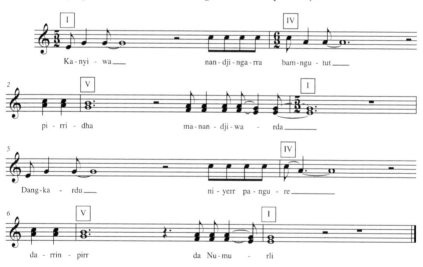

Kanyi-wa	This place
nandji ngarra bamngutut	Is where the bottle tree
pirridha	Once stood
manandji warda	Now it's gone

Dangkardu	Look
niyerr pangu-re	Look out over there
darrinpirr	On the floodplain
da Numurli	At Numurli[19]

Although the song was composed in Murriny Patha, the language of Wadeye itself, the Kungarlbarl clan's home country lies some distance to the north and east of Wadeye, on the floodplains of the Moyle River, and their traditional language is Marri Ngarr. The quoted part of the song features both the *bamngutut* (bottle tree), already mentioned as one of the important totems of the Kungarlbarl clan, and the important clan site named Numurli. (The song refers to a particular tree that used to stand at another clan site, but is no longer there.) As can be seen from the musical transcription of these two verses (ex. 7.1), the melody has a simple four-phrase structure, with use of harmony in thirds in the last half of each verse.[20]

Having completed this recording, I proceeded to my friends' house, where a group of family members, including four sisters of the deceased woman, their husbands, and some nieces and nephews, were waiting to record their own Kungarlbarl song, which had been composed by the sisters. Once again, a handwritten text and electronic piano were used to support the performance. Here is an extract from the second song recorded (translation by CLK, one of the composers):

Kanyi-wa	This one
da ngarra ngay-yu	Is my place
nandji ngarra bamngutut	Where the bottle tree
pirridha	Was standing up.
Manandji warda	It's not there any more
da ngarra ngay yu	At my place
da tjingarru	Oh my lovely place
da Arrntji	Arrntji [it's so beautiful].
Da tjingarru	Oh my lovely place
da darrinpirr	On the floodplain
da Numurli	That place is Numurli
da ngay-yu	That's my place.[21]

The similarities in wording and subject matter to the first song are obvious, though the tune is quite different (ex. 7.2).

A third song recorded from the same group had been composed by one of the sisters (CL) for her nephew. It mentioned similar Kungarlbarl places and totems, but specified in each verse that her nephew was singing for his mother's country. While one's primary affiliation is to the clan of one's father, rights and responsibilities are also inherited through one's mother, who in this case

Example 7.2. Musical transcription of two verses of the Kungarlbarl song composed by the deceased woman's sisters KL, PL, and CL, as performed at Wadeye, June 29, 2009. Recording and transcription by Linda Barwick. Also singing were family members RL, LP, LK, accompanied by JP playing electric piano. Transcription by Linda Barwick.

was a Kungarlbarl clan woman. In this way the songs prepared for the funeral acknowledged the relationship of relatives from both sides of the family.

We made several takes of some parts of the songs, and the next morning, before the funeral, I got together with my friends again, who directed some editing of the recording on my computer. Once satisfied, we burned the recordings to a CD, which was then given to the person in charge of the PA system at the church.

Family members, identified by t-shirts that had been screen-printed by the sisters with the image of the Kungarlbarl clan totem *ku kanandurturt* (crocodile) and the clan name Ma Thawurr (meaning "people of the tree" in Marri Ngarr language), were, as is usual in funerals at Wadeye, active participants in the service. Male relatives carried the coffin, covered with a large cloth bearing clan-specific designs, into the church at the beginning of the service, and at the end of the service carried it out again to the truck that would proceed at walking pace to the cemetery, followed by a procession of mourners. As has become the custom at funeral services in Wadeye, after the reading, family members took turns to approach the coffin, each bearing a plastic flower to leave on top of it (the flowers would eventually be replaced to ornament the grave). During these activities, and while the congregation lined up to take Holy Communion, the funeral songs recorded in advance were played. In addition to the three songs I had recorded, two other songs, composed and recorded by another relative on similar themes, were also played, one of which had been edited so that the recorded roar of the clan totem, the crocodile (the recording of which had been found in the music database), was mixed in as part of the song's introduction. Toward the end of the service, two hymns in Murriny Patha on conventional (non-clan-based) religious themes, were performed live.

The day after the funeral, I was approached by the deceased woman's brothers to record a fourth funeral song in her memory, even though the funeral was by now over. These men had not been able to participate in the original recording session because of the presence there of their sisters (a strong brother–sister avoidance is practiced at Wadeye). Brother–sister avoidance had also been evident in performance of the two song texts composed and performed by their sisters two days previously. On that previous occasion, whenever the song mentioned the name of a site that was also the given name of one of the brothers of the deceased woman, all the sisters omitted singing that word, and instead called on other relatives (nieces and nephews) to pronounce the name. Brother–sister avoidance was also practiced in the handling of the song recordings: when I subsequently prepared CDs of all the recordings for distribution to family members as keepsakes, I was asked to burn the song composed by the brothers onto separate CDs from those used for songs composed by the sisters, showing that the brother–sister avoidance continues into the digital realm. In the several years since this funeral, I have been contacted regularly to send additional copies of the CDs.[22]

In these funeral songs we can see a strong assertion of continuity with traditional clan-based social organization. Although composed to be heard as part of a church service, the songs make almost no mention of Christian themes; rather, they foreground the places and totems that signal traditional clan identity. Traditional modes of social organization and behavior (such as brother-sister avoidance, and acknowledgment of relationship to the clan country of one's mother) are also integrated into the performance and management of the recordings.

Nevertheless, there are also some quite striking divergences from traditional practice, and not just in musical style. The most important innovation is the creation and performance of songs by the same clan group as the deceased person. In ceremonial practice at Wadeye in at least the preceding forty years, this would never have happened. To explain why this innovation is so significant, we need to understand the history and function of the traditional tripartite ceremonial system.

The Tripartite Ceremonial System

As the Wadeye community grew in the 1950s and 1960s, a strategy was agreed upon among the elders of the various clans to increase social cohesion among disparate groups coming into the Mission. Following precedents and social structures that predated the Mission,[23] three mutually supporting "mobs" (groups) were formed from clans grouped by geography, language and culture.[24] Each mob within this tripartite ceremonial system created its own set of songs and dances, drawing on its ancestral stories concerning the important places and totems within the clan territory of the song composers. These ceremonial repertories were then adopted in a variety of public ceremonies, including rag-burning ceremonies for the disposal of the belongings of the deceased, funerals, and circumcision ceremonies, as well as more modern rites of passage such as openings of buildings, presentation of awards, and graduation ceremonies.[25]

Clans from the coastal areas to the north of Wadeye, who spoke a variety of different languages from the Marri language family (Marri Tjevin, Magatige, Marri Ammu, and Mendhe), were grouped into the Wangga mob, named after the traditional song styles that came from the northerly direction (around the mouth of the Daly river). The inland clans, speakers of Marri Ngarr, Ngen'giwumirri, Marrithiyel, and Ngan'gikurungurr, were grouped into the Lirrga mob, named after the traditional song styles of southwestern Arnhem Land (which lies in an easterly direction from Wadeye, near the present-day township of Katherine). The Murriny Patha-speaking clans in Wadeye and neighboring areas to the south were grouped into the Djanba mob, named after ceremonial styles from the Kimberley area far to the southwest of Wadeye.[26]

Three new repertories of song, all "in language," were composed in the period around 1960 when the tripartite ceremonial system was adopted (table 7.1).[27] For the Djanba mob, a newly-created repertory, also called *djanba*, was conceived by a Kardu Dimirnin man Robert Kolumboort, and later added to by, among others, his brothers Harry Luke Kolumboort and Lawrence Kolumboort, fellow Dimirnin clansman Joe Birrarri, and various members of the neighboring Yek Nangu clan including Johnny Ninnal. With few exceptions, *djanba* songs are in Murriny Patha language.[28] The *walakandha wangga*, named after the song-giving spirit beings that inhabit the country of the Marri Tjevin-speaking Nadirri and Perrederr clans (principal composers Nadirri clansmen Stan Mullumbuk, Thomas Kungiung, Les Kundjil and Philip Mullumbuk, with some songs from the neighboring Perrederr clan composer Wagon Dumoo) became the principal repertory for all Wangga mob clans.[29] For the Lirrga mob, the principal repertory performed at Wadeye became the *lirrga ma-muyil* in Marri Ngarr language (principal composers were the brothers Pius Luckan and Clement Tchinburrurr from the Marri Ngarr-speaking Wurdipuli or Rak Dirrangara clan).[30]

The mobs practiced a system of ceremonial reciprocity: each mob could be called upon to perform for one of the two other mobs, but as a rule would not

Table 7.1. Grouping of clans within the three mobs

Wangga mob	Lirrga mob	Djanba mob
Nadirri	**Wurdipuli**	**Dimirnin**
Perrederr	*Mardinga*	*Nangu*
Tjindi	Kungarlbarl	Maniny
Kuy	Kulinmirr	Kultjil
Yederr	Wakal Bengguny	Wakal Tjinang
Nganthawudi	Wuny	Kirnmu
Anggileni	Merrepen	

perform for the rites of passage of their own members. For example, the family of a Lirrga mob person could call upon either the Djanba mob or the Wangga mob to perform for the funeral or circumcision ceremony of their loved one. Thus, the songs and dances performed were not those of the ancestral country of the deceased person, but rather, came from the clan country of the leader of the ceremonial group performing. One reason for this is that the family of the focal person has other duties during the ceremony, and family members may also be too emotionally involved to perform during a funeral or rag-burning ceremony. This practice also functions to broaden the social networks of the clans, by strengthening bonds of mutual obligation.

Songs in each of these three main repertories shared certain features. As Marett has demonstrated, when sung in a rag-burning ceremony, these songs have the ability to draw the spirit of the deceased away from the everyday world and back to its home country, where it must join the company of the other ancestral dead. The songs were received in dream from ancestral song-giving spirits, and the texts often consisted of the utterances of these spirits.[31] Just as we saw in the funeral songs recorded in 2009, so, too, the traditional songs frequently name the key sites and totems of the clan of the composer and are full of expressions of longing for the home country.[32]

For example, one Marri Ngarr lirrga song (PL6)[33] composed by Pius Luckan contains the following text, which refers to the promontory Yenmura in Wurdipuli clan country:

wuyi ngina wuyi ngina	Our dear country, our dear country!
Yenmura Yenmura	Yenmura, Yenmura!
Wurdipuli Wurdipuli Wurdipuli	Wudipuli, Wudipuli, Wudipuli!
awu pulimi kumunnalderri kani	White eagle keeps swooping
Altjama Altjamaga	above the creek at Altjama

This song, in Marri Ngarr language, mentions the significant sites Yenmura and Altjama and the clan name (also a site) Wurdipuli, and refers to the activity there of the important clan totem *pulimi* (white-breasted sea eagle). In a parallel fashion, songs in the other two repertories include frequent references to the specific sites and totems of the clans of their own composers. Reflecting the common function of all three repertories—inducing the spirit of the deceased person to return to its home country—the songs frequently include expressions of homesickness or longing for home: in this song, the Marri Ngarr term *wuyi ngina* "my own dear country!" is used, but in *djanba*, the Murriny Patha cognate term *da tjingarru*[34] is used, and in *wangga*, the Marri Tjevin term *nidin ngina*.

It is important to note here that while the composer is usually the lead singer for the relevant mob, other members of the mob are active participants in the performance as dancers and secondary members of the musical ensemble (backup singers, and in the case of *wangga* and *lirrga*, didjeridu players). For mob members from clans other than those of the composer, the places, totems, and spirit beings celebrated in the songs are not their own. For example, members of the Kungarlbarl clan, who belong to the Lirrga mob, would dance to *lirrga* songs celebrating the Wurdipuli clan place Altjama and clan totem *pulimi* rather than their own clan places and totems, such as Kungarlbarl and *bamngutut*. Here we can observe a similar displacement to that we observed earlier, when *djanba* songs and dances celebrating Dimirnin clan sites, totems, and ancestors were performed to conduct the ghosts of the *lirrga*-owning deceased to their own clan country. In both cases, the clan sites and totems of the song composer stand in for those of the dancers and the group that commissioned the performance. The functional equivalence of the different clan groups is asserted, even while the particularity of each is celebrated.

Functional Innovation in the Funeral Songs

The situation with these new funeral songs is very different. The time displacement allowed by recording technology (a form of "schizophonia")[35] allows the family of the deceased to present their own songs and their own clan totems and places at the funeral. This would be impossible with live performance, not only because of the traditional reliance on the songs of another mob, but also because of the other duties that the family of the deceased have to perform in leading the mourning at the church service. New digital music technologies have allowed a fundamental shift in the musical practices around funerals at Wadeye, including the adoption of portable recorders to record new songs in advance of the funeral, the editing and production of CDs to use in the church or for distribution to family members, and the use of the computer database to search for previously recorded songs or sounds relating to the relevant clan to include in the mix.

Another notable innovation in the funeral songs is the prominence of women in composing and leading the singing of songs. In traditional *lirrga* and *wangga* performances, women never form part of the musical ensemble, though they may compose songs, which are then passed to their husbands or other kin to sing in ceremony, and they have a prominent role in the dancing. In *djanba* songs, the singing ensemble is normally led by men (though in the absence of male singers, senior women may take on this role), and the participation of a chorus of women is an integral part of the ensemble.[36] In newer Western-influenced song styles, there are clear gender differences according to music genre. Rock bands, especially heavy-metal bands, like the Nangu Band,[37] are made up almost exclusively of men, though there is at least one all-women group, the Emu Sisters, who compose and perform songs that are more pop-influenced.[38] Women are also prominent in the performance of hymns and church songs, both in Wadeye and elsewhere in Aboriginal Australia.[39]

The funeral songs, with their association with church music, and the use of soft pop style tunes and instrumentation, are clearly aligned with other modern genres dominated by women performers. Interestingly, in all the performances I recorded and observed, keyboards were played by men, with women (and some men) singing. In two cases at least, the keyboardists were the husbands of the women composers (and thus belonged to another clan). It is possible that this pattern reflects a reluctance of non-clan members to sing about Kungarlbarl totems and sites, but equally it may reflect local gender-specific musical practices, such as men-only use of didjeridu in ceremony.[40] Certainly the division of labor between the spouses mirrors a pattern common to the *djanba* and *wangga* traditions, where the wife of the song leader might be actively involved in supporting performances through composing songs, organizing the dancers, and (in the case of *djanba*) singing alongside her husband.

Producing the songs of one's own clan for these funeral ceremonies reduces reliance on other groups in the community, and arguably contributes to a weakening of the social networks of mutual obligation that the old tripartite ceremonial system had been designed to support. We have also seen how some new complications can arise through the practice of singing one's own clan songs, specifically in singing about sites that happen to be the name of an opposite-sex sibling. I have also observed the development of new practices around the recorded artefacts—the duplication of CDs as keepsakes for family members, and the addition of the recordings to the computer database. With live performances, such questions would rarely have arisen. Although live performances were frequently recorded and archived in the community's cultural collections, their efficacy and power lay in the moment of the ceremonial performance.

Repeated requests I have received to send copies of the recordings indicate that the traditional function of the funeral and postfuneral ceremonies like the now-waning practice of rag-burning—to allow the spirit of the deceased person to return to their ancestral country, and to free the family from grief—may be changing. Further unequivocal evidence of the transfer of focus from the ceremonial event itself to the recorded artefacts can be found in the request by the brothers of the deceased to record their own song in memory of their sister several days after the funeral itself. It is also likely that the recordings are being reused in funerals as other members of the clan pass away.

It seems, too, that recordings are being used as a resource for the composition of new songs. When working in the library to help maintain the music database, on several occasions I observed a noticeable increase in use of the database in the days before a funeral. Relatives come to listen to songs there, but mainly to get new copies of songs to take away. The database workstation provides a way for people to find and access appropriate songs independently for private study, providing musical and textual models and ideas to be reused in new songs. Once again, we may contrast this practice with the traditional public, embodied modes of learning songs through witnessing and dancing to live performance.

Among many other songs, the music database holds a number of recordings of songs by local Wadeye band formed in the 1980s named "Hot Wheels," which included a number of Kungarlbarl clan members. One of the songs in the computer database is their song "Kardu Thay," composed by Desmond Longmair and George Cumaiyi in about 1986, set to a tune based on the ABBA song "I have a dream."[41]

Even though the tune, musical setting, and genre of "Kardu Thay" are quite different from the Kungarlbarl funeral songs I recorded some twenty-three years later in 2009, parallels with the texts quoted above are clear, celebrating the same sites and totems, and even using the same turns of phrase (e.g., *niyerr pangu-re* "look over there," found in ex. 7.1). It seems quite likely that renewed circulation of this song and other pop-influenced band songs of the 1980s and 1990s (due to Alberto Furlan's digitization of the recordings in 2002–3 as part of his doctoral research, and subsequent placement in the music database) could have had an effect on the increasing activity in creating and performing funeral songs in the mid-to-late 2000s. More specifically, if the Kungarlbarl funeral songs I recorded in 2009 had indeed been directly influenced by Hot Wheels band songs accessed via the database, we could see this, too, as a continuation of traditional practices, since the repetition, borrowing or recasting of textual formulae from the cultural creations of previous generations has been an integral and highly valued part of the composition process. We might remember in this respect that new traditional songs are received via witnessing in dream the performances of ancestral ghosts.

Although in the case study reported here, members of the deceased's own family created the songs, it seems that there may be an emerging demand for specialist music production services to create clan songs for funerals in Wadeye. In 2010 I was told that nowadays the main activity of the Emu Sisters lies in composing and recording songs for funerals. Even though most of the women in this group belong to the Wurdipuli clan (part of the Lirrga mob, see table 7.1 above), they have composed songs on commission for various other clans to use in funerals, incorporating the names of the relevant totems and sites for the commissioning family. It may be no coincidence that several members of the Emu Sisters work in the Library and Knowledge Centre, with access to the music database as well as to other staff with expertise in musical instruments, digital recorders, digital sound-editing facilities, and the means to reproduce and distribute the CDs.

In contrast to the traditional songs, which required no technological infrastructure other than the ability to source or manufacture wooden instruments (clapsticks and didjeridu), the funeral songs as currently practiced at Wadeye have multiple dependencies: electricity; programmable electric pianos; recording, editing and playback equipment; the expertise to use a computer database to select CDs; the media (CD, DVD) and devices for playback (mp3 player, or since 2009, mobile phone)—the list goes on. Many homes in Wadeye lack the facilities to keep equipment or even a CD collection safe from dust, heat, humidity, and children. Consequently, most people rely on the community's cultural institutions (the library, museum, church, youth center and school) to house and maintain instruments, recording equipment, computer facilities, and so on. This institutional environment therefore provides the essential infrastructure enabling the production and development of funeral songs, and those clans that have better access to the institutions are in a better position to produce this repertoire. In a sense, the music technology infrastructure of these institutions has been hijacked, or diverted, from its ostensible purpose (education, training, collection maintenance) by the composers and performers of funeral songs.

Conclusion

In this chapter I have outlined some of the ways in which the practices of composition, performance, use, and dissemination of funeral songs have led to a loosening of social ties between mobs (through replacement of the inter-mob reciprocity of the tripartite ceremonial system), and even to loosening dependency on other clans within one's own mob (who formerly were needed to sing on behalf of your own clan). Music technologies have allowed a democratization of the means of making music, even a dispersal of the original social power and authority of the mob system, and possibly, a deprofessionalization of music making within the community.[42] At the same time the funeral songs contribute to a strengthening of family and internal clan networks, and to a strengthening of relationships with institutions and outsiders who control the means of production of the songs.

It is difficult to separate out the complex chains of causality that have inter-acted to produce the present situation. On the one hand, we can see these technologies as having fostered preexisting tendencies to clan autonomy through the time shift that enables clans now to produce their own music for funerals; on the other, we might blame these technologies for having destabi-lized or disrupted the precarious balance between clans established through live performance and the mutual dependencies of the tripartite ceremonial system. Have these music technologies been hijacked by the people of Wadeye to suit their own ends, or have they seduced the people of Wadeye into an unsustainable dependence on consumer goods and outsiders? Music technol-ogy is presently one of the many social means by which the tensions between autonomy and interdependence continue to play out in Wadeye.

Notes

1. My first thanks go to the Longmair and Kolumboort families, who invited me to participate in their funeral preparations. Mark Crocombe, Bernardine Kungul and other staff at the Wadeye Library and Knowledge Centre and the Kanamkek Yile Ngala Museum have been unfailingly helpful and provided me with much practical and personal support at Wadeye over the years. I also wish to thank Allan Marett, Michael Walsh, Joe Blythe, Lysbeth Ford, Nick Reid, and Alberto Furlan for their company and intellectual stimulation in the course of our project, and for assistance in translation of song texts, and the staff of Pacific and Regional Archive for Indigenous Sources in Endangered Cultures at the University of Sydney, especially Amanda Harris and Aidan Wilson, for technical and editorial support. The research was funded by the Australian Research Council grant DP0450131 "Preserving Australia's Endangered Heritages: Murrinhpatha Song at Wadeye."

    For information on *djanba*, see the Wadeye Song Database: Linda Barwick et al., "Wadeye Song Database" (University of Sydney, 2010). For information on the project, see Linda Barwick et al., "Murriny Patha Song Project Website," University of Sydney, accessed September 2, 3016, http://azoulay.arts.usyd.edu.au/mpsong/.

2. Pamela Wilson and Michelle Stewart, "Indigeneity and Indigenous Media on the Global Stage," in *Global Indigenous Media: Cultures, Poetics, and Politics*, ed. Pamela Wilson and Michelle Stewart (Durham, NC: Duke University Press, 2008): 12, 14.

3. Faye Ginsburg, "Rethinking the Digital Age," in *Global Indigenous Media: Cultures, Poetics, and Politics,* ed. Pamela Wilson and Michelle Stewart (Durham, NC: Duke University Press, 2008): 289–93; see also Tony Bennett and Valda Blundell, "First Peoples," *Cultural Studies* 9, no. 1 (1995): 5; Wilson and Stewart, "Indigeneity and Indigenous Media on the Global Stage," 31.

4. John Taylor, "Demography of the Thamarrurr Region," ed. John Taylor, *Social Indicators for Aboriginal Governance: Insights from the Thamarrurr Region, Northern Territory* (Canberra: ANU E-Press, 2004), http://press.anu.edu.au/publications/series/centre-aboriginal-economic-policy-research-caepr/social-indicators-aboriginal.

5. There are two different orthographies of the language in use. This paper adopts the orthography developed by Joe Blythe for our project. For full details, see Joe Blythe, "Orthography Adopted by the Murriny Patha Song Project," *Project Orthography,* Australian Research Council Discovery Project DP0450131 2004-8, 2006, http://azoulay.arts.usyd.edu.au/mpsong/language/language/orthography.html.

6. Lysbeth Ford, Aloysius Kungul, and Judith Jongmin, "A Sociolinguistic Survey of Wadeye: Linguistic Behaviour of the Marri Ngarr, Magati Ke, Marri Amu and Marri Tjebin" (paper presented at the Top End Linguistic Society meeting, Darwin, 2000). See also Michael Walsh, "The Murinypata Language of North-West Australia" (PhD diss., Australian National University, 1976); Chester Street, *An Introduction to the Language and Culture of the Murrinh-Patha* (Darwin, NT: Summer Institute of Linguistics, Australian Aborigines Branch, 1987).

7. Australian Institute of Aboriginal and Torres Strait Islander Studies (AIATSIS) and Federation of Aboriginal and Torres Strait Islander Languages (FATSIL), *National Indigenous Languages Survey Report 2005* (Canberra: Department of Communications, Information Technology and the Arts, 2005).

8. William E. H. Stanner, *On Aboriginal Religion,* Oceania Monograph 11 (Sydney, NSW: University of Sydney, 1963, 1989); see also Johannes Falkenberg, *Kin and Totem: Group Relations of Australian Aborigines in the Port Keats District* (Oslo: Oslo University Press, 1962); Theresa Ward, *The Peoples and Their Land around Wadeye: Murrinh Kanhi-Ka Kardu I Da Ngarra Putek Pigunu* (Port Keats, NT: Wadeye Press, 1983); R. John Pye, *The Port Keats Story* (Darwin, NT: J. R. Coleman, 1980).

9. New governance structures introduced in 2003 (Thamarrurr Regional Council) had clan-based representation, but were replaced in the NT Intervention in 2009. See Tobias Nganbe and Dominic McCormack, "Education in Wadeye and the Thamarrurr Region: Challenges and Responsibilities across the Generations," Bowden McCormack Lawyers and Advisers, September 2009, http://www.bowden-mccormack.com.au/WebsiteContent/articles-papers/education-wadeye.pdf; Alberto Furlan, "Songs of Continuity and Change: The Reproduction of Aboriginal Culture through Traditional and Popular Music" (PhD diss., University of Sydney, 2005); Bill Ivory, "*Kunmanggur,* Legend and Leadership: A Study of Indigenous Leadership and Succession Focussing on the Northwest Region of the Northern Territory of Australia" (PhD diss., Charles Darwin

University, 2009), https://espace.cdu.edu.au/eserv/cdu:13227/Thesis_CDU_13227_Ivory_B.pdf.

10. Allan Marett et al., "The National Recording Project for Indigenous Performance in Australia: Year One in Review," in *Backing Our Creativity: The National Education and the Arts Symposium,* September 12–14, 2005 (Surry Hills, NSW: Australia Council for the Arts, 2006).

11. The clan is also known as "Kardu wakal thay" or "Ma thawurr." *Kardu wakal thay* means "descendants of the tree" in Murriny Patha, the language spoken by all clan members now; *ma thawurr* is the cognate term (literally, "people of the tree") in Marri Ngarr, the ancestral language of the clan, which is now known by only a few elderly members of the clan. See Ward, *The Peoples and Their Land around Wadeye.*

12. Baptismal names are used for government records, and are the names used here, because the clan names are more private in nature.

13. Reasons behind these changes and some practical consequences for community governance and education are discussed in Furlan, "Songs of Continuity and Change"; John Taylor, *Demography as Destiny: Schooling, Work and Aboriginal Population Change at Wadeye,* Caepr Working Paper no. 64 (2010) (Canberra: Australian National University Centre for Aboriginal Economic Policy Research, 2010); Ivory, "Indigenous Community Governance Project."

14. Linda Barwick, "Tempo Bands, Metre and Rhythmic Mode in Marri Ngarr 'Church Lirrga' Songs," *Australasian Music Research* 7(2003): 67–83.

15. For a history of contact with popular music and the formation and evolution of guitar bands in Wadeye, see Furlan, "Songs of Continuity and Change," 216–20. In the early-to-mid 1970s, the lay missionary Lesley Reilly (née Rourke) made recordings of many of these groups, which in later years she was often asked to copy and circulate to family members (personal communication to Linda Barwick, 2003). Her collection is now deposited with the Australian Institute of Aboriginal and Torres Strait Islander Studies (collection REILLY_L01) and the digitized song files are also held in the database of the Wadeye Library and Knowledge Centre.

16. Helen Molnar, "The Broadcasting for Remote Areas Community Scheme: Small vs. Big Media," *Media Information Australia,* no. 58 (1990): 147–54.

17. Linda Barwick et al., "Communities of Interest: Issues in Establishing a Digital Resource on Murrinh-Patha Song at Wadeye (Port Keats), NT," *Literary and Linguistic Computing* 20, no. 4 (2005): 383–97.

18. Furlan recounts that formal song writing workshops for the creation of religious songs in Murriny Patha were organized by missionary linguists Chester Street and Lynette Street in Darwin, and that later secular songs on "cultural" themes were composed on the same principles. Furlan, "Songs of Continuity and Change," 219–20.

19. The text is based on a handwritten original used in the performance, written in Murriny Patha by MK, which I was invited to photograph to keep alongside the recording, and has been transliterated into the orthography used by the Murriny Patha song project. The translation is my own. Reproduced with permission.

20. The musical style of the song, including the use of the electric piano, resembles some of the Murriny Patha hymns composed in the 1970s and 1980s, which are still performed in the church at Wadeye. See *Nhinhi Pekpeknhingka* and other recordings by Chester and Lynne Street with the Wadeye Choir. Chester Street and Lynette Street, *Nhinhi Pekpeknhingka* (Seven Hills, NSW: Global Recordings Network, 1983), cassette recording, also available online.

21. Reproduced with permission.

22. This happens even though the songs are available within the community through the music database in the town library. Asking me to provide them acknowledges my role and relationship with the family.

23. For the traditional trade routes of the *mayern kulu* and the *mayern mandjigat*, see Falkenberg, *Kin and Totem*, 23.

24. Furlan, "Songs of Continuity and Change," 132; see also Allan Marett, Linda Barwick, and Lysbeth Ford, *For the Sake of a Song: Wangga Songmen and Their Repertories* (Sydney: Sydney University Press, 2013), 38; Allan Marett, *Songs, Dreamings and Ghosts: The Wangga of North Australia* (Middletown, CT: Wesleyan University Press, 2005), 24, 59; Barwick, "Tempo Bands, Metre and Rhythmic Mode," 68.

25. For extensive discussion of the ceremonial occasions and social functions of *wangga* and other repertories in the Daly region, see Marett, *Songs, Dreamings and Ghosts*; Marett, Barwick, and Ford, *For the Sake of a Song*, chapter 1. For discussion of the extraregional links of these repertories, see Linda Barwick, "Musical Form and Style in Murriny Patha Djanba Songs at Wadeye (Northwest Australia)," in *Analytical and Cross-Cultural Studies in World Music*, ed. Michael Tenzer and John Roeder (Oxford: Oxford University Press, 2011), 316–54.

26. The song-giving spirits of Kardu Dimirnin country are also called *djanba*, and are frequently mentioned in *djanba* song texts. It seems likely that this name for the song-giving ancestral spirits is relatively recently coined, however, since it was not documented by Falkenberg, whose fieldwork was carried out in the early 1950s, before the creation of the tripartite ceremonial system.

27. "In language" means "in the everyday spoken languages of the composers," rather than in the unintelligible spirit languages that were formerly in common use for *wangga* and other song repertories in this area. The creation of songs in comprehensible language was a major innovation that had far-reaching consequences. See Marett, *Songs, Dreamings and Ghosts*. See also Linda Barwick et al., "Arriving, Digging, Performing, Returning: An Exercise in Rich Interpretation of a *Djanba* Song Text in the Sound Archive of the Wadeye Knowledge Centre, Northern Territory of Australia," in *Oceanic Music Encounters: The Print Resource and the Human Resource; Essays in Honour of Mervyn Mclean*, ed. Richard M. Moyle (Auckland: University of Auckland, 2007), 13–24; Michael Walsh, "A Polytropical Approach to the 'Floating Pelican' Song: An Exercise in Rich Interpretation of a Murriny Patha (Northern Australia) Song," *Australian Journal of Linguistics* 30, no. 1 (2010): 117–30.

28. Two other public dance-song genres belonging to Yek Nangu and Kardu Dimirnin people (*malgarrin*, composed by Kardu Dimirnin clansman

Mulindjin; and *wurltjirri*, composed by Nangu clansman Tchimararr) were also performed on ceremonial occasions by the Djanba mob.

29. Wagon Dumoo was a member of the neighboring Marri Tjevin-speaking Perrederr clan. Another rarely performed repertory for the Wangga mob was the *Ma-yawa wangga* (named after the song-giving spirit beings of the Marri Ammu-speaking Rak Tjindi clan (principal composers Charlie Brinken and Maurice Tjakurl Ngulkur).

30. Two other *lirrga* repertories were held by composers resident some distance away at Nauiyu Nambiyu community at Daly River. One, also in Marri Ngarr language, was composed by Jimmy Nambatu (Rak Mardinga clan), while the other repertory, composed by Ngen'giwumirri clansman Long Harry Kilimirri, comprised songs mainly in untranslatable spirit language, some modeled on Western Arnhem Land kun-borrk songs from the *Midjdjarn, Diyama* and *Karrbarda* song sets encountered by the composer while working in Western Arnhem Land. See Lysbeth Ford, "Marri Ngarr Lirrga Songs: A Linguistic Analysis," *Musicology Australia* 28 (2005–6), 26–58; Linda Barwick, "Marri Ngarr Lirrga Songs: A Musicological Analysis of Song Pairs in Performance," *Musicology Australia* 28 (2005–6), 1–25.

31. Allan Marett, "Ghostly Voices: Some Observations on Song-Creation, Ceremony and Being in Northwest Australia," *Oceania* 71, no. 1 (2000): 18–29.

32. Barwick et al., "Arriving, Digging, Performing, Returning," 16; Walsh, "A Polytropical Approach," 120–22.

33. Text transcription and glossing by Lysbeth Ford. See Ford, "Marri Ngarr Lirrga Songs," 39.

34. In the second Kungarlbarl funeral song cited above, the Murriny Patha term *da tjingarru* is used, translated by Colleen Longmair as "my country is a beautiful place."

35. Steven Feld, "From Schizophonia to Schismogenesis: On the Discourses and Commodification Practices of 'World Music' and 'World Beat,'" in *Music Grooves*, ed. Charles Keil and Steven Feld (Chicago: University of Chicago Press, 1994), 258–59. Originally coined by Murray Schafer, the word *schizophonia* indicates the "split between an original sound and its electroacoustical transmission or reproduction" (R. Murray Schafer, *The Tuning of the World* [New York: Alfred K. Knopf, 1977], 90). The time displacement to which I refer here is but one inevitable consequence of the "acoustic dislocations and respatializations" of "sounds split from sources" explored by Feld.

36. Barwick, "Musical Form and Style in Murriny Patha Djanba Songs," 330.

37. Nangu Band, *Red Sunset* (Alice Springs, NT: Central Australian Aboriginal Media Association, 1998), Audio compact disc, CAAMAnangu.

38. Although they have no commercially available recordings, the Emu Sisters, like many other local Wadeye bands, have recorded many songs for local distribution through the database at the Library and Knowledge Centre.

39. Fiona Magowan, "Shadows of Song: Exploring Research and Performance Strategies in Yolngu Women's Crying-Songs," *Oceania* 72(2001): 89–104; Diane Austin-Broos, "Whose Ethics? Which Cultural Contract? Imagining Arrernte Traditions Today," *Oceania* 71 (2000): 189–200; Muriel Swijghuisen

Reigersberg, "Applied Ethnomusicology, Music Therapy and Ethnographically Informed Choral Education: The Merging of Disciplines during a Case Study in Hopevale, Northern Queensland," in *Applied Ethnomusicology: Historical and Contemporary Approaches*, ed. Klisala Harrison, Elizabeth Mackinlay, and Svanibor Pettan (Newcastle upon Tyne: Cambridge Scholars, 2010), 51–75.

40. Linda Barwick, "Gender 'Taboos' and Didjeridus," in *The Didjeridu: From Arnhem Land to Internet*, ed. Karl Neuenfeldt (Sydney, NSW: John Libbey in association with Perfect Beat Publications, 1996), 89–98.

41. For the full text of the song, see Furlan, "Songs of Continuity and Change," 388, "Hot Wheels Band 02."

42. As noted by Furlan, since the 1980s, young people's social groups at Wadeye have come to be organized around affiliation to bands ("Songs of Continuity and Change," 221). The interrelationships between these groupings and the ceremonial mob system outlined in this chapter is far too complex to address here, but interested readers are directed to the research of John Mansfield, "The Social Organisation of Wadeye's Heavy Metal Mobs," *Australian Journal of Anthropology* 24, no. 2 (2013): 148–65.

Chapter Eight

The Politics of Virtuality

Sámi Cultural Simulation through Digital Musical Media

Thomas R. Hilder

The virtual is something that is almost, but not quite, "real," as Rob Shields writes in his study of virtuality.[1] Etymologically related to the term *virtue*, he elucidates, it has in various cultural and historical contexts been linked to dreams, rituals, and the visual arts. In the digital era, virtuality has come to be associated almost exclusively with online communities and simulating technologies. Today, virtuality is often considered negatively, as a form of escapism that deceives and deludes, amplified by a larger trope of the apparent alienating, antihuman, dystopian facets of technology.[2] This sentiment has most famously been articulated by Jean Baudrillard, who writes in *Simulacra and Simulation* that we have entered the age of "simulacra," a "hyperreal order" in which the perceived world is simply a vast assemblage of simulations that obscure deeper political and social realities.[3] However, contemporary anxieties about simulation are part of a longer history of a disdain for the "virtual," fueled by the legacy of Enlightenment thought, colonial practice, and nineteenth-century empiricism, fixated on the observable, tangible, and measurable world.[4]

Baudrillard's theory itself rests upon a problematic notion of Indigenous people as passive victims of a world obsessed with the authentic and "real" and denies the possibility of Indigenous people adopting media technologies for their own cultural and political purposes.[5] Moreover, it overlooks how notions of realms beyond the visible human world are common within many cultures, including numerous Indigenous cosmologies.[6] Following the literature of virtuality,[7] this chapter takes issue with Baudrillard's *Simulacra and Simulation* by exploring how digitally assisted cultural simulation can enable powerful means of Indigenous cultural revival, musical transmission, and political articulation. I focus on the Sámi, the Indigenous people of Northern Europe, and investigate how digital technology—in museums, educational software, and CD production—has become part of the complex and dynamic fabric of Indigenous cultures, in turn transforming notions of Indigenous subjectivity, cultural belonging, and political activism. In particular, I inspect how digital cultural simulation can help to revive a Sámi Indigenous cosmology, within which the human world exists alongside the realms of the spirits and the dead. How do Indigenous artists and activists resist notions of a world subsumed by the "hyperreal order"? In what ways are Indigenous traditions and digital media complementary and mutually constitutive, capable of transforming notions of human embodiment, imagination, and cultural signification? How might digital Indigenous music point beyond hegemonic understandings of the "real" and "virtual"?

At its core, my chapter highlights the importance of virtual worlds and the contemporary technologies that help make them perceivable as a fundamental and powerful element in Indigenous expressive culture, in what I term the *politics of the virtual*. In particular, I draw on Michelle Raheja's notion of the "virtual reservation" in her book *Reservation Reelism: Redfacing, Visual Sovereignty, and Representations of Native Americans,* a notion that denotes the creative space forged by Native American filmmaking for resisting cultural erasure, asserting Indigenous agency, and articulating alternative concepts of time, space and spirituality.[8] Critical of "technological dystopianism" but wary of adopting a narrative of "technological utopianism," my chapter seeks a more nuanced account of different ways of understanding digital media and thus revealing alternative modes of experiencing and living in global modernity.

Media have long provided a tool for political disempowerment of the Sámi by the emerging Nordic states, from the dissemination of the Bible in the seventeenth century to the emergence of national Nordic broadcasting corporations in the twentieth century. At the same time, transcriptions of oral traditions from the seventeenth century, ethnographic writing from the nineteenth century, and technologies of sound recording from the early twentieth century have served the means of cultural activists, folklorists, and linguists (both Sámi and non-Sámi) in their attempt to preserve what they perceived as a threatened culture.[9] Writing and printing also became tools with which Sámi activists in the early twentieth century could express and disseminate their political beliefs.[10] In the post–World War II era, state modernization and welfare provisions, which aimed to homogenize national communities, enabled a wider Nordic public to access and utilize media for their own cultural mobilization.[11]

Sámi language programs on the Norwegian national broadcasting corporation, NRK (Norsk Rikskringkasting) which began in 1946, developed into the transnational institution NRK Sápmi that today offers news readings, cultural programs, and children's entertainment on radio, television, and the Internet.[12] In the 1970s, several Sámi language newspapers were established in Norway along with book publishers that focused on Sámi language literature.[13] Meanwhile, a Sámi music industry emerged in the mid-1980s with the establishment of two record labels, DAT and Iđut, which aimed to support Sámi musicians.[14] These institutions have played a key role in wider Sámi political resistance and cultural revival over the last forty years.[15] In this way, the technologies of modernity, which had served to disempower minority populations, became the very tools that enabled Indigenous mobilizations and the building of a transnational Sámi community, Sápmi, across Norway, Sweden, Finland, and the Russian Kola Peninsula.[16] The rapid arrival and transformations of digital media technologies has impacted Sámi society by transforming cultural memory, notions of Indigenous subjectivity, and processes of self-determination, as well as by offering new opportunities for musical creativity, distribution, and education. As folklorist Coppélie Cocq has argued, Sámi digital platforms offer significant sites for cultural revitalization and new opportunities for the transmission of oral traditions.[17] Living in the rich and welfare-generous Nordic states where there is great access to digital media and playing a significant role in the global Indigenous movement, the Sámi thus provide an important case for exploring digital Indigeneity.

Sámi musical performance has been a way of engendering notions of pan-Sámi-ness, and its revival from the late 1960s has itself been assisted by musical media.[18] While a variety of musical traditions have been practiced by Sámi communities, it was *joik*, a distinct unaccompanied vocal tradition formerly linked to shamanic rituals, that became central to the Sámi musical revival. Owing to its ability to engender belonging within a Sámi community, its former suppression through Christianization and assimilation, and its uniqueness within Nordic expressive culture, *joik* became a powerful way of resisting state oppression, articulating Sámi identity, and reviving Sámi languages and Indigenous cosmologies.[19] *Joikers* and musicians began to experiment by incorporating *joik* into popular music forms, adding instrumental accompaniment, performing on stage, and releasing recordings. Alongside musical festivals, education projects, and funding programs, media institutions (such as Sámi record labels, NRK Sápmi, and more recently the Internet) have supported the emergence of a lively and diverse Sámi music scene. A Sámi musical revival became a way of drawing on the past to shape the present, and tradition and technology were engaged in a dynamic interplay, whereby tradition was both restored and transformed.[20] Today, Sámi musical performance encompasses "traditional" and "modern" *joik*, pop, techno, jazz, heavy metal, rap, and classical music that in some way incorporates a Sámi language or deals with Sámi themes. Not only has the music of the Sámi revival, like the wider Sámi mobilization, often relied heavily on the technologies of modernity; there is also a strong predilection for and experimental use of music technologies within Sámi musical performance and CD production.[21] As I shall argue, the employment, exploitation, and foregrounding of the possibilities of digital musical media has not only transformed Sámi musical performance; it has also opened up many creative opportunities for articulations of Sámi Indigeneity.

In this chapter, I focus on the opportunities afforded by digital technologies to simulate and thereby strengthen Sámi cultural revival by analyzing the digital mediascapes of Sámi Indigeneity and drawing on offline as well as online ethnographic research. In the first section, I introduce Sápmi Park and trace a history of the practices of exhibiting Sámi culture through the medium of the museum. Here, I discuss discourses of simulation and simulacra in postmodern theory and ideas of the "world as exhibition" in postcolonial studies. In the second section, I focus on the software program *Juoiggas!* by the Sámi *joiker* and producer Johan Sara Jr., and analyze the potential of digital media to simulate Sámi culture in order to nurture forms of cultural transmission, building on notions of digital orality in Sámi online contexts as explored by Cocq. In the final section, I focus on the album *Sacred Stone* by the Sámi group Vajas, looking at ways in which music production can simulate aspects of a Sámi environment and cosmology. Here, I introduce more recent debates concerning the "virtual" and Donna Haraway's notion of the "cyborg" to question the binaries *humans/technology, virtual/reality*.[22] I conclude by discussing both a Sámi Indigenous cosmology, within which there is a fluid relationship between the material world and realms of the spirits and the dead, and ontologies of *joik*, which seem to contradict the subject-object distinction within semiotic theory, upon which ideas of simulation are based.[23] Highlighting the ways in which technologies have become embedded within, and in turn transform traditional practice, I argue that simulations through Sámi musical performance can offer interesting perspectives on articulations of Indigeneity in digital modernities.

While issues of music and virtuality have received increased attention, my chapter addresses more closely debates in Indigenous studies and media theory.[24] In *Manifest Manners: Postindian Warriors of Survivance*, literary scholar Gerald Vizenor discussed simulation in Indigenous contexts.[25] Drawing on Baudrillard, he argued that cultural representations of Native Americans, embodied in the figure of the "Indian," marked "the absence of the real tribes" and formed part of a "literature of dominance" that erases Native Americans in the popular imagination; but he also posited the "postindian"—the contemporary Native American artist, activist or academic who articulates Indigenous "survivance" and "resistance" through alternative cultural media, orality and performance.[26] Drawing on Vizenor, Raheja argues that Native American filmmaking is like a "virtual reservation," "a field onto which an alternative vision of the world can be projected; as a meeting space for tribal intellectuals and scholars to workshop, debate, and define new projects for sustaining Indigenous knowledges; and as a network of computer-assisted transnational Indigenous communities who exchange and create information."[27] Within the field of virtuality studies, Shields writes, "digital virtualities offer themselves as *deterritorialized* spaces of escape from norms" that provide "a haven for those who are otherwise labelled deviant or who feel the restriction of social and moral discipline too strongly."[28] Virtual reality, he continues, "is a training ground not only in particular ways of seeing but in ways of imagining fictional, distant and alternative realities."[29] Likewise, the anthropologist Tom Boellstorff, drawing on his ethnographic fieldwork in Second Life, posits, "in virtual worlds we can be virtually human, because in them humans . . . discover new possibilities for human being."[30] These perspectives highlight the potential for technologies of virtuality for Indigenous resistance to global modernities, reviving Indigenous cosmologies, and for proposing alternative ways of being human in a digital age.

The "World as Simulation": Exhibiting Sámi Culture

Sápmi Park is located in Norway's Sámi administrative capital, Karasjok, in the county of Finnmark. Drawing on and challenging classic representations of "Sámi-ness," Sápmi Park offers an entertaining and interactive introduction to Sámi culture by Sámi for international visitors to the Norwegian Arctic tundra.[31] One part of the park is an outdoor exhibition of Sámi tents (*lávvu*) and turf huts (*guohti*) where Sámi dressed in traditional costumes (*gákti*) teach visitors how to throw a lasso over reindeer antlers, recount traditional stories, and perform *joiks* over cups of freshly boiled coffee. A *lávvu*-shaped main building houses the rest of the park's attractions: an exhibition of contemporary Sámi art; a souvenir shop with an on-site silversmith; and the Karasjok tourist information office. The highlight of the park is the multimedia and multisensorial exhibition, Sápmi Magic Theatre, in a small auditorium located at the end of a corridor.[32] Here, visitors are treated to a three-dimensional presentation, *Stalubákti* (Mountain of the spirits), accompanied by a Sámi *noaidi*, or shaman, whose face is seen as an apparition through a fireplace simulated before them. Above a drum that sounds like a heartbeat, a drone, and a chorus of *joiks*, he recounts a story of another side of Sápmi "that you can only see with your heart."[33] The presentation is a simulation of the myth of creation and the realms of the human, dead, and spirits, according to a Sámi cosmology, as collected from oral sources by the exhibition's main producer, the Swedish Sámi artist Åsa Simma.[34] The beating drum is revealed to be the sound of a

reindeer's heart buried in the ground at the beginning of time to provide sus-
tainance to the earth. Further *joiking* heralds an introduction to the Sámi oral
tradition of *joik*. The Sámi "songs of life," he explains, are like "magical books,"
some of which express different emotions and are comparable to images of
humans and animals, while others allow you to travel into the landscape and
dreams. As the fire fades, the audience is asked about the possibility of life
after death. Rising vocal lines depict the Northern Lights, the ancestors, who
dance on the ceiling above the audience. The presentation concludes with the
drum rhythm once again, the heartbeat in the earth which, we are told, will
offer guidance in times of need. As a simulation of Sámi culture, Sápmi Park
provides my own point of departure for discussing Sámi virtuality.

The digital exhibition—employing strategies of representation, simulation,
and multisensorial immersion common in digital virtuality—invites an analysis
within a longer history of modes of representation and simulation in Sámi and
wider (post)colonial contexts.[35] In *Colonising Egypt*, Timothy Mitchell provides
a compelling argument, drawing on Said (*Orientalism*) and Heidegger ("The
Age of the World View") about the ways in which imperial discourses and practices were characterized by a particular notion of what he terms the "world-
as-exhibition."[36] Tracing the growing number of attempts to recreate the
"Orient" through exhibitions since the nineteenth century, Mitchell proposes
that the striving for verisimilitude in exhibits was central in the construction of
the modern detached subject, the rendering of the world as a constellation of
objects, which in turn gave the semblance of an external reality—society, culture, and political order. Just as the very simulation of reality within the exhibition often left visitors with confusion about what was representation and what
was reality, Europeans who traveled to the Middle East experienced reality as
though it were an exhibition, set up to index a larger if unobtainable truth.[37]
From Mitchell's texts, we thus learn how, through imperial practices such as
exhibitions, a gap was created in the eyes of the modern subject between the
signifier and signified, the object world and some external reality, and thus
how the lived-in world seemed to adopt the appearance of a mere simulation.[38] While Mitchell bases his study on particular cases from the Middle East
and North Africa, his theoretical observations into wider imperial phenomena
can offer insights into Sámi and other Indigenous contexts.

Inspecting a longer history of exhibitions of Sámi culture reveals how this
notion of "world as exhibition," or rather, "world as simulation" might have
emerged. A history of exhibiting Sámi culture extends back to the early nineteenth century, when Sámi were invited to perform at so-called live-people
exhibitions (*Volkerschau*) in European and North American urban centers, as
has been explored by Cathrine Baglo.[39] As part of these exhibitions, Sámi were
asked to act as if they were living their everyday lives in their natural environment. Often a *lávvu* would be erected on site, reindeer would be included as

part of the show, and Sámi were asked to *joik*.[40] As Baglo argues, while such exhibitions highlighted the power hierarchies of the time, it should be remembered that Sámi were never completely devoid of agency in these enterprises, and many Sámi used these experiences as a chance to travel.[41] Nonetheless, presenting live Sámi as exhibits alongside the reindeer, costumes and tents, rendered them as objects that somehow stood for an abstract notion of a Sámi "way of life."[42] That such events, including those at the Nordland-Austellung and Passage-Panoptikum in Berlin in 1911, often served as sites for conducting ethnographic analysis highlights how live human exhibitions were crucial in shaping and confirming theories—particularly notions of culture—within the ethnographic disciplines.[43] Endeavoring to simulate the "reality" of a Sámi livelihood, the exhibition itself created an imaginary but unobtainable "authentic Sámi culture." For the nostalgic spectator, however, this Sámi culture had supposedly already begun to disappear, owing to the destructive force and mass-mediated nature of modernity.

Such processes can be witnessed within the ethnographic museum, which became the primary medium for representing Sámi culture to a wider public in the twentieth century. The Norsk Folkemuseum (The Norwegian Museum of Cultural History) in Oslo, for example, is a large museum with outdoor and indoor exhibits, incorporating displays of material culture as well as live performances. Anxious to portray the nation in all its diversity, the museum includes a section, albeit difficult to find, within the main building dedicated to Sámi culture. This section begins with a darkened circular room framed by imposing blue exhibition cabinets and a central display securely fenced by glass panes. Within the central display we see another classic representation of a "traditional" Sámi scene: two model Sámi dressed in winter costumes next to a reindeer transporting two baby sleighs over the snowy landscape in front of a *lávvu*. Encircling this are smaller cabinets with an array of ethnographic memorabilia. In one cabinet we see a small model of a *guohti* above a hand-drawn picture from a traveler's book of what it might have looked like in another time. In another, we see artifacts used for hunting arranged on a furry white carpet meant to represent snow and among trunks of birch trees suggestive of a forest. A sacred stone stands in front of another wall with an ethnographic visual depiction of a sacrificial ceremony at a sacred site (*sieidi*). Next to the exhibits are texts of varying lengths that attempt to describe the displays and set the artifacts in a wider cultural, social, and religious context. This particular representational strategy was part of a wider trend during the rise of capitalism in museum exhibitions, which, as Mitchell argues, "came to resemble more and more the commercial machinery of the rest of the city."[44] Indeed, museum exhibitions and shopping malls for the growing bourgeoisie in urban centers enabled the emergence of modern consumerist subjectivity, for which a concatenation of objects somehow signified a larger truth.[45] The medium of the museum like the Norske Folkemuseum, thus, helped to preserve for posterity a "true" Sámi culture, a representation which began to seem, like the urban landscapes within which they were situated, somehow too "real." Moreover, the very placement of Sámi artifacts within an ethnographic museum cemented the nostalgic notion that Sámi culture could now, in modernity, exist only as a form of simulation.

Questions concerning the creation of modern subjectivity, the fetishization of objects, and the sense of a simulated world have a long history. A line of cultural critics influenced by Marxist theory have warned of the effects of industrial labor, cultural production, and mass consumerism; most famously, Horkheimer and Adorno argued that these phenomena enabled the rise of Nazism and North American capitalist consumerism by deceiving the masses with regard to wider political and social truths.[46] Baudrillard offered another pessimistic outlook on contemporary cultural production and mass consumption enabled through communication technologies. In his famous text *Simulacra and Simulation*, Baudrillard discusses how in the second half of the twentieth century society entered a new era of advanced capitalism, bringing about a new relationship between the world we perceive and that which exists. The surplus of signifiers within this system purport to be reality but in actuality form a simulacrum that simply indexes itself. Using the example of Disney World, Baudrillard argues that the external world to which the theme park supposedly refers is not actually real but "belong[s] to the hyperreal order and to the order of simulation."[47] As he explains, "What every society looks for in continuing to produce, and to overproduce, is to restore the real that escapes it."[48] Within this condition there emerges a fixation on the real and a longing, fueled by nostalgia, for authenticity.[49] Thus, for Baudrillard, the (post)modern subject is deceived by simulation and is no longer able to perceive reality. As Teimouri has argued, Baudrillard's postmodern theory intersects with the work of postcolonial theorists such as Said and Mitchell, who have attempted to reveal the "Orient" as simply a simulacrum that refers only back onto itself and not to an actual reality.[50] As Mitchell argues, within this system, "the world appears to the observer as a relationship between picture and reality, the one present but secondary, a mere representation, the other only represented, but prior, more original, more real."[51] Like Baudrillard, Mitchell speculates that "perhaps the sequence of exhibitions became so accurate and so extensive, no one ever realized that the 'real world' they promised was not there."[52] Within Indigenous studies, scholars such as Vizenor have likewise drawn on Baudrillard to argue how popular representations of Indigenous people—what Ramos termed the "hyperreal Indian"—work to marginalize and erase contemporary Indigenous populations.[53]

Do exhibition spaces like Sápmi Park cement the ubiquity of simulation and simulacra and further remove us from reality? Does Sápmi Park, with its display of cultural exotica and its tourist shop, simply provide a site for the mass consumption of an imagined Sámi culture? Or conversely, does it challenge our own sense of reality and virtuality? Drawing on Baudrillard, Mitchell, and Vizenor, I question what it means for Indigenous cultural expression if, for the (post)modern subject, the lived-in, mass-mediated, and consumerist world is a mere simulacrum, an all-encompassing simulation that is somehow falsifying and potentially dangerous. If we take seriously the words of the Sámi *noaidi* in the Mountain of the Spirits, what might it mean to perceive a Sápmi "that you can only see with your heart?" Before offering answers to these questions, I now inspect further ways in which digital simulations have been used by Sámi artists and cultural activists for purposes of cultural revival and transmission. I build, in particular, on discussions by Cocq about revitalization, place, representation, simulation, interactivity, and orality in Sámi Internet platforms for language learning, storytelling, and educational websites.

Digitally Simulating Culture: *Joik* Education

Juoiggas! is a computer program that assists in learning how to *joik*. Launched in 2008, the software is available both on CD-ROM and on the Internet. Produced by *joiker*, composer, producer, and pedagogue Johan Sara Jr. and his brother, graphic designer and computer programmer Mikkel Sara, *Juoiggas!* features the *joiks* of nine respected *joikers* from North Sápmi. The software is marketed through the Karasjok-based Sámi online platform *E-Skuvla* (literally, e-school), which offers Internet pedagogical material and distance education packages, mainly for Sámi language learning for children of all ages. On opening the *Juoiggas!* software, the user can choose between three languages (North Sámi, Norwegian, English) and is given an introduction to *joik*, music theory, and each of the nine *joikers* through textual descriptions, transcriptions, and photos. Using the menu bar at the bottom of the page (in the form of notes on a staff), one can go through twenty-five different *joiks* (some from Sara's own compositions) arranged in increasing complexity. On each page, one is presented with a transcription of the *joik* in Western notation as well as a short description of the *joik*. By pressing the play function, one can then listen to the *joik* sung with accompanying instruments and a metronome, while a vertical line on the transcriptions moves horizontally along the staff, following the notes. It is intended that the user imitate the voice of the *joiker* while playing back the melody. Other functions allow one to mute the metronome, instruments, and vocal parts individually or in combination. This allows users to attempt to replicate the *joiker*'s voice, following the transcription without the other accompanying aids. Another function enables any section of the *joik* to be repeated over and over again, thus allowing for more focused practice. In these ways, *Juioggas!* attempts to exploit many features of digital technologies in order to simulate "traditional" forms of *joik* transmission. As traditional contexts for *joik* transmission are fragile, and examples of *joik* within school curricula are limited, the software allows for new possibilities of *joik* education.

The visual imagery of *Juoiggas!* itself plays with notions of visual simulation. On launching the program, we are drawn into the world of *Juoiggas!* via a graphic sequence before we arrive at the language menu. This sequence follows a sparkling, silver, but somehow unidentifiable form as it moves swiftly across a translucent silvery-blue surface covered with musical notation. Through the curves of the notation, and the increasingly unsteady movement of the shape, the surface takes on the appearance of a rolling infinite digital landscape, alluding to notions of an assemblage. The written notes become in this digital universe raw numerical data, mere representations forming a larger simulated sonic and visual space. In this way, the user is made to feel as if they are surfing on a digital landscape of sonic and visual dimensions that will enable them to explore at their will the endless possibilities of *joik* expression. Indeed, these references to familiar digital imagery capitalize on common tropes of digital freedom and limitlessness. Like all digital media imagery, nonetheless, the celebration of its digital nature is only part of its aim. The silvery-blue color scheme and the rolling glistening surface suggests a landscape reminiscent of an expansive North Sápmi tundra. The moving object therefore takes on the semblance of a snowmobile, used by contemporary Sámi in inner-Finnmark areas as both a reindeer herding vehicle and a sport vehicle. As the object gathers speed, it begins to bounce around until, on reaching the end of the assemblage, it is launched up into a black sky and splinters into ice particles. The displaced particles circle in slow motion until they finally explode apart in real time. This explosion reveals, above what looks like a night seascape, the title of the program written in a font that appears, in its 3D form and shining surface, to have been carved out of blocks of ice. The digital and traditional setting presented by *Juoiggas!* is accompanied by a musical soundscape consisting of disembodied, haunting, electronic synthesized sounds and *joik* vocals on high reverb that pan in and out of the sonic texture. That *Juoiggas!* foregrounds both its electronic and its natural qualities highlights the desire for digital simulation to blur the boundaries between the real and the virtual.

Cocq has discussed how Sámi digital environments have been key to contemporary articulations of Indigenous place and imagining a Sámi homeland.[54] By emphasizing classic images of North Sámi tundra landscapes, she argues, these websites often construct an idealized, "remote" and "exoticized" Sápmi landscape.[55] The tundra has long symbolized in the wider Nordic imagination the homeland of the Sámi, not only because it provides the expansive terrain needed for reindeer herding. When Sámi reindeer-herding rights to land on the tundra are threatened, there are often hard-fought protests and legal cases. Most famously, in 1979 plans by the Norwegian authorities to build a dam on the Alta-Kautokeino River which would flood a large area of rein-deer-herding tundra and the town of Masi led to a hunger strike in front of Norwegian Parliament that captivated national as well as international inter-est.[56] The development did go ahead, albeit in altered form to save the town of Masi, but the government enquiry following the protests led to the recognition of the Sámi as Indigenous within the Norwegian constitution. Masi, like other more famous nearby towns, such as Kautokeino and Karasjok, has been a site of intense cultural resistance to state assimilation and one of the areas where *joik* has survived the strongest. Located in the heart of the Finnmark tundra in Norwegian North Sápmi, Masi is also the hometown of Johan Sara Jr. and where his studio is based. It is no surprise, then, that the *joiks* featured on *Juoiggas!* all come from North Sápmi areas in Norway between Kautokeino and Tana, as the software itself discloses. One of the *joiks*, "Virdnejávri" by Piera Balto, also testifies to the political struggle surrounding the Alta-Kautokeino River. As the text under the *joik* explains, the *joik* is of a lake along the river, which since the development no longer has its natural shape. In these ways, the simulation of a Sámi tundra in *Juoiggas!*, like the sites Cocq analyzes, helps to locate the software and *joik* itself as something distinctly Sámi, with particular articulations of Indigenous belonging to place.

Simulations of nature are also relevant when considering the transmission of *joik*. The tundra is itself often said to be the home of *joik*. Some see the tundra as having providing a space beyond the reaches of society and church when *joik* was made shameful through Christianization and cultural assimila-tion. Others see *joik* as "belonging" to the tundra, associated with such tradi-tional practices as reindeer herding, and regard it as some kind of "song of nature."[57] In these ways, it is often believed that the tundra forms one of the most important spaces for the teaching and learning of *joik*. Some *joiks* are to people, others to places and natural phenomena, including animals. These are themselves well represented within the *Juoiggas!* catalog, which features numer-ous birds, mosquitoes, lakes, and a river. "An ode to nature," is written unas-sumingly in the description under the *joik* "Virdnejávri." As *Juoiggas!* explains in the introduction, the *joik* is embedded in the nature-based traditions of Sápmi. Indeed, some of the *joiks* are suggestive of a wider nature-based cos-mology of the Sámi and environmental philosophy of Johan Sara Jr. Under the *joik* "Johka," taken from Sara's album *Boska*, the text emphasizes the cen-trality of water (*johka*) for life on earth. According to a *joik* philosophy, one doesn't *joik* about something but one *joiks* it into being.[58] Thus, performing these *joiks* in another sense make present the very lakes and river of their title, thus adding another level of simulation to *Juoiggas!* Furthermore, interest in water and its sonic dimension has been explored in two recent CD projects by Sara: *Rievdadus* (Transmission), and *Voi_ice in Cube*. On *Rievdadus* a track entitled "Vuolggán Juostá" (Somewhere I start) follows the acoustic sounds, which Sara digitally manipulated and rearranged in his studio, of a river as it emerges from the drops of melting ice and makes its way down to the roaring sea.[59] Meanwhile, *Voi_ice in Cube* is a more abstract digital exploration of Sara's own vocal experiments within various snow and ice acoustic environments.[60] The interest in digital simulation pursued in *Juoiggas!* is indeed emblematic of Sara's wider exploration of the boundaries between the natural and digital, where reality and the virtual seemingly become one.

But simulation in *Juoiggas!* works in perhaps a more significant way. The nine *joikers* who feature on the program are all respected *joikers* within the North Sámi community; they all have a range of experiences performing *joik* on local, international, and international stages; recording CDs; or doing educational and political work. The late Inga Juuso (1945–2014) is described in the program as having a deep connection to Sámi culture, a highly skilled *joik* technique, and a strong commitment to teaching *joik* to younger generations in her unique role as appointed *joiker* within the education organization Musikk i Troms (Music in the Troms Province). *Juoiggas!* includes two person *joiks* by Juuso, "Hento Risten" and "Anden Inger Maria." As has been theorized within media studies, the transportation of visual and sonic dimensions of people across time and space via communication technologies enables forms of "telepresence." The sonic representations of Inga Juuso and the other eight *joikers* through *Juoiggas!* mean that *joik* education can take place within the classroom, at home, or anywhere with Internet access, even without the physical presence of a "cultural bearer." *Juoiggas!* in this sense provides a simulation of traditional forms of *joik* transmission that works across both geographical distances and generational boundaries.

Cocq, drawing on McLuhan and Ong, has discussed the potential connections between preprint and digital cultures with respect to orality in Sámi digital storytelling, a phenomenon that also resonates with *Juoiggas!*[61] Part of the revival of *joik* has been the urge to develop ways of teaching *joik* to younger generations. This is both a response to the ways many traditional contexts for *joik* learning have become threatened and an opportunity to explore new learning contexts in contemporary Sámi society. Numerous *joikers* and musicians have published books in which *joiks*, sometimes alongside or as part of a story, are printed in musical notation with their texts in order to encourage children to sing along.[62] *Med Joik som Utgangspunkt* (Starting with *joik*), published in 2004 by the Sámi composer and producer Frode Fjellheim, is an anthology of *joiks* from different Sámi regions based on sound archival sources and famous *joikers*.[63] Its notational and textual renderings of the *joiks* with commentary on vocal technique and philosophy and an accompanying CD provided a model for *Juoiggas!* Fjellheim himself uses his textbook within *joik* workshops, projects with Sámi choirs, and his own course in *joik* at Høgskolen i Nord-Trøndelag

(Nord Trøndelag University College) to teach people of different backgrounds and ages in Norway how to *joik*. What *Juoiggas!* does is attempt to replicate this holistic teaching methodology without the physical presence of *joikers* by exploiting the opportunities of digital media. Users are free to take their own path through the *joik* repertoire presented on the program. While these opportunities for interactivity may not equal complex music software such as GarageBand or Sibelius, they do offer important opportunities of *joik* learning.[64] Cocq has also observed that, through interactive multimedia functions, Sámi Internet platforms can create narratives that "resemble an oral performance."[65] Indeed, the interactive functions together with the convergence of sonic, visual and textual aspects, all work to offer a holistic platform for *joik* education that attempts to simulate other traditional oral, embodied, and newly developed oral and textual methods of *joik* transmission.[66]

But where does this leave the gap between simulation and reality? Concerned to highlight continuity between digital simulation and our perception of the real world, Cocq explains that "a digital environment is not a simulation—it refers to a real place and its materiality."[67] Nonetheless, she contends, "the production of a digital Sápmi results in the creation of a place based on imagination, and sometimes in the alteration of reality. It exemplifies how digital places reshape real places and how the real becomes less authentic than fiction."[68] For Cocq, thus, Sámi digital platforms are part of Baudrillard's hyperreal order, in which simulation plays into the trap that seeks to "restore the real that escapes it."[69] Taking a closer look at Baudrillard's theory, however, reveals that it relies on particular assumptions about contemporary global society, and indeed notions of Indigeneity. Part of our fixation on the real, Baudrillard argues, stems from ethnological discourses about Indigenous people who were the first victims of simulacra.[70] Indigenous people (whom Baudrillard refers to as Indians, or ironically as "Savages") became simulacra through the work of anthropologists, who either represent Indigenous culture in texts and museum exhibitions or work to protect Indigenous cultures through efforts to prevent contact or through cultural repatriation.[71] For Baudrillard, the desire to see representations of Indigenous people is symptomatic of how contemporary society yearns for the authentic but essentially unobtainable real: "The Indian returned to the ghetto, in the glass coffin of the virgin forest, again becomes the model of simulation of all possible Indians *from before ethnology*."[72] It is this aspect of his theory that has attracted scholars in Indigenous studies, such as Ramos, Vizenor, and Raheja, not only to apply notions of simulacra and hyperreality in their critiques of popular imaginations of Indigenous people but also to critique Baudrillard's writing.[73] Vizenor uses the figure of the "postindian" as a model for Indigenous resistance against colonial representatios of Native Americans: "The postindian arises from the earlier inventions of the tribes only to contravene the absence of the real with theatrical performances; the theatre of tribal consciousness is the recreation of the real, not the absence of the real in the simulations of dominance."[74] Indeed, anthropological discourses have moved on since the 1990s, and Baudrillard ignores a much longer history of Indigenous people exploiting communication media for their own cultural and political ends.[75] If, however, we consider Indigenous people as active participants within contemporary global culture, how might the varied uses of digital technologies and the diverse cultural meanings they may impart alter our understanding of cultural production and signification? Might there be, as Vizenor's text would suggest, another potential interpretation of Sámi employments of digital media that resists Baudrillard's "hyperreal order"?[76] Indeed, how might an analysis of Sámi uses of digital media reveal an alternative interpretation, a reading that forces us to reconsider our understandings of the real and the virtual? I now offer a study of the music of the Sámi group Vajas, drawing on scholarship of virtuality and Haraway's cyborg. In particular, I draw on Raheja who, also rejecting Baudrillard, highlights the potentials of Native American film through virtuality to propose alternative notions of space, time, and spirituality.[77]

Humanizing Technology: Sámi Sonic Works

Vajas was a group based in Tromsø formed out of a collaboration between Kristin Mellem, Nils Johansen, and Ánde Somby. They became popular in the Sámi music scene through performances at various Sámi festivals and the release of their one and only album, *Sacred Stone*, in 2007. Through the diverse musical backgrounds of the group's members, Vajas offered new expressions of Sámi musical aesthetics as well as articulations of Indigeneity. Kristin Mellem is a violinist and composer from the coastal community in Kåfjord, in North Troms, Norway. Through her collaboration with various artists from the north Nordic region and composition for Beaivváš Sámi Našonálateáhter (Sámi National Theatre), she has drawn on her own Sámi and Kven heritage.[78] Nils Johansen, meanwhile, is a keyboardist, composer, and producer from Tromsø who is famed for being one half of the duo Bel Canto with Anneli Drecker since the late 1980s. Meanwhile, Ánde Somby is a lawyer, academic, activist, and *joiker* from Sirbma in northeast Finnmark, Norway. He has played an important role in Sámi political mobilization (e.g., participating in the famous Alta-Kautokeino River protests in front of Norwegian Parliament in 1979) and Sámi musical revival (e.g., cofounding one of the first Sámi record companies, DAT, in 1985). Digital media has itself become an important resource for his creative and political expression. He often uses his Facebook wall (set to global access) to comment on current local and global political debates, while his SoundCloud account allows him to share his latest *joiks,* as well as older digitized recordings, with a wider public. The tracks on *Sacred Stone* provide commentary on Sámi oppression, call for pan-Indigenous solidarity, and revive a Sámi Indigenous religion. Somby's impassioned and exploratory vocals, the folksy and plaintive violin lines played by Mellem, and the intricate and polished electronics of Johansen create a unique soundscape that explores acoustic and electronic aesthetics. Listening to *Sacred Stone* is almost like entering a virtual world where one encounters animals, aspects of the climate, and *noaidi* in the Sápmi environment. Ramnarine has discussed this CD in relation to issues of shamanism, spirituality and ecology; and in her analyses of the use of *joik* and acoustic sounds in electronically mediated compositions by Nils Aslak Valkeapää and the Sámi film *Ofelaš*, she argues for the significance of contemporary Sámi media productions to articulate issues concerning the sacred, the environment, and postcoloniality.[79] As the media theorist Mark Post has argued, CD recordings are copies of sounds that never existed as an original, thus creating a sonic simulacra.[80] In relation to Indigenous cultural production, Raheja posits Native American film as "a supplemental arena of the possible that initiates and maintains a dialectical relationship between multiple layers of Indigenous knowledge systems—from the dream world to the topography of real and imagined landscapes."[81] In a similar vein, I elucidate how Vajas's digital manipulation of acoustic sounds and their simulation of natural sounds through digital technologies revives aspects of a Sámi Indigenous cosmology and causes us to question the difference between the virtual and the real.

Right from the beginning of *Sacred Stone*, the listener is led into a simulated environment. The opening track is entitled "Borššáš" (North Sámi for "Sparkling Creek") and is a *joik* to a small stream. At first we hear synthesized sounds on one note that feels like a steady pulse and tonal center, though the note gradually changes in timbre. Shortly after these synthesized sounds begin, we hear the acoustic sounds of water flowing gently in the background, suggesting the creek itself. Other layers of synthesized patterns emerge in the musical texture in higher and lower registers, forming different rhythmic patterns and suggesting alternative pulses, and panning back and forth, from left to right. These synthesized notes, although distinctly electronic in timbre, come to suggest the sparkling of the creek in the sun, as the title of the track suggests. Meanwhile, longer synthesized notes offer both a sense of harmony around the tonal center (in the mixolydian mode) and a sense of physical space. This sense of space is reinforced through undistinguishable sounds in high reverb in the background of the sonic texture that might be birds twittering or water dripping in some sort of water cavern. It is at this moment that Somby's vocals enter, performing into being the sparkling creek itself through his playful *joik* poetry.[82] His voice, while giving a human dimension to the musical texture, nonetheless, also plays sonic tricks. There appears to be added reverb on his voice, which adds to the sense of an expansive space, and his voice becomes multiplied at the end of lines where he simply sings vocables, giving the impression that he is surrounded by a choir of *joikers*. At the same time, there are sporadic motives played on a bass that add to the feeling of spontaneity and motion. As Somby vocalizes each stanza of the *joik*, drums and cymbals break into the musical texture and later develop a steady rhythm to give the overall track a sense of momentum, alluding to the increasing pace of the flow of water. Meanwhile the synthesized notes emerge and recede in and out of the musical texture to enhance the effect of glistening water. This glistening water is not only suggested sonically but is itself featured on the graphics of the album cover and sleeve, where bluish-gray and white formations appear like ice above small rocks and a dark bluish stream. The vitality of this stream is further evoked through the *joik* text ("bubbles," "wells," "caressing"). As the musical textures fade, we are left with the splashing sound of water as it continues down the creek.

One of the potentials of digital media musical production as utilized by Vajas is creating a sense of environment. Through evoking the sounds of a stream, the *joik* "Boršŝáš" brings the stream to life and transports the listener to a sonic world in nature. Nature is also evoked on several other tracks on *Sacred Stone*. Sounds of a crow open the second track, entitled "Pubbagarjá" (Pub-Crow), thus rendering sonically the protagonist of the *joik*. Meanwhile, the third and title track of the album, "Sieidi Geaḍgi" (Sacred stone), immediately sets the scene of a harsh Sápmi landscape by incorporating the sounds of swirling wind. In his study of the use of recording technologies, Paul Greene discusses how studio production can be used to create a sense of place that can localize musical sounds in the face of globalizing technologies.[83] The challenges and potentials of studio work and CD production have been discussed by Beverley Diamond, who notes the strong predilection by Sámi artists to incorporate recordings of everyday soundscapes in their music.[84] Indeed, Vaja's technique is by no means new in the repertoire of Sámi music. Nils-Aslak Valkeapää's *Goase Dušše* (The bird symphony), as Ramnarine has discussed, and *Eanan, Eallima Eatni* (The earth, mother of life) both incorporate the sounds of birdcalls from Sápmi.[85] Likewise, the digital manipulation of sounds of water and ice in recent CD projects by Johan Sara Jr. mentioned in the previous section can be seen as a continuation of such a tradition.[86] Ramnarine has argued that this turn to acoustic environments in Nils Aslak Valkeapää's compositions can reveal much about issues of human agency, environmentalism, and human–nature relations, but these examples can also be interpreted in terms of virtuality.[87] They suggest the enactment of "telepresence," whereby the listener is transported to a Sámi environment through sonic simulation. The apparent increasing opportunities of sonic verisimilitude offered by digital technologies enhances listeners' experience of these virtual soundscapes.

Aspects of a Sámi Indigenous religion are also made manifest in *Sacred Stone*. On the track "Boldon Noaiddit" (Burned shamans) we hear the sounds of someone trudging through snow and the mysterious rattling of a wooden object. The musical texture grows with pensive, meandering piano melodies accompanied by pizzicato cello intoning two alternating minor-mode chords. Somby then intones pitchless lyrics in a way that suggests Sprechstimme, meditating on the past hunt of Sámi *noaidi* and the suppression of Indigenous spiritual life. Hints of percussive sounds add to the texture before melodic fragments of a violin become foregrounded to suggest an ominous waltz. One could interpret the snow steps as those of a *noaidi* with a rattling frame drum in hand taking refuge from a Lutheran world evoked through the classical instruments with a reverb that suggest the acoustical realm of a church. In these ways, the sonic simulations of place and space reinforce the historical narrative and political expression of the track. A similar effect is created in other Sámi music, namely Wimme's track "Oainnahus" (Vision) from the CD *Gierran* (Enchantment). The musical textures of *joik*, bass clarinet, synthesizer and digitally manipulated acoustic recordings take the listener on a journey through an enigmatic and unnerving soundscape. Sounds of a distant choir hint again at Christianity, and a clarinet intones a hymnlike melody that sounds like it is straight out of the score of a horror film. Meanwhile, we hear snippets of a lonely fiddler, a synthesized oscillating bass, and Wimme's tormented *joiking* as if he is on his own trance-induced shamanic journey. Indeed, simulations of *noaidi* trance are also suggested in the track "Áigi Vássá" (Time doesn't stop) on Ulla Pirttijärvi's album *Máttaráhku Askái* (In our foremothers' arms). It opens with a low-pitched drone with a haunting timbre that emerges out of silence. Vocalizations of a *joik* that oscillate around one pitch, low in Pirttijärvi's range, can then be heard close in the foreground of the sonic texture. Through the creative studio work by Frode Fjellheim, the vocals appear to multiply, grow in intensity, and circle around the listener through panning left to right. After building to a climax, the vocals die away to leave the drone before it fades to inaudibility. These examples highlight the ways in which sonic simulation enable forms of cultural revival of a Sámi Indigenous religion. It might seem that there is nothing remarkable in these examples or in the digital techniques they employ to create the overall sonic effects. Closer inspection of discourses about Sámi traditional practice and debates concerning virtuality, nonetheless, make for a more interesting reading.

Indeed, to understand the types of sonic simulation in Vajas, it is first necessary to explore more thoroughly current theories of virtuality, theories that themselves question the division between the virtual and the real. Tracing a longer history of ideas of virtuality and acknowledging its importance in other cultures, Shields has argued that the virtual is "another register or manifestation of the real"[88] through which, as Maria Bittarello writes, "we make sense of actuality."[89] Nonetheless, Shields asserts, the positivistic trends in science since the eighteenth century separated the "materialism of empirical reality and the idealism of abstract thought."[90] Furthermore, Boellstorff explains that pessimistic associations of virtual reality with advanced capitalism presuppose that technologies distance humanity from reality.[91] Boellstorff argues, however, that the virtual is just as natural as reality and that, since cultural perception is itself a form of mediation, perceived reality is always somehow virtual: "It is in being virtual that we are human."[92] As Shields writes, virtual media "create the illusion of presence through props, simulations, partial presences . . . and rituals which invoke the past and make absent others present. They aid metaxis from the virtual to the actual by giving concrete presence to intangible ideas."[93] The synthesized sounds in *Sacred Stone*, although perceived to be artificial, do indeed take on the quality of something natural. Furthermore, they give presence to those elements—water, animals, humans—as part of traditional creative practice and an Indigenous Sámi cosmology.

Moreover, as Shields contends, "the greatest power of digital virtuality . . . has been in providing a matrix in which new modes of being and practices of becoming could be experimented with."[94] Such modes of being and practices of becoming have indeed been alluded to by Vajas's lead singer. The intimate vocal quality of Somby on *Sacred Stone* is suggestive of his own philosophical and aesthetic goals that explore the virtual. Reflecting on his work with Vajas and his future artistic ambitions, Somby related to me:

> I am so fascinated by what lies at the boundaries of the voice. . . . I have always been the one who has wanted to be at the boundary, and then look to what is beyond, look out and not in. And that, I believe, is what *joik* is going to do more of, both in relation to attempting to do something with *joik*'s lyrical dimension and also to do something more with expression. . . . Because it is a sort of strange vision that, if I manage to make such a *joik* which is beyond that which the voice can manage to express, I can then go to the computer and I can say to it [the computer] "Now I have made a *joik* which the human voice can't *joik* by itself. Have you, for example, the ability to sing so deep beyond the possibility of the human voice but that it nonetheless still becomes a *joik*?" . . . And that means, just in a practical sense, simply that I think *joik* is a very exciting mode of expression which has so many universes which have not yet been discovered.[95]

This striking quote highlights the potential of digital media to assist and transform Sámi traditional knowledge and creative expression. Ramnarine argues that the incorporation of natural sounds in the compositions of Nils Aslak Valkeapää articulates a "postcolonial environmental ethic" in which humans are a part of nature.[96] Likewise, Somby's creativity blurs the boundaries of the human and technology, of the real and the virtual. Indeed, by striving for the possibilities of technology for the human, Somby alludes to the posthuman-ist discourse of Haraway's technologically enhanced human, the cyborg.[97] The cyborg was a way for Haraway to highlight how technologies have always been part of human bodies and endeavors and how technologies can be a way of subverting patriarchy and colonialism. She writes, "Cyborg writing is about the power to survive, not on the basis of original innocence, but on the basis of seizing the tools to mark the world that marked them as other." "Feminist cyborg stories," she explains, "have the task of recoding communication and intelligence to subvert and control."[98] She continues, "These machine/organ-ism relationships are obsolete, unnecessary. For us, in imagination and in other practice, machines can be prosthetic devices, intimate components, friendly selves."[99] For Somby, the computer itself becomes one such "friendly self" in his attempt to explore new possibilities of *joik* expression. Indeed, as the musi-cal examples by Vajas highlight, digital technologies have already assisted in Somby's attempt to overcome the problematic division of humans and technol-ogy, of the real and of the virtual.

The Politics of Virtuality: Concluding Thoughts

Notions of the real and virtual are significant when considering the Sámi, not simply because of current opportunities for Sámi digital simulation, but also because such notions intersect with understandings of alternative realms beyond the lived-in, material world of a Sámi Indigenous cosmology. While the-ories concerning the beliefs and practices within a Sámi Indigenous religion differ, a Sámi cosmology is often thought to consist of three realms—the liv-ing (middle world), the dead (underworld), and the gods (upper world)[100]—though it has also been argued that there were simply two, the visible and the invisible world.[101] The realms, while distinct, were also related, since Sámi gods were often linked to phenomena in a Sámi environment and astrology (the sun, wind, and thunder) and the landscape was considered sacred.[102] Indeed, it was believed that the realms of the dead and the gods could be accessed through particular liminal places within the physical landscape.[103] Specific sacred mountains were an entrance point into the world of gods, rivers car-ried the souls of humans to the realm of the dead, and springs allowed for dead ancestors to reenter the material world as spirits.[104] Also important were special rock formations that became sacred sites, known as *sieidi*, which served as gateways to the other realms.[105] Rituals were enacted at these sites, includ-ing animal sacrifices, to engage the world of gods in acts of reciprocity with the human realm.[106] A key figure in Sámi society was the *noaidi*, who acted as a mediator between the distinct realms.[107] Through trance-inducing rituals, a *noaidi* could travel into the realm of the dead, in order to free the captured souls of the living to heal illness, in other times of crisis, and to prophesy the future.[108] It is believed that the Sámi drum played a crucial role in *noaidi* rituals, helping the *noaidi* fall into trance.[109] The different illustrations on the skins of the few surviving drums often resemble representations of the realms of the living, dead and gods, thus providing a kind of "cognitive map" for the *noaidi*'s spirit during trance.[110] Meanwhile, sources suggest that *joik* was a means to induce trance and to communicate with the spiritual realm.[111] It is this cosmology that the presentation at Sápmi Park simulated. As Shields reminds us, the virtual—as embodied in memories, dreams, visions—has in numerous cultures played an important role in understanding the real, and could be made tangible through ritual.[112] In reference to the ancient Greeks as well as Siberian shamanism, Bittarello posits that invisible and visible worlds "co-exist," mutually affect one another, and thus are equally real.[113] Thus, we could consider a Sámi Indigenous cosmology as consisting of invisible (virtual) and visible (actual) realms that together formed a lived reality. The virtual could manifest itself in and influence the actual world, while humans could also perceive and, through shamanism, shape aspects of the virtual world. Thus, the actual world existed side-by-side with, and was mutually dependent upon, the virtual world.

Such a cosmology could offer alternative perspectives for considering forms of simulation and virtuality within contemporary Sámi expressive culture. This is especially so considering the revival of certain aspects of Indigenous Sámi cosmology within contemporary Sámi cultural performance. *Sacred Stone* is littered with references to a Sámi cosmology and itself utilizes many aspects of Sámi traditional culture. As we have seen, the track "Boršoáš" (Sparkling creek) simulates, through the text, the vocals, and the intricate digital production, the sounds and images of a trickling stream. Listening to the track can be a way of presencing the creek in front of us, just as live *joik* performance might.[114] At the same time, the bubbling water hints at its source, a spring, where, in a Sámi Indigenous cosmology, souls of the dead could reenter the physical world as spirits. Likewise, the *sieidi* that is brought to life on the track "Sieidi Gea*d*gi" (Sacred stone) is also the site at which humans attempt to communicate with the invisible world through sacrificial ceremonies and trance. Allusions to another world are also plentiful within the text (e.g., "The home from the ones from the other side"; "She could give pieces of images"). Meanwhile, simulations of a Sámi landscape, with snow and ice, feature prominently on *Juoiggas!* Water also becomes thematized through the *joiks* to a lake and river ("Virdnejávri" and "Johka"), both of which, as their accompanying text highlights, remind us of the fragility of life on earth and the connection between humans and sacred nature. On the one hand, these examples elucidate the importance of digital media for enabling simulation in order to support the revival of Sámi traditional practices and cosmologies. On the other, they also play with notions of alternate realities central to a Sámi Indigenous cosmology, thus transforming "traditional" practice. This is most evident at Sápmi Park, where the presentation *Stalubákti* (The mountain of the spirits) takes the visitor on a journey into Sámi traditional beliefs, mythology, and shamanism. What we experience, however, is not simply a simulation of a virtual world. The *noaidi* in the fire asks us to suspend our disbelief and imagine, just for a short while, how the world through a Sámi cosmology might appear. Rivers are the veins of a reindeer, forests the fur, and stars the eyes. Likewise, the sonorous Northern Lights are the ancestors, and *joiking* enables one to travel into alternative realities. Bitarello has written about the importance of imagination and spirituality (e.g., myths) for helping us not only to make meaning out of perceived reality but also to envision better realities.[115] And Shields has written about the importance for digital virtual technologies to assist the imagination in perceiving aspects of the world which positivist empirical science have made redundant.[116] As such, *Stalubákti* and the other examples show how uses of digital media have the potential, through immersive, embodied and multisensorial simulation, to remind us what is missing in empirical accounts of the world and to render aspects of imaginary and utopian worlds visually and sonically perceptible within the actual world. In particular, *Stalubákti* asks us, through a Sámi cosmology, to perceive Sápmi beyond what it may appear like in the actual physical world, indeed urging us to the look at a world "that you can only see with your heart." It is these aspects of Sámi expressive culture that Vizenor might call simulations of "shadows, memories, and visions" that articulate resistance to a hyperreal erasure of Indigenous people.[117]

These ideas also have implications for how we might more generally reconsider pessimistic views and theories of digital media, especially virtuality and simulation. Boellstorff, drawing on Massumi, writes that the virtual emerges from "a perceived gap between experience and 'the actual.' . . . This gap between virtual and actual is critical: were it to be filled in, there would be no virtual worlds, and in a sense no actual world either."[118] Here, Boellstorff renders the gap between the "virtual" and the "actual" as a utopian space. This is in stark contrast to Baudrillard's lamentation of the loss of the "real" in an era of simulacrum. Although Boellstorff denies that the attempt to approach the real through virtuality is a sign of Baudrillardian nostalgia, he believes that this gap is a prerequisite for human perception of our world.[119] Vizenor, however, questions the assumption of semiotic theory and subject-object distinctions in accounts of Indigenous culture.[120] And according to a Sámi philosophy, such a gap may not be so necessary at all. As we have seen, according to ontologies of *joik*, one does not *joik* about someone, one *joiks* someone.[121] Through the act of *joiking*, the person, animal, or place who is *joiked* is made present. According to some commentators, this is an act of memory; according to the *noaidi* in *Stalubákti* joiks are "pictures of people."[122] Thus, as Ramnarine has argued, semiotic theory, whereby an arbitrary sign (a construct of the human imagination) stands for something signified (a part of lived reality), no longer holds.[123] Within a *joik* philosophy, the sign (in this case the *joik*) *is* the signified (person, animal, or place, etc.). Moreover, as Nils Aslak Valkeapää and Ánde Somby have described, *joiks* have no beginning or end, but continue to resonate in nature whether someone vocalizes them or not, and whether we can perceive them or not.[124] Ramnarine has interpreted these aspects of *joik* performance as highlighting the interconnection of humans and environment.[125] Such an ontology also highlights the idea that there are other ways of evaluating digital technologies and simulation. It raises important questions about notions of experienced and imagined realities, problematizes standard distinctions between subjects and objects, and opens up new ways of thinking about embodiment. In these ways, a Sámi cosmology could provide a model for reconsidering totalizing and dystopian theories of contemporary digital culture and simulation. Indeed, it shows that, despite the increasing ubiquity of digital technologies around the world, there are alternative ways of thinking about, experiencing, and utilizing global digital culture.

Refashioning digital media and reconsidering virtuality is, I emphasize, a political exercise. As we have seen, the emergence of a "world as simulation" was created through practices and processes central to imperialism. Likewise, the binary real/virtual within which the virtual was considered negatively was a product of Enlightenment science. Uses of digital technologies for simulation in Sámi cultural and musical contexts have been utilized to revive Sámi Indigenous cosmologies and Sámi cultural traditions, including *joik*. The experimental uses of technology should not be seen as somehow being a "less real" simulation of culture, as nostalgic ethnographic accounts might have us believe. As Somby's vocal vision elucidates, they can be seen as both intrinsic to, and transformative aspects of tradition. Indeed, as Haraway has argued, the humanization of technologies can be a way of resisting patriarchy and colonialism.[126] Moreover, forms of simulation employed within Sámi expressive culture themselves question and play with the distinction between the real and the virtual, and this in itself draws on a Sámi cosmology in which notions of invisible realms were central to understanding lived reality in the physical world. The virtual, scholars have argued, does not necessarily have to be seen as distinct from reality, but rather as existing alongside, permeable with, and dependent upon the lived-in world. It is in the sphere of the virtual that humans can adopt new ways of relating to the object world, develop alternative understandings of embodiment and orality, and explore diverse ways of imagining and perceiving reality. Raheja argues for the importance of filmic virtuality for Indigenous resistance and cultural revival: "The virtual reservation does not stand in opposition to or as a substitute for the material world, but creates a dialogue with it. It helps us see things in the material world in a different dimensionality, thus enhancing our understanding of online and virtual as well as off-line and off-screen communities."[127] Moreover, as Shields contends, "the virtual troubles any simple negation because it introduces multiplicity into the otherwise fixed category of the real. As such the tangible, actually real phenomena cease to be the sole, hegemonic examples of 'reality.'"[128] Such a view gives space to new ways of thinking about the contemporary digital world. The politicized nature of virtual technologies is also recognized by Boellstorff, who urges us to advance "a politics that sees virtual worlds as one site for social struggle and justice."[129] A deeper study of Sámi and other Indigenous understandings of virtuality and uses of digital technology would not only enable us to appreciate complex ways of resisting totalizing notions of reality in the contemporary digital world, but also lead to understand better different ways of living and experiencing global modernities.[130]

Notes

1. Rob Shields, *The Virtual* (London: Routledge, 2003).
2. Tom Boellstorff, *Coming of Age in Second Life: An Anthropologist Explores the Virtually Human* (Princeton, NJ: Princeton University Press, 2008), 26–27, 32.
3. Jean Baudrillard, *Simulacra and Simulation* (Ann Arbor: University of Michigan Press, 1994), 1–42.
4. Shields, *The Virtual*, 37, 44.
5. Michael Meadows, "Re-claiming a Cultural Identity: Indigenous Media Production in Australia and Canada," *Continuum* 8, no. 2 (1994): 270–92.
6. Shields, *The Virtual*, 37; Bittarello, "Another Time, Another Space: Virtual Worlds, Myths and Imagination," *Journal For Virtual Worlds Research* 1, no. 1 (2008): 13–14; Bittarello, "Mythologies of Virtuality: 'Other Space' and 'Other Dimension' from Ancient Myths to Cyberspace," in *The Oxford Handbook of Virtuality*, ed. Mark Grimshaw (Oxford: Oxford University Press, 2014), 97.
7. Shields, *The Virtual*; Boellstorff, *Coming of Age in Second Life*; Bittarello, "Another Time, Another Space" and "Mythologies of Virtuality."
8. Michelle H. Raheja, *Reservation Reelism: Redfacing, Visual Sovereignty, and Representations of Native Americans in Film* (Lincoln: University of Nebraska Press, 2010), 203.
9. See Richard Jones-Bamman, "'As Long as We Continue to Joik, We'll Remember Who We Are': Negotiating Identity and the Performance of Culture: The Saami Joik" (PhD diss., University of Washington, 1993), 235–63.
10. See Vuokko Hirvonen, *Voices from Sápmi: Sámi Women's Path to Authorship*, trans. Kaija Anttonen (Kautokeino, NO: DAT, 2008), 66–80.
11. For an overview of this history, see Sari Pietikäinen, "'To Breathe Two Airs': Empowering Indigenous Sámi Media," in *Global Indigenous Media: Cultures, Poetics, and Politics*, ed. Pamela Wilson and Michelle Stewart (Durham, NC: Duke University Press, 2008), 200–201.

12. See Odd Mathis Hætta, *Dá Lea Sámi Radio: Nrk Sámegiel Sáddagat 1946–1980* (Karasjok, NO: Davvi Girji, 2003).

13. John T. Solbakk, "Sami Mass Media: Their Role in a Minority Society," in *Sami Culture in a New Era: The Norwegian Sami Experience*, ed. Harald Gaski (Karasjok, NO: Davvi Girji, 1997), 172–98.

14. Thomas R. Hilder, *Sámi Musical Performance and the Politics of Indigeneity in Northern Europe* (Lanham, MD: Rowman & Littlefield, 2015), 164–67.

15. Sari Pietikäinen, "Sami in the Media: Questions of Language Vitality and Cultural Hybridisation," *Journal of Multicultural Discourses* 3, no. 1 (2008): 26.

16. Ibid., 28; Pietikäinen, "'To Breathe Two Airs,'" 199; See also Pamela Wilson and Michelle Stewart, "Indigeneity and Indigenous Media on the Global Stage," in *Global Indigenous Media: Cultures, Poetics, and Politics*, ed. Pamela Wilson and Michelle Stewart (Durham NC: Duke University Press, 2008), 3.

17. Coppélie Cocq, "Anthropological Places, Digital Spaces, and Imaginary Scapes: Packaging a Digital Sámiland," *Folklore* 124, no. 1 (2013): 1–14; Coppélie Cocq, "From the Árran to the Internet: Sami Storytelling in Digital Environments," *Oral Tradition* 28, no. 1 (2013): 125–42.

18. Hilder, *Sámi Musical Performance and the Politics of Indigeneity*.

19. Jones-Bamman, "'As Long as We Continue to Joik, We'll Remember Who We Are'"; Richard Jones-Bamman, "From 'I'm a Lapp' to 'I Am Saami': Popular Music and Changing Images of Indigenous Ethnicity in Scandinavia," in *Ethnomusicology: A Contemporary Reader*, ed. Jennifer C. Post (London: Routledge, 2006), 351–67; Hilder, *Sámi Musical Performance and the Politics of Indigeneity*.

20. For more on revival, see Tamara E. Livingston, "Music Revivals: Towards a General Theory," *Ethnomusicology* 43, no. 1 (1999): 66–85.

21. See also Jones-Bamman, "'As Long as We Continue to Joik, We'll Remember Who We Are,'" 388–90.

22. Donna J. Haraway, "The Cyborg Manifesto: Science, Technology, and Socialist-Feminism in the Late Twentieth Century," in *Simians, Cyborgs and Women: The Reinvention of Nature*, ed. Donna J. Haraway (New York: Routledge, 1991), 149–81.

23. See also Tina K. Ramnarine, "Acoustemology, Indigeneity, and Joik in Valkeapää's Symphonic Activism: Views from Europe's Arctic Fringes for Environmental Ethnomusicology," *Ethnomusicology* 53, no. 2 (2009): 190–92.

24. For an introduction to the topic of music and virtuality (which was published in the final phases of editing of this book), see Sheila Whiteley and Shara Rambarran, eds. *The Oxford Handbook of Music and Virtuality* (Oxford: Oxford University Press, 2016).

25. Gerald Vizenor, *Manifest Manners: Postindian Warriors of Survivance* (Hanover, NH: Wesleyan University Press, 1994).

26. Ibid., 55; See also Raheja, *Reservation Reelism*, 252.

27. Raheja, *Reservation Reelism*, 153. In this book, Raheja also draws on Vizenor.

28. Shields, *The Virtual*, 60.

29. Ibid., 65.

30. Boellstorff, *Coming of Age in Second Life*, 238.

31. I discuss Sápmi Park to open up a discussion on tradition and modernity in Hilder, *Sámi Musical Performance and the Politics of Indigeneity in Northern Europe*, 71–72.

32. This exhibition was produced and created by Sápmi KS and BRC Imagination Arts, with Åsa Simma as writer and cultural advisor and Nils Gaup as media consultant.

33. Åsa Simma wrote the narration for this simulation.

34. Åsa Simma, personal communication, Berlin, February 11, 2015.

35. There are numerous other examples of online Sámi exhibitions, which employ aspects of virtuality, hyperlink, and the convergence of visual, sonic and textual culture, such as Sápmi—Becoming a Nation, at Tromsø University Museum, accessed September 2, 2016, http://sapmi.uit.no/.

36. Timothy Mitchell, *Colonising Egypt* (Cambridge: Cambridge University Press, 1988), 13.

37. Ibid., 21.

38. Ibid., 62.

39. Cathrine Baglo, "På Ville Veger: Levende Utstillinger Av Samer I Europa Og Amerika" (PhD diss., University of Tromsø, 2011). For a critical discussion of museum histories in Scandinavia, see Mark B. Sandberg, *Living Pictures, Missing Persons: Mannequins, Museums, and Modernity* (Princeton, NJ: Princeton University Press, 2003).

40. See Susanne Ziegler, "Wax Cylinder Recordings of Sami Music in the Berlin Phonogramm-Archiv," *European Meetings in Ethnomusicology* 12 (2007): 213–16.

41. Baglo, "På Ville Veger," 22–23.

42. Ibid., 202–42.

43. Ibid., 170–201; Ziegler, "Wax Cylinder Recordings of Sami Music."

44. Mitchell, *Colonising Egypt*, 10.

45. Ibid., 11.

46. Max Horkheimer and Theodor W. Adorno, *Dialectic of Enlightenment*, trans. John Cumming (London: Verso, 1997), 120–67.

47. Baudrillard, *Simulacra and Simulation*, 12.

48. Ibid., 23.

49. Ibid., 6–7.

50. Mahdi Teimouri, "On the Question of Overlap between the Post-colonial and the Postmodern," *Sarjana* 27, no. 2 (2012): 2/3; Mitchell, *Colonising Egypt*, 31.

51. Mitchell, *Colonising Egypt*, 60.

52. Ibid., 10.

53. Alcida Rita Ramos, "The Hyperreal Indian," *Série Antropologia*, no. 135 (1992): 1–17; Vizenor, *Manifest Manners: Postindian Warriors of Survivance*; Raheja, *Reservation Reelism: Redfacing, Visual Sovereignty, and Representations of Native Americans in Film*.

54. Cocq, "Anthropological Places, Digital Spaces, and Imaginary Scapes: Packaging a Digital Sámiland."

55. Ibid., 9–10.

56. See Odd Terje Brantenberg, "The Alta-Kautokeino Conflict: Saami Reindeer Herding and Ethnopolitics," in *Native Power: The Quest for Autonomy and*

Nationhood of Indigenous Peoples, ed. Jens Brøsted et al. (Bergen, NO: Universitetsforlaget, 1985), 23–48.

57. Ola Graff, "Samisk Joik: Viddas Egen Musikk? Ei Betrakning over Joikens Forhold Til Naturen," [Sámi joik: The tundra's own music? A consideration of joik's relation to nature.] *Musikk Fokus* 1991, no. 7 (1991): 18–22.

58. Ánde Somby, "Joik and the Theory of Knowledge," accessed September 2, 2016, http://www.stavacademy.co.uk/mimir/joik.htm. For further discussion of this phenomenon, see Ramnarine, "Acoustemology, Indigeneity, and Joik," 190–92.

59. For further discussion of this CD, see Hilder, *Sámi Musical Performance and the Politics of Indigeneity*, 135–41.

60. For discussion of acoustic ecologies in Sámi compositions by Nils Aslak Valkeapää, see Ramnarine, "Acoustemology, Indigeneity, and Joik,"

61. Cocq, "From the Árran to the Internet: Sami Storytelling in Digital Environments," 127–28; See also Paddy Scannell, *Media and Communication* (Los Angeles, CA; London: SAGE, 2007), 135–36.

62. See, for example, Ulla Pirttijärvi, *Hoŋkoŋ Dohkká* [The Hong Kong doll] (Kautokeino, NO: DAT, 1996).

63. Frode Fjellheim, *Med Joik Som Utgangspunkt* [With joik as a point of departure] (Trondheim, NO: Vuelie, 2004).

64. See also Cocq, "From the Árran to the Internet," 132.

65. Ibid., 133.

66. See also Thomas R. Hilder, "Repatriation, Revival and Transmission: The Politics of a Sámi Cultural Heritage," *Ethnomusicology Forum* 21, no. 2 (2012): 161–79.

67. Cocq, "Anthropological Places, Digital Spaces, and Imaginary Scapes," 11.

68. Ibid.

69. Baudrillard, *Simulacra and Simulation*, 23.

70. Ibid., 8–9.

71. Ibid., 7–11.

72. Ibid., 8. Italics in original.

73. See Ramos, "The Hyperreal Indian"; Vizenor, *Manifest Manners* 4–5; Raheja, *Reservation Reelism*, 36, 53, 136–38; Teresa Strong-Wilson, "Turtles All the Way: Simulacra and Resistance to Simulacra in Indigenous Teachers' Discussion of Indigenous Children's Literature," *Children's Literature in Education* 39, no. 1 (2008): 53–74; Colin Perrin, "Approaching Anxiety: The Insistence of the Postcolonial in the Declaration on the Rights of Indigenous Peoples," *Law and Critique* 6, no. 1 (1995): 55–74; Stephen Muecke, "Cultural Activism: Indigenous Australia 1972–94," in *Trajectories: Inter-Asia Cultural Studies*, ed. Kuan-Hsing Chen (1998): 299–313. For a critique of notions of Indigenous "authenticity," see also Gareth Griffiths, "The Myth of Authenticity," in *De-Scribing Empire*, ed. Chris Tiffin and Alan Lawson (London: Routledge, 1994), 70–85. Baudrillard articulates his stance on Indigeneity more explicitly in Richard G. Smith, "The Catastrophe of Paradox Questions and Answers on Hyperreal America with Jean Baudrillard," *Space and Culture* 5, no. 2 (2002): 96–102.

74. Vizenor, *Manifest Manners*, 5.

75. See Meadows, "Re-claiming a Cultural Identity." For another critique of Baudrillard's notion of the simulacra with regard to TV advertisements, see Mark Poster, *The Mode of Information: Poststructuralism and Social Context* (Cambridge: Polity Press, 1990), 61–68.

76. Vizenor, *Manifest Manners*.

77. Raheja, *Reservation Reelism*, 145–89.

78. The Kven are a Finnish-speaking national minority in Northern Norway.

79. Tina K. Ramnarine, "Singing Sacred Stones: Music, Spirituality, and Ecology in Europe's Arctic Fringes," presented at the Society for Ethnomusicology Annual Conference (Middletown, CT, 2008); Ramnarine, "Acoustemology, Indigeneity, and Joik in Valkeapää's Symphonic Activism"; Tina K. Ramnarine, "Sonic Images of the Sacred in Sámi Cinema: From Finno-Ugric Rituals to Fanon in an Interpretation of Ofelaš (Pathfinder)," *Interventions* 15, no. 2 (2013): 239–54.

80. Poster, *The Mode of Information*, 9.

81. Raheja, *Reservation Reelism*, 153.

82. For further discussion of Somby and issues of presencing that which is *joiked* through *joik* performance, see Ramnarine, "Acoustemology, Indigeneity, and Joik," 191.

83. Paul D. Greene and Thomas Porcello, *Wired for Sound: Engineering and Technologies in Sonic Cultures* (Middletown, CT: Wesleyan University Press, 2005), 8–9.

84. Beverley Diamond, "'Allowing the Listener to Fly as They Want to': Sámi Perspectives on Indigenous CD Production in Northern Europe," *World of Music* 49, no. 1 (2007): 23–48. See also Diamond's chapter in this volume.

85. See Ramnarine, "Acoustemology, Indigeneity, and Joik."

86. Hilder, *Sámi Musical Performance and the Politics of Indigeneity*, 135–41.

87. Ramnarine, "Acoustemology, Indigeneity, and Joik."

88. Shields, *The Virtual*, 46.

89. Bittarello, "Mythologies of Virtuality," 108.

90. Shields, *The Virtual*, 37.

91. Boellstorff, *Coming of Age in Second Life*, 20.

92. Ibid., 5.

93. Shields, *The Virtual*, 41.

94. Ibid., 13.

95. Ánde Somby, personal interview, March 12, 2008, Tromsø.

96. Ramnarine, "Acoustemology, Indigeneity, and Joik," 210.

97. Donna J. Haraway, *Simians, Cyborgs and Women: The Reinvention of Nature* (New York: Routledge, 1991).

98. Haraway, "The Cyborg Manifesto," 175.

99. Ibid., 178.

100. Åke Hultkrantz, "Religion and Environment among the Saami: An Ecological Study," in *Circumpolar Religion and Ecology: An Anthropology of the North*, ed. Takahashi Irimoto and Takako Yamada (Tokyo: University of Tokyo Press, 1994), 354–55.

101. Håkan Rydving, "Synliga Och Osyngliga Lanskap: Några Samiska Eksempel," in *Ting Og Tekst*, ed. Else Mundal and Anne Ågotnes (Bergen, NO: Bryggens Museum, 2002), 65–77.
102. Hultkrantz, "Religion and Environment among the Saami," 354–56.
103. Inga-Maria Mulk and Tim Bayliss-Smith, "Liminality, Rock Art and the Sami Sacred Landscape," *Journal of Northern Studies* 2007, no. 1/2 (2007): 91–118.
104. Ibid., 105–8.
105. Ibid.
106. Ibid., 98.
107. Ibid., 95–96.
108. Louise Bäckman, "The Dead as Helpers?: Conceptions of Death amongst the Saamit (Lapps)," *Temenos: Nordic Journal of Comparative Religion* 14 (1978): 25–52.
109. Bo Sommarström, "Pointers and Clues to Some Saami Drum Problems," in *Saami Pre-Christian Religion: Studies on the Oldest Traces of Religion among the Saamis*, ed. Louise Bäckman and Åke Hultkrantz (Uppsala, SE: Almqvist & Wiksell, 1985), 139–56.
110. Juha Pentikäinen, "The Shamanic Drum as a Conitive Map: The Historical and Semiotic Study of the Saami Drum in Rome," in *Mythology and Cosmic Order*, ed. René Gothoni and Juha Pentikäinen (Pieksämäki, FI: Studia fennica, 1987), 17–36.
111. Ola Graff, "Joik Og Runebomme. Hvilken Betydning Hadde Joikinga I De Før-Kristne Seremoniene?" (Tromsø, NO: Universitetsmuseet i Tromsø, 1996).
112. Shields, *The Virtual*, 37.
113. Bittarello, "Mythologies of Virtuality," 97.
114. Ramnarine, "Acoustemology, Indigeneity, and Joik," 191.
115. Bittarello, "Another Time, Another Space," 13–14.
116. Shields, *The Virtual*, 37–38.
117. Vizenor, *Manifest Manners*, 63.
118. Boellstorff, *Coming of Age in Second Life*, 19; Brian Massumi, *Parables for the Virtual: Movement, Affect, Sensation* (Durham, NC: Duke University Press, 2002), 30.
119. Boellstorff, *Coming of Age in Second Life*, 238, 243.
120. Vizenor, *Manifest Manners*, 74–78.
121. Somby, "Joik and the Theory of Knowledge."
122. Johan Turi, (*Turi's*) *Book of Lappland*, trans. E. G. Nash (London: Cape, 1931), 202.
123. See Ramnarine, "Acoustemology, Indigeneity, and Joik," 190–91.
124. Elina Helander and Kaarina Kailo, eds., *No Beginning, No End: The Sami Speak Up* (Edmonton: Canadian Circumpolar Institute Press, 1998), 87; Somby, "Joik and the Theory of Knowledge"
125. Ramnarine, "Acoustemology, Indigeneity, and Joik," 190–92.
126. Haraway, "The Cyborg Manifesto," 155.
127. Raheja, *Reservation Reelism*, 153.
128. Shields, *The Virtual*, 21.
129. Boellstorff, *Coming of Age in Second Life*, 248.

130. I would like to acknowledge Shzr Ee Tan and Henry Stobart as well as the anonymous reviewers for their feedback on this chapter. I am especially grateful to Nicholas Baer for his discussions on media and offering comments on an earlier draft of this chapter and to Daniel O'Gorman for discussions on Baudrillard.

Selected Bibliography

Alexenberg, Mel. *The Future of Art in a Postdigital Age: From Hellenistic to Hebraic Consciousness.* Chicago: Intellect, 2011.

Anaya, James S. *Indigenous Peoples in International Law.* 2nd ed. Oxford: Oxford University Press, 2004.

Appadurai, Arjun. *Modernity at Large: Cultural Dimensions of Globalization.* Minneapolis: University of Minnesota Press, 1996.

————. "Disjuncture and Difference in the Global Cultural Economy." *Public Culture* 2 (1990): 1–24.

Baily, John. "Modi Operandi in the Making of 'World Music' Recordings." In *Recorded Music: Performance, Culture and Technology,* edited by Amanda Bayley, 107–24. Cambridge: Cambridge University Press, 2010.

Barber, Benjamin. *Strong Democracy: Participatory Politics for a New Age.* Berkeley: University of California Press, 1984.

Barbero, Jesús Martin. *Communication, Culture and Hegemony. From the Media to Mediations.* London: SAGE, 1993.

Barsh, Russel Lawrence. "Indigenous Peoples in the 1990s: From the Object to Subject of International Law." *Harvard Human Rights Journal* 7, no. 2 (1994): 33–86.

Barwick, Linda. "Gender 'Taboos' and Didjeridus." In *The Didjeridu: from Arnhem Land to Internet,* edited by Karl Neuenfeldt, 89–98. Sydney: John Libbey in association with Perfect Beat Publications, 1996.

Barwick, Linda. "Marri Ngarr Lirrga Songs: A Musicological Analysis of Song Pairs in Performance." *Musicology Australia* 28 (2006): 1–25.

Barwick, Linda. "Musical Form and Style in Murriny Patha Djanba Songs at Wadeye (Northwest Australia)." In *Analytical and Cross-Cultural Studies in World Music,* edited by Michael Tenzer and John Roeder, 316–54. Oxford: Oxford University Press, 2011.

Barwick, Linda, Nicholas Reid, and Lysbeth Ford. "Communities of Interest: Issues in Establishing a Digital Resource on Murrinh-Patha Song at Wadeye (Port Keats), NT." *Literary and Linguistic Computing* 20, no. 4 (2005): 383–97.

Barz, Gregory F., and Timothy J. Cooley, eds. *Shadows in the Field: New Perspectives for Fieldwork in Ethnomusicology.* 2nd ed. New York: Oxford University Press, 2008.

Battiste, Marie, and James [Sa'ke'j] Youngblood Henderson. *Protecting Indigenous Knoweldge and Heritage: A Global Challenge.* Purich's Aboriginal Issues Series. Saskatoon, SK: Purich, 2000.

Baudrillard, Jean. *Simulacra and Simulation,* trans. of *Simulacres et Simulation* by Sheila Glaser. Ann Arbor: University of Michigan Press, 1994.

Beebe, Roger, and Jason Middleton, eds. *Medium Cool: Music Videos from Soundies to Cellphones*. Durham, NC: Duke University Press, 2007.

Bigenho, Michelle. *Sounding Indigenous: Authenticity in Bolivian Music Performance*. New York and Basingstoke: Palgrave, 2002.

Bigenho, Michelle. *Intimate Distance: Andean Music in Japan*. Durham: Duke University Press, 2012.

Bijsterveld, Karin, and José van Dijck, eds. *Sound Souvenirs: Audio Technologies, Memory and Cultural Practices*. Amsterdam: Amsterdam University Press, 2009.

Bjönberg, Alf. "Learning to Listen to Perfect Sound: Hi-Fi Culture and Changes in Modes of Listening, 1950–80." In *The Ashgate Research Companion to Popular Musicology*, edited by Derek B. Scott. Farnham, UK: Ashgate, 2009.

Boellstorff, Tom. *Coming of Age in Second Life: An Anthropologist Explores the Virtually Human*. Princeton, NJ: Princeton University Press, 2008.

Bolter, Jay. *Remediation: Understanding New Media*. With Richard Grusin. Cambridge: MIT Press, 1999.

Born, Georgina. "Digitising Democracy." *Political Quarterly* 76, no. 1 (2005): 102–23.

———. "On Musical Mediation: Ontology, Technology and Creativity." *Twentieth-Century Music* 2, no. 1 (2005): 7–36.

Born, Georgina, and Kyle Devine. "Music Technology, Gender, and Class: Digitization, Educational and Social Change in Britain." *Twentieth-Century Music* 12, no. 2 (2015): 135–72.

Brady, Erika. *A Spiral Way: How the Phonograph Changed Ethnography*. Jackson: University Press of Mississippi, 1999.

Brown, Michael F. *Who Owns Native Culture?* Cambridge, MA: Harvard University Press, 2003.

Browner, Tara. *Heartbeat of the People: Music and Dance of the Northern Pow-wow*. Urbana: University of Illinois Press, 2002.

———. "Making and Singing Pow-Wow Songs: Text, Form and the Significance of Culture-Based Analysis." *Ethnomusicology* 44, no. 2 (2000): 214–33.

Buckingham, David, Maria Pini, and Rebekah Willett. "'Take Back the Tube!': The Discursive Construction of Amateur Film and Video Making." *Journal of Media Practice* 8, no. 2 (2007): 183–201.

Canessa, Andrew, ed. *Natives Making Nation: Gender, Indigeneity, and the State in the Andes*. Tucson: University of Arizona Press, 2005.

Canessa, Andrew. "Who Is Indigenous? Self-Identification, Indigeneity, and Claims to Justice in Contemporary Bolivia." *Urban Anthropology and Studies of Cultural Systems and World Economic Development* 36, no. 3 (2007): 195–237.

Cascone, Kim. "The Aesthetics of Failure: Post-digital Tendencies in Contemporary Computer Music." *Computer Music Journal* 24, no. 4 (2000): 12–18.

Castells, Manuel. *The Rise of the Network Society*. 2nd ed. Oxford: Wiley-Blackwell, 2010.

Chadwick, Andrew. *Internet Politics: States, Citizens, and New Communication Technologies*. New York: Oxford University Press, 2006.

Chanan, Michael. *Repeated Takes: A Short History of Recording and its Effects on Music*. London: Verso, 1997.

Clifford, James. "Indigenous Articulations." *The Contemporary Pacific* 3, no. 2 (2001): 468–90.

———. *The Predicament of Culture: Twentieth-Century Ethnography, Literature, and Art.* Cambridge, MA: Harvard University Press, 1988.

———. "Traditional Futures." In *Questions of Tradition,* edited by Mark Salber Phillips and Gordon Schochet, 152–68. Toronto, ON: University of Toronto Press, 2004.

Cobo, Martinéz. "Report to the Un Sub-Commission on the Prevention of Descrimination of Minorities." United Nations, 1986.

Collins, John. "The Problem of Oral Copyright: The Case of Ghana." In *Music and Copyright,* edited by Simon Frith, 146–58. Edinburgh: Edinburgh University Press, 1993.

Crowdy, Denis. "Studios at Home in the Solomon Islands." *The World of Music* 49, no. 1 (2007): 143–54.

Denzin, Norman K. *Performative Ethnography: Critical Pedagogy and the Politics of Culture.* Thousand Oaks, CA: SAGE, 2003.

Dery, Mark. *Escape Velocity: Cyberculture at the End of the Century.* New York: Grove Press, 1996.

Diamond, Beverley. "'Allowing the Listener to Fly as They Want to': Sámi Perspectives on Indigenous CD Production in Northern Europe." *The World of Music* 49, no. 1 (2007): 23–48.

———. "Media as Social Action: Native American Musicians in the Recording Studio." In *Wired for Sound: Engineering and Technologies in Sonic Cultures,* edited by Paul D. Greene and Thomas Porcello, 118–37. Middletown, CT: Wesleyan University Press, 2005.

———. "The Music of Modern Indigeneity: From Identity to Alliance Studies." *ESEM* 12 (2007): 169–90.

———. "Native American Contemporary Music: The Women." *The World of Music* 41, no. 2 (2002): 11–39.

Doctorow, Cory. *Content: Selected Essays on Technology, Creativity, Copyright, and the Future of the Future.* San Francisco, CA: Tachyon Publications, 2008.

Doyle, Peter. *Echo and Reverb: Fabricating Space in Popular Music Recording, 1900–1960.* Middletown, CT: Wesleyan University Press, 2005.

Dueck, Byron. *Musical Intimacies and Indigenous Imaginaries: Aboriginal Music and Dance in Public Performance.* New York: Oxford University Press, 2013.

Dunbar-Hall, Peter, and Chris Gibson. *Deadly Sounds, Deadly Places.* Sydney: UNSW Press, 2004.

Dyson, Laurel Evelyn, Max Hendriks, and Stephen Grant, eds. *Information Technology and Indigenous People.* London: Information Science Publishing, 2007.

———. "Preface." In *Information Technology and Indigenous People,* edited by Laurel Evelyn Dyson, Max Hendriks and Stephen Grant, x–xxii. London: Information Science Publishing, 2007.

Ellen, Roy, Peter Parkes, and Alan Bicker, eds. *Indigenous Environmental Knowledge and Its Transformations: Critical Anthropological Perspectives.* Amsterdam: Harwood Academic Publishers, 2000.

Ellis, Clyde. *A Dancing People: Powwow Culture on the Southern Plains*. Lawrence: University Press of Kansas, 2003.

Ellis, Clyde, Luke E. Lassiter, and Gary H. Dunham, eds. *Powwow*. Lincoln: University of Nebraska Press, 2005.

Everett, Anna, and John Thornton Caldwell, eds. *New Media: Theories and Practices of Digitextuality*. New York: Routledge, 2003.

Feld, Steven. "From Schizophonia to Schismogenesis: On the Discourses and Commodification Practices of 'World Music' and 'World Beat.'" In *Music Grooves*, edited by Charles Keil and Steven Feld, 257–89. Chicago: University of Chicago Press, 1994.

Forte, Maximilian C., ed. *Indigenous Cosmopolitans: Transnational and Transcultural Indigeneity in the Twenty-First Century*. New York: Peter Lang, 2010.

Frith, Simon. "Art Versus Technology: The Strange Case of Popular Music." *Media, Culture & Society* 8, no. 3 (1986): 263–79.

———. "Introduction." In *Music and Copyright*, edited by Simon Frith, iv–xiv. Edinburgh: Edinburgh University Press, 1993.

———. "Music and Morality." In *Music and Copyright*, edited by Simon Frith, 1–21. Edinburgh: Edinburgh University Press, 1993.

Gauntlett, David, and Ross Horsley, eds. *Web Studies*. London: Edward Arnold, 2004.

Gibson, Chris, and Peter Dunbar-Hall. "Nitmiluk: Place and Empowerment in Australian Aboriginal Popular Music." *Ethnomusicology* 44, no. 1 (2000): 39–64.

Giddings, Seth, and Martin Lister, eds. *The New Media and Technocultures Reader*. London: Routledge, 2011.

Ginsburg, Faye. "Rethinking the Digital Age." In *Global Indigenous Media: Cultures, Poetics, and Politics*, edited by Pamela Wilson and Michelle Stewart, 287–305. Durham, NC: Duke University Press, 2008.

Ginsburg, Faye, Lila Abu-Lughod, and Brian Larkin. "Introduction." In *Media Worlds: Anthropology on New Terrain*, edited by Faye Ginsburg, Lila Abu-Lughod, and Brian Larkin, 1–36. Berkeley: University of California Press, 2002.

Greaves, Tom, ed. *Intellectual Property Rights for Indigenous Peoples: A Sourcebook*. Oklahoma City: Society for Applied Anthropology, 1994.

Greene, Paul D. "Wired Sound and Sonic Cultures." In *Wired for Sound: Engineering and Technologies in Sonic Cultures*, edited by Paul D. Greene and Thomas Porcello, 1–22. Middletown: Wesleyan University Press, 2005.

Greene, Shane. *Customizing Indigeneity: Paths to a Visionary Politics in Peru*. Stanford, CA: Stanford University Press, 2009.

Guy, Nancy. "Trafficking in Taiwan Aboriginal Voices." In *Handle with Care: Ownership and Control of Ethnographic Materials*, edited by Sjoerd R. Jaarsma, 195–209. Pittsburgh, PA: University of Pittsburgh Press, 2002.

Habermas, Jürgen. *The Structural Transformation of the Public Sphere: An Inquiry into a Category of Bourgeois Society*. Translated by Thomas Burger. Boston, MA: MIT Press, 1991.

Hall, Gillette, and Harry Patrinos. *Indigenous Peoples, Poverty, and Development*. Cambridge: Cambridge University Press, 2012.

Haraway, Donna J. "The Cyborg Manifesto: Science, Technology, and Socialist-Feminism in the Late Twentieth Century." In *Simians, Cyborgs and Women: The Reinvention of Nature*, edited by Donna J. Haraway, 149–81. New York: Routledge, 1991.

Hayles, Katherine N. *How We Became Posthuman: Virtual Bodies in Cybernetics, Literature, and Informatics*. Chicago: University of Chicago Press, 2008.

Hayward, Philip, ed. *Sound Alliances: Indigenous Peoples, Cultural Politics, and Popular Music in the Pacific*. London: Cassell, 1998.

Hilder, Thomas. "Repatriation, Revival and Transmission: The Politics of a Sámi Cultural Heritage." *Ethnomusicology Forum* 21, no. 2 (2012): 161–79.

———. *Sámi Musical Performance and the Politics of Indigeneity in Northern Europe*. Lanham, MD: Rowman & Littlefield, 2015.

Himpele, Jeff. *Circuits of Culture: Media, Politics and Indigenous Idenity in the Andes*. Minneapolis: University of Minnesota Press, 2008.

Hoefnagels, Anna. "Powwow Songs: Traveling Songs and Changing Protocol." *The World of Music* 44, no. 1 (2002): 127–36.

Hoefnagels, Anna, and Beverley Diamond, eds. *Aboriginal Music in Contemporary Canada*. Montreal: McGill Queen's University Press, 2012.

Horkheimer, Max, and Theodor W. Adorno. *Dialectic of Enlightenment*. 1944. Translated by John Cumming. London: Verso, 2010.

Hutchby, Ian. "Technologies, Texts and Affordances." *Sociology* 35, no. 2 (2001): 441–56.

Ivison, Duncan, Paul Patton, and Will Sanders. "Introduction." In *Political Theory and the Rights of Indigenous People*, edited by Duncan Ivison, Paul Patton and Will Sanders, 1–21. Cambridge: Cambridge University Press, 2000.

———. *Political Theory and the Rights of Indigenous Peoples*. Cambridge: Cambridge University Press, 2000.

Jameson, Fredric. "Notes on Globalization as a Philosophical Issue." In *The Cultures of Globalization*, edited by Fredric Jameson and Masao Miyoshi, 54–80. Durham, NC: Duke University Press, 1998.

Jameson, Fredric, and Masao Miyoshi, eds. *The Cultures of Globalization*. Durham, NC: Duke University Press, 1998.

Jenkins, Henry. *Convergence Culture: Where Old Media and New Media Collide*. New York: New York University Press, 2006.

Katz, Mark. *Capturing Sound: How Technology Has Changed Music*. Berkeley: University of California Press, 2010.

Koch, Grace. "Music and Land Rights: Archival Recordings as Documentation for Australian Aboriginal Land Claims." *Fontes Artis Musicae* 55, no. 1 (2008): 155–64.

Kymlicka, Will. "Theorizing Indigenous Rights." *The University of Toronto Law Journal* 49, no. 2 (1999): 281–93.

Landau, Carolyn, and Janet Topp Fargion. "We're All Archivists Now: Towards a More Equitable Ethnomusicology." *Ethnomusicology Forum* 21, no. 2 (2012): 125–40.

Landzelius, Kyra. "Introduction: Native on the Net." In *Native on the Net: Indigenous and Diasporic Peoples in the Virtual Age*, edited by Kyra Landzelius. London: Routledge, 2006.

———. *Native on the Net: Indigenous and Diasporic Peoples in the Virtual Age*. London: Routledge, 2006.

Lange, Patricia. "Video-Mediated Nostalgia and the Aesthetics of Technical Competencies." *Visual Communication* 10, no. 1 (2011): 25–44.

Langlois, Tony. "Pirates of the Mediterranean: Moroccan Music Video and Technology." *Music, Sound, and the Moving Image* 3, no. 1 (2009): 71–85.

Lessig, Lawrence. *Remix: Making Art and Commerce Thrive in the Hybrid Economy*. London: Penguin, 2008.

Leuthold, Steven. "An Indigenous Aesthetic? Two Noted Videographers: George Burdeau and Victor Masayesva." *Wicazo Sa Review* 10, no. 1 (1994): 40–51.

———. *Indigenous Aesthetics: Native Art, Media, and Identity*. Austin: University of Texas Press, 1998.

Lipsitz, George. *Dangerous Crossroads: Popular Music, Postmodernism and the Poetics of Place*. New York: Verso, 1994.

Lister, Martin, Jon Dovey, Seth Giddings, Iain Grant, and Kieran Kelly, eds. *New Media: A Critical Introduction*. London: Routledge, 2003.

Livingston, Tamara E. "Music Revivals: Towards a General Theory." *Ethnomusicology* 43, no. 1 (1999): 66–85.

Lysloff, René T. A. "Mozart in Mirrorshades: Ethnomusicology, Technology, and the Politics of Representation." *Ethnomusicology* 41, no. 2 (1997): 206–19.

Lysloff, René T. A., and Leslie C. Gay Jr. "Introduction: Ethnomusicology in the Twenty-First Century." In *Music and Technoculture*, edited by Rene T. A. Lysloff and Leslie C. Gay Jr, 1–22. Middletown, CT: Weslyan University Press, 2003.

Magowan, Fiona. "'The Land Is Our Märr (Essence); It Stays Forever': The Youthu-Yindi Relationship in Australian Aboriginal Traditionaland Popular Music." In *Ethnicity, Identity and Music: The Musical Construction of Place*, 135–55. Oxford: Berg, 1994.

———. "Shadows of Song: Exploring Research and Performance Strategies in Yolngu Women's Crying-Songs." *Oceania* 72 (2001): 89–104.

Magowan, Fiona, and Karl Neuenfeldt, eds. *Landscapes of Indigenous Performance: Music, Song and Dance of the Torres Strait and Arnhem Land*. Canberra: Aboriginal Studies Press, 2005.

Manuel, Peter. *Cassette Culture: Popular Music and Technology in North India*. Chicago: University of Chicago Press, 1993.

Manovich, Lev. "Database as Symbolic Form." *Convergence: The International Journal of Research into New Media Technologies* 5, no. 2 (1999): 80–99.

———. *The Language of New Media*. Cambridge, MA: MIT Press, 2001.

Marett, Allan. "Ghostly Voices: Some Observations on Song-Creation, Ceremony and Being in Northwest Australia." *Oceania* 71, no. 1 (2000): 18–29.

Marett, Allan. *Songs, Dreamings and Ghosts: The Wangga of North Australia*. Middletown, CT: Wesleyan University Press, 2005.

Marett, Allan, Linda Barwick, and Lysbeth Ford. *For the Sake of a Song: Wangga Songmen and their Repertories*. Sydney, NSW: Sydney University Press, 2013.

McLuhan, Marshall. *The Gutenberg Galaxy: The Making of Typographic Man.* London: Routledge & Paul, 1962.

Meintjes, Louise. *Sound of Africa: Making Music Zulu in a South African Studio.* Durham, NC: Duke University Press, 2003.

Miller, Vincent. *Understanding Digital Culture.* Los Angeles: SAGE, 2011.

Mills, Sherylle. "Indigenous Music and the Law: An Analysis of National and International Legislation." *Yearbook of Traditional Music* 28 (1996): 57–86.

Milner, Greg. *Perfecting Sound Forever: An Aural History of Recorded Music.* New York: Faber & Faber, 2009.

Minde, Henry. "The Challenge of Indigenism: The Struggle for Sami Land Rights and Self-Government in Norway 1960–1990." In *Indigenous Peoples: Resource Management and Global Rights,* edited by Henry Minde, Ragnar Nilsen and Svein Jentoft, 75–106. Delft, NL: Eburon, 2003.

———. "The Destination and the Journey: Indigenous Peoples and the United Nations from the 1960s through 1985." In *Indigenous Peoples: Self-Determination, Knowledge, Indigeneity,* edited by Henry Minde, Harald Gaski, Svein Jentoft and Georges Midré, 49–86. Delft, NL: Eburon, 2008.

———. "The Making of an International Movement of Indigenous Peoples." *Scandinavian Journal of History* 21, no. 3 (1996): 221–46.

Minde, Henry, Ragnar Nilsen, and Svein Jentoft, eds. *Indigenous Peoples: Resource Management and Global Rights.* Delft, NL: Eburon, 2003.

Morozov, Evgeny. *The Net Delusion: How Not to Liberate the World.* London: Allen Lane, 2011.

Nakamura, Lisa. *Cybertypes: Race, Ethnicity and Identity on the Internet.* New York: Routledge, 2002.

Negus, Keith. *Music Genres and Corporate Cultures.* New York: Routledge, 1999.

Neuenfeldt, Karl. "'Bring the Past to Present': Recording and Reviving Rotuman Music via a Collaborative Rotuman/Fijian/Australian CD Project." *The World of Music* 49, no. 1 (2007): 83–103.

———. "Notes on the Engagement of Indigenous Peoples with Recording Technology and Techniques, the Recording Industry and Researchers." *The World of Music* 49, no. 1 (2007): 7–21.

———. "An Overview of Case Studies of Contemporary Native American Music in Canada, the United States of America and on the Web." *The World of Music* 44, no. 1 (2002): 7–10.

Peers, Laura, and Alison K. Brown, eds. *Museums and Source Communities: A Routledge Reader.* London: Routledge, 2003.

Pietikäinen, Sari. "Sami in the Media: Questions of Language Vitality and Cultural Hybridisation." *Journal of Multicultural Discourses* 3, no. 1 (2008): 22–35.

———. "'To Breathe Two Airs': Empowering Indigenous Sámi Media." In *Global Indigenous Media: Cultures, Poetics, and Politics,* edited by Pamela Wilson and Michelle Stewart. Durham, NC: Duke University Press, 2008.

Porcello, Thomas. "Afterword." In *Wired for Sound: Engineering and Technologies in Sonic Culture,* edited by Paul D. Greene and Thomas Porcello, 269–81. Middletown, CT: Wesleyan University Press, 2005.

———. "Music Mediated as Live in Austin: Sound Technology and Recording Practice." In *Wired for Sound: Engineering and Technologies in Sonic Cultures*, edited by Paul D. Greene and Thomas Porcello, 269–82. Middletown, CT: Wesleyan University Press, 2005.

Posey, Darrell Addison, and Graham Dutfield. *Beyond Intellectual Property: Toward Traditional Resource Rights for Indigenous Peoples and Local Communities*. Ottawa: International Development Research Centre, 1996.

Poster, Mark. *The Mode of Information: Poststructuralism and Social Context*. Cambridge: Polity Press, 1990.

———. *The Second Media Age*. Cambridge: Polity Press, 1995.

Pratt, Mary Louise. *Imperial Eyes: Travel Writing and Transculturation*. 2nd ed. New York: Routledge, 2008.

Railton, Diane, and Paul Watson. *Music Video and the Politics of Representation*. Edinburgh: University of Edinburgh Press, 2011.

Ramnarine, Tina K. "Acoustemology, Indigeneity, and Joik in Valkeapää's Symphonic Activism: Views from Europe's Arctic Fringes for Environmental Ethnomusicology." *Ethnomusicology* 53, no. 2 (2009): 187–217.

Rheingold, Howard. *The Virtual Community: Homesteading on the Electronic Frontier*. 2nd ed. Cambridge, MA: MIT Press, 2000.

Romero, Raúl R. *Debating the Past: Music, Memory, and Identity in the Andes*. Oxford: Oxford University Press, 2001.

Said, Edward W. *Orientalism*. London: Routledge & Kegan Paul, 1978.

Salazar, Juan Francisco. "Imperfect Media: The Poetics of Indigenous Media in Chile." University of Western Sydney, 2004.

Saugestad, Sidsel. "Discussion: On the Return of the Native." *Current Anthropology* 45, no. 2 (2004): 263–64.

Scales, Christopher A. "The Politics and Aesthetics of Recording: A Comparative Canadian Case Study of Powwow and Contemporary Native American Music." *World of Music* 44, no. 1 (2002): 41–59.

———. *Recording Culture: Powwow Music and the Aboriginal Recording Industry on the Northern Plains*. Durham. NC: Duke University Press, 2012.

Schiwy, Freya. "Decolonizing the Frame: Indigenous Video in the Andes." *Framework* 44, no. 1 (2003): 116–32.

———. *Indianizing Film: Decolonization, the Andes, and the Question of Technology*. New Brunswick, NJ: Rutgers University Press, 2009.

Seeger, Anthony. "Ethnomusicologists, Archives, Professional Organisations, and the Shifting Ethics of Intellectual Property." *Yearbook for Traditional Music* 28 (1996): 87–105.

Seeger, Anthony, and Shubha Chaudhuri, eds. *Archives for the Future: Global Perspectives on Audiovisual Archives in the 21st Century*. Calcutta: Seagull, 2004.

Shaw, Karena. *Indigeneity and Political Theory: Sovereignty and the Limits of the Political*. London: Routledge, 2008.

Shields, Rob. *The Virtual*. London: Routledge, 2003.

Shilling, Chris. *The Body in Culture, Technology & Society*. London: SAGE, 2005.

Small, Christopher. *Musicking: The Meanings of Performing and Listening*. Middletown, CT: Wesleyan University Press, 1998.

Smith, Linda Tuhiwai. *Decolonizing Methodologies: Research and Indigenous Peoples.* London: Zed Books, 1999.

Snickars, Pelle and Patrick Vonderau, eds. *The YouTube Reader.* Stockholm: National Library of Sweden, 2009.

Solbakk, John T. "Sami Mass Media—Their Role in a Minority Society." In *Sami Culture in a New Era: The Norwegian Sami Experience,* edited by Harald Gaski, 172–98. Karasjok, NO: Davvi Girji, 1997.

Spivak, Gayatri Chakravorty. "In Other Worlds: Essays in Cultural Politics." New York: Methuen, 1987.

Sterne, Jonathan. *The Audible Past: Cultural Origins of Sound Reproduction.* Durham, NC; Duke University Press, 2003.

———. *MP3: The Meaning of a Format.* Durham, NC: Duke University Press, 2012.

Stobart, Henry. "Rampant Reproduction and Digital Democracy: Shifting Landscapes of Music Production and 'Piracy' in Bolivia." *Ethnomusicology Forum* 19, no. 1 (2010): 27–56.

———. "Constructing Community in the Digital Home Studio: Carnival, Creativity and Indigenous Music Video Production in the Bolivian Andes." *Popular Music* 30, no. 2 (2011): 209–26.

———. "'Justice with My Own Hands': The Serious Play of Piracy in Bolivian Indigenous Music Videos." In *Postcolonial Piracy: Media Distribution and Cultural Production in the Global South,* edited by L. Eckstein and A. Schwarz, 215–42. London: Bloomsbury, 2014.

———. *Music and the Poetics of Production in the Bolivian Andes.* Aldershot, UK: Ashgate, 2006.

Sunstein, Cass R. *Republic.Com.* Princeton, NJ: Princeton University Press, 2003.

Swijghuisen Reigersberg, Muriel. "Applied Ethnomusicology, Music Therapy and Ethnographically Informed Choral Education: The Merging of Disciplines during a Case Study in Hopevale, Northern Queensland." In *Applied Ethnomusicology: Historical and Contemporary Approaches,* edited by Klisala Harrison, Elizabeth Mackinlay and Svanibor Pettan, 51–75. Newcastle upon Tyne: Cambridge Scholars, 2010.

Tan, Shzr Ee. *Beyond "Innocence": Amis Aboriginal Song in Taiwan as an Ecosystem.* Farnham, UK: Ashgate, 2012.

Taylor, Diana. *Performing Cultural Memory in the Americas.* Durham, NC: Duke University Press, 2003.

Taylor, Timothy D. *Global Pop: World Music, World Markets.* New York: Routledge, 1997.

———. "A Riddle Wrapped in a Mystery: Transnational Music Sampling and Enigma's 'Return to Innocence.'" In *Music and Technoculture,* edited by Rene T. A. Lysloff and Leslie C. Gay Jr, 64–92. Middletown, CT: Wesleyan University Press, 2003.

———. *Strange Sounds: Music, Technology & Culture.* New York: Routledge, 2001.

Theberge, Paul. *Any Sound You Can Imagine: Making Music/Consuming Technology.* Middletown, CT: Wesleyan University Press, 1997.

Tucker, Joshua. *Gentleman Troubadours and Andean Pop Stars: Huayno Music, Media Work, and Ethnic Imaginaries in Urban Peru.* Chicago: University of Chicago Press, 2013.

Turino, Thomas. *Moving Away from Silence: Music of the Peruvian Altiplano and the Experiment of Urban Migration.* Chicago: University of Chicago Press, 1993.

———. *Music as Social Life: The Politics of Participation.* Chicago: University of Chicago Press, 2008.

Van Dijk, Jan A. G. M. *The Network Society.* London: SAGE, 2012.

Vernallis, Carol. *Experiencing Music Video: Aesthetics and Cultural Context.* New York: Columbia University Press, 2004.

Vesna, Victoria. "Database Aesthetics." *AI & Society* 14, no. 2 (2000): 155–56.

Warwick, Jacqueline. *Girl Groups, Girl Culture: Popular Music and Identity in the 1960s.* New York: Routledge, 2013.

Whiteley, Sheila, and Shara Rambarran, eds. *The Oxford Handbook of Music and Virtuality.* Oxford: Oxford University Press, 2016.

Williams, Frederick. *The Communications Revolution.* Beverly Hills: SAGE, 1982.

Williams, Raymond. *Television: Technology and Cultural Form.* London: Routledge, 2003.

Wilson, Pamela, and Michelle Stewart, eds. *Global Indigenous Media: Cultures, Poetics, and Politics.* Durham, NC: Duke University Press, 2008.

———. "Indigeneity and Indigenous Media on the Global Stage." In *Global Indigenous Media: Cultures, Poetics, and Politics,* edited by Pamela Wilson and Michelle Stewart, 1–35. Durham, NC: Duke University Press, 2008.

Zemp, Hugo. "The/an Ethnomusicologist and the Record Business." *Yearbook for Traditional Music* 28 (1996): 36–56.

Zagorski-Thomas, Simon. "The Stadium in Your Bedroom: Functional Staging, Authenticity and the Audience-Led Aesthetic in Record Production." *Popular Music* 29, no. 2 (2010): 251–66.

Contributors

LINDA BARWICK is professor and associate dean (research) at the Sydney Conservatorium of Music, University of Sydney. Her research focuses on Australian indigenous and immigrant musics and the digital humanities, particularly on the archiving and repatriation of ethnographic field recordings as a site of interaction between researchers and cultural heritage communities. She has studied community music practices through fieldwork in Australia, Italy, and the Philippines. Themes of her research include the analysis of musical action in place, the language of song, and the aesthetics of cross-cultural musical practice. She has helped develop the cross-institutional research infrastructure facility PARADISEC (the Pacific and Regional Archive for Digital Sources in Endangered Cultures) since its inception.

BEVERLEY DIAMOND is an honorary research professor at Memorial University of Newfoundland, where she founded the Research Centre for the Study of Music, Media, and Place (MMaP). She has contributed to Canadian cultural historiography, feminist music research, and Indigenous studies. Her research on Indigenous expressive culture has explored constructs of technological mediation, transnationalism, and, most recently, concepts of reconciliation and healing. Publications include *Native American Music in Eastern North America* (2008) and the coedited anthologies *Aboriginal Music in Contemporary Canada: Echoes and Exchanges* (2012) and Music and Gender (2000). Diamond has been recognized with a Trudeau Fellowship (2009–12), the Social Sciences and Humanities Research Council of Canada Gold Medal (2014), and fellowship in the Royal Society of Canada (2008) and the Order of Canada (2013).

THOMAS R. HILDER is postdoctoral fellow in musicology at the Grieg Academy, Department of Music, University of Bergen, with training in ethnomusicology at Royal Holloway, University of London (PhD, MMus). Focusing on popular music repertories of Northern Europe, his interdisciplinary research responds to current debates in postcolonial studies, digital media, gender theory, and transnationalism. He is the author of *Sámi Musical Performance and the Politics of Indigeneity in Northern Europe* (2015).

FIORELLA MONTERO-DIAZ is a lecturer in ethnomusicology at Keele University and the administrator and archivist of the British Forum for Ethnomusicology. Her research is on music hybridity, race, class, the elites and social conflict in contemporary Lima, Peru. Recent publications include "Singing the War: Reconfiguring White Upper-Class Identity through Fusion Music in Post-war Lima" in *Ethnomusicology Forum.*

JOHN-CARLOS PEREA received his PhD in Music (ethnomusicology) from the University of California, Berkeley, in 2009, and is currently an assistant professor of American Indian studies in the College of Ethnic Studies at San Francisco State University. He is the author of *Intertribal Native American Music in the United States* (2014). Perea's essays have also been published in MUSICultures, the Encyclopedia Britannica, and the Grove Dictionary of American Music.

HENRY STOBART is reader in music and ethnomusicology in the Music Department of Royal Holloway, University of London. He has been studying indigenous music in the Bolivian Andes for nearly thirty years, undertaking extensive field research in both rural and urban settings. His books include *Music and the Poetics in the Bolivian Andes* (2015) and the edited volume *The New (Ethno)musicologies* (2008).

SHZR EE TAN is a senior lecturer at Royal Holloway. Theoretical approaches she has engaged with include aspirational cosmopolitanism in sound art and Sinophoe music scenes, the instrumentalisation of nostalgia in cultural ecosystems, and gender performance. Recent work includes an article on the YouTube Symphony Orchestra in *The Oxford Handbook of Music and Virtuality,* an essay in (and co-editing of) *Gender in Chinese Music* (2013) plus a monograph, *"Beyond Innocence": Amis Aboriginal Song in Taiwan as an Ecosystem* (2012).

RUSSELL WALLACE is a composer, producer, and traditional Lil'wat singer. Wallace's music has been part of a number of soundtracks (film, video, television) and theater/dance productions. He was the composer in residence for the Aboriginal Dance Program from 1996 to 2003 at the Banff Centre for the Arts. He has produced CDs that have been nominated for awards at the Junos, the Canadian Aboriginal Music Awards, and the Native American Music Awards in the United States. His education includes diplomas in theatre and performing arts from Vancouver Comunity College, information technology from Capilano University, and a major in creative writing at the University of British Columbia, where he also took courses in ethnomusicology. Currently, Wallace works and teaches at the Native Education College, Capilano University, and works for the Office for Aboriginal Peoples at Simon Fraser University in British Columbia.

Index

aesthetics, 19, 32, 99, 128, 131,
133–36; audiovisual aesthetics, 15;
electronic aesthetics, 190; individual
and collective aesthetics, 15; local
aesthetics, 106; "low-tech" aesthetics,
128; media aesthetics, 129; musical
aesthetics, 11, 189; production
aesthetics, 108; recording aesthetics,
106, 107; video aesthetics, 132

activism, 3, 5, 11; American Indian
activism, 54; cultural activism, 131;
cyberactivism, 41, 48; Indigenous
activism, 2, 5; Indigenous musical
activism, 12, 40; local activism,
5; political activism, 5, 177;
transnational activism, 3, 14

Adorno, Theodor, 6, 183

affordance, 15, 133, 137, 150

agency, 8, 55, 86, 88–89, 93n46, 106,
134, 182; human agency, 6, 38, 191;
Indigenous agency, 13, 177; political
agency, 86, 131; social agency, 87

amateur, 32, 45, 128, 135–37, 153n43

anthropology, 112. *See also* ethnography

Appadurai, Arjun, 6, 29, 75

archive, 3, 14, 15–17, 38, 53, 55, 59,
63–64, 67, 115, 170, 173; aural
history archive, 17, 55; digital
archive, 2, 16, 35; media archive, 54;
music archive, 68; personal archive,
59; sound archive, 17; tape archive,
60. *See also* database

assemblage, 2, 176, 185

Audacity, 67

audience, 4, 12, 29, 32–33, 35–37,
43–44, 46, 99, 107, 112, 120,
131–34, 139–40, 147–48, 181;
non-Indigenous audience, 12,
47–48; regional audience, 128;
transnational audience, 8, 12, 107,
134

audiocassette, 16, 138, 150n5;
audiocassette recorder, 55;
audiocassette technology, 63. *See also*
cassette

authenticity, 42, 47–48, 78, 79, 82–85,
88–89, 117, 154n52, 176, 182–83,
188; Indigenous authenticity, 13,
148, 201n73; strategic inauthenticity,
113

authorship, 7, 12, 13, 17–18, 133

Baudrillard, Jean, 8, 19, 176–77, 179,
183–84, 188–89, 196, 202n75

blog, 29, 31, 36–37, 44, 47, 86; blogger,
33, 87; community blog, 34; music
blog, 33

body, 2, 8, 20, 103, 110, 131–32; human
body, 8, 20

Boellstorff, Tom, 180, 193, 196, 198

Boss BR-600, 64–65

camera, 38, 47, 131, 140–46, 154n52,
155n68; camera person, 131;
cameraman, 141; camerawork, 134;
video camera, 138

capitalism, 182; advanced capitalism,
183, 193; capital, 134; capitalist
economies, 18; capitalist
exploitation, 87; global capitalism,
5–6, 130; late capitalism, 6, 106;
political capital, 131. *See also* culture